The Other Side of Curriculum
Lessons from Learners

Lois Brown Easton

HEINEMANN
Portsmouth, NH

Heinemann
A division of Reed Elsevier Inc.
361 Hanover Street
Portsmouth, NH 03801–3912
www.heinemann.com

Offices and agents throughout the world

Some of the material in Chapter 5 under the heading Varying the Conditions for Learning in a Mastery System was previously published in "If Standards Are Absolute . . . ," in *Education Week,* vol. 19, no. 31 (April 12, 2000), pp. 50–53. Reprinted by permission.

Library of Congress Cataloging-in-Publication Data
Easton, Lois Brown.
    The other side of curriculum : lessons from learners / Lois Brown Easton.
      p. cm.
    Includes bibliographical references and index.
    ISBN 0-86709-562-8 (alk. paper)
      1. Curriculum planning—Colorado—Case studies. 2. Experiential learning—Colorado—Case studies. 3. Eagle Rock School. I. Title.

  LB2806.15 .E29 2002   2001039920
  375'.001'09788—dc21

Editor: Leigh Peake
Production: Lynne Reed
Cover design: Jenny Jensen Greenleaf
Typesetter: House of Equations, Inc.
Manufacturing: Steve Bernier

Cover photograph is of Marion Blakeney, Eagle Rock graduate.

Printed in the United States of America on acid-free paper
06 05 04 03 02 DA 1 2 3 4 5

To Judith Decker Gilbert (1940–1997), whose understanding of learning led to Eagle Rock's curriculum and has influenced curriculum in Colorado, throughout the country, and around the world.
"I can do this," she said, and she did.

Contents

Foreword

Roland S. Barth

Educators are gifted and talented at finding reasons why good ideas and practices in other schools cannot possibly work in their school. But the transferal to other settings of the good ideas and practices so evident at the Eagle Rock School do not depend on the financial support of a business, selective admission of students, or the small number of students in classes. Indeed ample evidence suggests that these kinds of structural changes have precious little to do with improved student performance. To the contrary, what other schools can take away from Lois Easton's portrayal here of the Eagle Rock School are ideas. Many rich, revolutionary ideas.

These ideas are difficult to convey through conventional language. You must be there to understand. Therefore, you are about to embark on a most unusual field trip to a most remarkable school. I know, because I have taken this field trip. This excursion will reveal not only what the school looks like, its history, and its organization, but also the central ideas that underlie its very existence. Real students will be your guides, and the ideas of Eagle Rock will emanate from their words as well as from those of the author.

Eagle Rock is a "lab school." But unlike most lab schools, which are associated with universities, Eagle Rock is affiliated with a motor company. In the current heated debate over school reform, business people and educators take highly divergent positions. Few partnerships between business and education survive, much less produce noteworthy outcomes. This successful, decade-long effort on the part of Honda Motor Company and the Eagle Rock School is to be celebrated—and then examined carefully. Lessons learned can be applied elsewhere, perhaps in your school, perhaps in your business.

What is being test-driven here is a very different way of teaching, of learning, and of disclosing what is learned. In this school the adults are every bit as much engaged in learning as the students. Indeed, Eagle Rock is nothing less than an attempt to create a community of learners. The primary vehicle for this ambitious lesson plan is the curriculum. This is, above all, a book about curriculum—what we want youngsters to know and to be able to do, and how to get them to know and do it.

The world of schools is replete with different conceptions of curriculum. Yet, the organizing principle of the curriculum behind most pedagogy in most schools might be called the "transmission of knowledge." The proper business of schools is to transmit to students as much as possible of what is deemed desirable knowledge. The proper function of students is to learn as much of this knowledge as fast as possible between September and June and to display its acquisition on demand, usually through standardized tests. Students are evaluated on the basis of how much knowledge they have acquired how quickly and how able they are to demonstrate this acquisition to teachers. The model assumes the primacy of didactic teaching. Most schools and most teachers are as wedded to this model today as they were a hundred years ago.

Unfortunately, the transmission-of-knowledge model of learning is beset with tragic flaws. First of all, it is futile to attempt to transmit to students in a few months everything we think they should know. Secondly, evidence suggests that students retain perhaps five percent of this knowledge after a few weeks. After a few years, what they remember is inconsequential. A third flaw in the model is that it does not engage the learner very fully for very long. Nor does the model fit the learning style of the majority of students. Finally, the model begets a host of undesirable side effects, from cheating to dropping out. The transmission-of-knowledge model leads neither to high standards nor to high test scores, both of which are now so desperately sought.

The students at Eagle Rock have long histories of being exposed to transmitted knowledge in schools. For most of them the model has failed and has caused them to fail. What they encounter at Eagle Rock is a different model, a different curriculum, and a different pedagogy based on an experiential model of learning. Some of the central ideas I find embedded in the curriculum at the school are:

- Students as teachers.
- Self-directed learning.
- Learning experiences that have personal meaning in students' lives.
- The power of storytelling in promoting learning.
- High expectations for students who have been low performers.
- Learning assessed by the learner and by others invested in the learning.
- Learning that is transformational as well as informational.
- The school as a community of learners.

The curriculum at the Eagle Rock School is, above all, a personal growth curriculum, a curriculum that fosters learner-centered learning.

The adults do not own and devise this curriculum. It is created by adults working in concert with the idiosyncratic life of each student. This is a curriculum that arises from the values, principles, and beliefs that are at the very core of the school's remarkable culture. In a very real sense the ever-emerging culture of the school shapes the ever-emerging curriculum of the school. To be sure, there are warts associated with this curriculum, for the school, like each of its students and educators, is a work in progress.

Clearly, our nation's schools need alternative models of teaching and learning. What you are about to read describes one attempt to create such an alternative model, along with how the model works and its consequences for students and adults alike. This assortment of vignettes coalesces into one grand story—the mission of the Eagle Rock School. By telling their stories to others, teachers and students alike come to reflect on their school experiences, analyze them, clarify them—and learn from them. And so do we.

The Other Side of Curriculum: Lessons from Learners is a detailed, powerful portrayal of another way of thinking about curriculum, about teaching, about learning, and about organizing schools. I can think of no teacher, administrator, curriculum administrator, staff developer, or parent—or student, for that matter—who will not find the ideas embedded in these rich stories provocative. And for those of you who would transform your schools into communities of learners, I can think of no more helpful companion.

Have a splendid field trip!

Preface

I remember the first curriculum I constructed. It was in the seventies. Along with many other teachers from my district, I went to a curriculum workshop hosted by the nearby university. There we learned all about behavioral objectives. My orderly mind loved constructing them:

Given X,
the student will do Y
to Z proficiency
through action A.

Sometimes we added the number of times this performance would be successfully repeated. We even stated by when this behavior would be accomplished.

After the class, we all returned to our classrooms and wrote the district curriculum. I don't know for whom we constructed that curriculum. The resulting black binders resided on a bookshelf in my classroom until I left the school five years later. I remember that the eighth-grade English curriculum was at least 150 pages long, however, and that I never (or almost never) consulted it. Yet I was known as a pretty good teacher, and my students seemed to learn. Although I actually liked doing those objectives (all right—I admit I also liked diagramming sentences), I knew this curriculum did not have much to do with learning.

The second curriculum I constructed was for a textbook company. I had sent the editors some interdisciplinary, interactive units I'd created for my students, and they "hired" me (my "salary" was an advance on royalties) to be the in-house senior author of a new language arts series. Unfortunately, it was strongly suggested that our team adhere closely to what competitive companies were including in their textbooks and that we pay strict attention to the curricular requirements of important adoption states like Texas and California. I was so disappointed that for months I kept my units in the trunk of my car, ready to flee with them to a more hospitable environment. Although the textbooks we finally developed did pay some attention to interdisciplinary units (each chapter started out with a theme and then dealt with oral language, reading, grammar, usage, mechanics, and writing related to that theme), they never sold well. (I like to believe they were ahead of their time!) I never did figure out for whom we wrote that curriculum, either—perhaps the sales department. What bothered me more was that what the teacher was to say for each lesson was written in blue in the teacher's manual . . . as if she could not think for herself.

The next curriculum I designed was during the time of Madeline Hunter of the UCLA School of Education. Some of you may remember her "essential elements of instruction." In a series of curriculum workshops, I refreshed my memory about behavioral objectives. This time, however, they seemed to have a purpose. They were related to learning, albeit from a teacher's point of view—what a teacher was supposed to do. Again, my orderly mind relished the job, and I got pretty good at things like behavior, level of performance, and conditions. Not to mention anticipatory set and monitoring and adjusting. Again, we produced thick tomes of objectives, and these served the fine function of propping up the flimsier books on my classroom bookshelf.

I wrote my fourth curriculum when I worked for a state department of education. This time, I worked with language arts teachers from around the state, and we consulted the leading language arts professional groups. We wrote what teachers in that state should do in order to teach what those groups said should be taught. I look back on that curriculum with some respect. Although our document was a revision of something called the "Essential Skills"—and we couldn't dump the name—we wrote very broad outcomes from the point of view of what the student would be able to do at the end of instruction. (We wanted to get away from multitudinous little skills at each grade level, which had been common in earlier curricula. I'll never forget one for kindergarten: *The student will show a sense of humor.* Would I have been promoted to first grade?) Our curriculum had only five big writing outcomes and five big reading outcomes, and, guess what, they related to each other (making possible a connection between reading and writing)! We did the same with listening and speaking. Even though this was a state curriculum and meant to be adopted or adapted by districts and then by schools, it seemed more learner friendly, written with learners in mind.

After helping a new high school create curriculum related to the premises of the Coalition of Essential Schools, I got to observe a number of other schools in the Coalition create their own curriculum documents from the ground up. These efforts were heading in the right direction.

Then I came to Eagle Rock, where learners were front and center. As you will read in this book, staff, including but not limited to administrators (who, anyway, are also teachers at Eagle Rock) developed curriculum with learners and their learning foremost in mind. Sure, they consulted their own content discipline's recommendations and attended to the Colorado State Model Content Standards. But the curriculum was written with learning in mind. Furthermore, it was tried out in various iterations to see what effect it would have on learners—and then rewritten. As I write this, in early 2001, we are on our tenth edition of the curriculum—and we opened our doors in the fall of 1993. It's not that we can't make up our minds; it's that we have learned so much about curriculum and student learning from trying out each iteration.

You'll encounter some "new old" concepts of curriculum in this book—that is, their new meaning and application are slightly different from their old meaning and application—because we are considering curriculum from the viewpoint of the learner. The real experiences of our staff and students have helped us each step of the way, and we want to share them with you. If you visit Eagle Rock—and we hope you can—you'll be smack-dab in the middle of similar experiences. If all you can do is read this book, the stories will help you understand how we understand curriculum.

About This Book

Each chapter begins with a story or stories about what really happens at Eagle Rock. You will meet real Eagle Rock students and staff members and eavesdrop on Eagle Rock learning experiences. The power of storytelling is immense, and you may find that the stories remain with you even when the concepts don't. Each story is followed by a detailed discussion of the concept it illustrates, sometimes with references to other places, resources, and materials that you can consult to find out more. Finally, each chapter ends with an invitation to explore your own stories related to the concept through a series of questions you can ask yourself or use with colleagues to see how the concept applies in your own setting.

Each chapter, therefore, follows this general outline:

1. Stories. True tales about Eagle Rock students and staff learning.

2. Discussion. This is a written rendition of how we might talk together about a "learning story" if you were visiting Eagle Rock rather than reading this book. Sometimes I muse about the story. Sometimes I include background information and related details. Sometimes I ask questions the story raises in my mind and, I hope, in yours. Then I alert you to important aspects of the related concept, sometimes with references to outside sources.

3. Questions to consider. These questions stimulate you to think about what you can do to make your own curriculum a curriculum for learning. One good way to begin is to gather and analyze a number of artifacts related to your current curriculum: graduation or grade-level requirements; the scope and sequence of a grade-level cluster; course descriptions or syllabi; curriculum guide(s); a blank transcript or report card; the state standards for which you are responsible; course requirements (readings, assignments, final products); sample units, assignments, and assessments; video- or audiotapes of students learning in a classroom; letters to parents about classroom requirements; a report made to the board of education about curriculum; newspaper articles about learning in your school or district; an accreditation self-study; course evaluations; interviews with staff members, students, parents, and

community members. Imagine that you are examining these arti-
facts for the first time and describe what you see in them:
- What do they say about your beliefs about learning?
- What do they say about your learning environment?
- What do you value in terms of curriculum, instruction, and
  assessment?

Then, use these artifacts to document your responses to questions that
will encourage you to consider not only the specifics of the changes
you might want to make but broader issues as well:

- In what ways are you already implementing this concept? What
  evidence do you have that it makes a difference in terms of student learning?

- What or who might block your making this change? How could
  you address these concerns?

- What policies might affect your implementation of this change?
  How can you address any state or district policies that might block
  the change you want to make? Are waivers possible? Under what
  conditions?

- What incentives are there for making the change? Who will support the change? Who will be the first to implement it?

- How can you communicate with various constituencies about what
  you want to do before you do it? How will you address the issues
  they raise? How will you continue to communicate with these
  constituencies as you proceed with your change?

- What role can students play in making the change you desire?
  parents? the district? the state?

- What professional development will be needed? What ongoing
  support will be needed?

- How will you know that the change is affecting learning? What
  data will you gather, and how will you analyze and use your data?

- How will you communicate what you are learning about the effect
  of your change?

Chapter 1, "About Eagle Rock," is an overview of our school:

- A history of the school and background information.

- A description of the students (student profile as well as information on admissions processes and criteria).

- The culture of Eagle Rock (philosophy and beliefs, as well as the
  structures, governance policies, and activities that support the
  philosophy).

- The program.
- The daily schedule.
- The Professional Development Center.
- Our curriculum format.

The remaining chapters each describe a concept that led to and is embedded in the Eagle Rock curriculum, followed by questions that help readers make the translation to their own contexts.

Chapter 2, "Curriculum Emanates from the Culture," discusses how curriculum should arise out of the values, principles, and beliefs that form the culture of the school. Eagle Rock's culture (known by the code 8 + 5 = 10) has been described as that of a "learning community." This chapter looks at what that designation means. It also presents some concrete ideas for creating a culturally embedded curriculum, including how to make curriculum manageable so that it supports the culture. You'll visit an Eagle Rock classroom in which culture is taught directly. The questions for you to consider are: *What is your culture? How is it represented? How is curriculum related to culture in your school? What do you do about outside influences such as state and district standards? How is your culture taught and reinforced through curriculum? How well does your curriculum function in your culture? How transparent is it? How could you make your curriculum more attuned to and promoting of culture?*

Chapter 3, "Curriculum Includes Instruction and Assessment," considers the close links required among curriculum, instruction, and assessment if real learning is to occur and be measured. The separation of the three key acts of teaching and learning is artificial, but it helps to deal with each individually in order to unite them better. If learning is to occur, a seamless relationship must be established so that curriculum is instruction, and instruction is assessment, and assessment is curriculum. One affects all the others. You'll go into four Eagle Rock classrooms to examine curriculum, instruction, and assessment and see how they blend together. You'll also look at the concepts of "less is more" and "backwards planning." The questions for you to consider are: *How do you understand curriculum, instruction, and assessment at your school? How coherent is the relationship of one to another? How could you use a "less is more" approach to curriculum? Would "backwards planning" work at your school? What would be the benefits of a more coherent approach to CIA?*

Chapter 4, "Curriculum Is Learner Centered," introduces you to Loula, an Eagle Rock graduate who really struggled to learn. This chapter considers the differences among three approaches to education: teacher centered, student centered, and learner centered. It makes a case that schools need to be learner centered and discusses four reasons, using student examples to make important points about what learners need. It introduces Eagle Rock's regular presentations of learning (POLs), a practice developed more fully in Chapter 5. The questions for you to consider are: *How would you describe your current school: teacher centered? student centered? learner centered? Who is doing the learning in your school now? How do you provide for the whole person in your current curriculum (and related instruction and assessment)? What curriculum processes or instructional methods allow learning to focus on what the learner needs? Who has the most power over learning in your school?*

Chapter 5, "Curriculum Is Competency Based," distinguishes a time-based curriculum from a competency-based one. Carnegie units or credits are the conventional markers for a time-based curriculum; course titles and grades indicate content and achievement. A competency-based system has more integrity in terms of attesting to what students can do and how well. In this chapter you'll meet Jeremy, former gang member now going to college to learn signing. You'll see how he has to prove himself through his graduation POL. You'll learn more about presentations of learning and take a hard look at standards and how they might fit into a competency-based system. You'll explore the necessity of varying the conditions for learning so that all students can learn. You'll also learn how a competency-based system affects students and staff. The questions for you to consider are: *What are the advantages if your school or district moves to a competency-based system? What are the barriers, and how can they be overcome? How can state standards fit into a competency-based system, even support it? What conditions need to vary—and how—if all students are held to high expectations?*

Chapter 6, "Curriculum Helps Learners Become Self-Directed," tells the story of James, an Eagle Rock graduate, who discovered a "secret" about learning. You'll meet him through a sequence of his presentations of learning, including his graduation POL. This chapter addresses, from the viewpoint of a number of students, what self-directed learning is and what conditions are necessary for accomplishing it. You'll learn how curriculum can sponsor self-directed learning, examine how important choice is to self-directed learning, and discover how to encourage choice making through curriculum. The questions for you to consider are: *To what extent do you help students become self-directed? How can you inspire more self-directed learning, and what are the advantages and disadvantages of doing so? How can you incorporate more choice into your school, program, and curriculum?*

Chapter 7, "Curriculum Is for the Whole Student," expands the concept of curriculum to include personal growth. You'll listen to Melanie's personal growth presentation of learning and read about two portfolios she constructed to document her personal growth. While academic growth is very important at Eagle Rock, we have learned that personal growth is as important and sometimes needs to come first, before academic growth can be accomplished. This is a scary concept, especially for public schools. You'll read how we foster personal growth and consider how your school could do so, too. *What do you think students, staff members, and parents would say about a personal growth curriculum? To what extent do you now have such a curriculum? What are the advantages and disadvantages of instituting personal growth as a curriculum component?*

Chapter 8, "Curriculum Encourages a Constructivist Approach," explores whether curriculum–instruction–assessment (CIA) decisions can implement a theory of learning. This chapter relates to Chapter 6 but focuses more specifically on the constructivist theory of learning and how Eagle Rock attempts to help students construct their own meaning. You'll meet Danny, an Eagle Rock graduate, as he reminisces about a learning experience he shaped for himself while here. The theory of constructivism is explored, and various Eagle Rock learning scenarios provide examples of how we've tried to implement the theory. The questions for you to consider are: *What do you know about constructivism? To what extent do you implement it in your school—and why do you want to implement or enhance it at your school? What are the barriers to doing so? What are the benefits?*

Chapter 9, "Curriculum Is Meaningful," puts an interdisciplinary approach to curriculum in the larger context of making curriculum meaningful and reminds readers of several ways presented in this book that help educators make curriculum meaningful. The chapter describes the fifties unit, an exciting interdisciplinary all-school curriculum culminating in a production of *Grease*. You'll meet Eagle Rock graduate Jena and discover the effect this unit had on her learning. The chapter also tells you one way to categorize the many forms of interdisciplinary curriculum, identifies some conditions that make interdisciplinary learning possible, and suggests some steps educators can take to create interdisciplinary learning. The questions for you to consider are: *What makes your current curriculum meaningful? How would a more interdisciplinary approach enhance meaningfulness? What conditions are necessary for a successful interdisciplinary approach? What steps might you take to implement a more meaningful curriculum?*

Chapter 10, "Curriculum Is for Learning," is a summary. Do these seven concepts of curriculum really help learners learn? You'll meet Ruth and Marchello, very different people and very different learners, who graduated together in March 2000. What evidence is there that Eagle Rock's curriculum helped them learn? Was it important to them that curriculum emanated from the culture? that curriculum, instruction, and assessment were coherent? that curriculum was learner centered and competency based and encouraged self-directed learning? How did the Eagle Rock curriculum provide for them as whole students? How did it help them construct meaning? And finally, how meaningful was the curriculum to them? This is the ultimate test of the concepts. Do they really help young people learn? How do we need to keep working at Eagle Rock to help students learn? The questions for you to consider are: *How can you institute a process of curriculum review and change? What factors need to be considered if you undertake such a wholesale process?*

Introduction

Reforming, restructuring, and reinventing were the three R's of the nineties, and this revisionism will likely characterize the new century as well. Few district administrators are sitting back complacently, gleefully smacking their hands together, and saying, "Been there, done that. We've reinvented our educational system, restructured the district, and reformed our schools. We're finished." Each year, new knowledge about how people learn, new ideas that lead to new thinking, and new strategies for helping students learn point toward curriculum renovation, prompting us to ask anew: *What should students know and be able to do? What shall we teach? How can we best teach what we believe students should know and be able to do? How can we help students learn? How will we know that students have learned?*

These questions get expressed in very specific ways:

1. How much of the curriculum comes from the outside (that is, national and state mandates or guidelines) and how much from the inside (the community and the school culture)?

2. How can curriculum be learner centered, rather than student or teacher centered?

3. How can decisions be made about when students are ready to move from grade to grade or when they are ready to graduate?

4. Who should create curriculum? Who should know the curriculum? Where do power and authority for curriculum lie?

5. What part do standards play in curriculum? Where does curriculum development begin—with standards or somewhere else?

6. How is curriculum translated into the everyday learning lives of students and teachers?

7. How does the curriculum represent learning theory? What should it say about instruction? about assessment? How do all of these concepts fit together in a curriculum?

8. What effect does curriculum have on students? teachers? others?

9. What implications are there within curriculum for the conditions of learning?

10. What aspects of student development are within the purview of curriculum? only academics? academics and personal growth?

11. How do schools foster lifelong learning?

12. How can curriculum be meaningful?

This book discusses a number of concepts about learning as they relate to these and similar questions. If you want some direction in this regard, you've come to the right place.

Most of the examples you'll find here come from the curriculum I know best—the one used at Eagle Rock School and Professional Development Center. Eagle Rock is a professional development school, a school designed to experiment with many ideas about education in a very public way, so that others can learn from the experiments. Many such schools have influenced education, ranging from early experimental schools like John Dewey's, in Chicago, to those in place today: Ted Sizer's Coalition of Essential Schools, Henry Levin's Accelerated Schools, James Comer's School Development Program, Robert Slavin's Success for All, John Goodlad's Partnerships for Educational Renewal, and the New American Schools. At less visible levels, there are numerous local "lighthouse" schools, model programs, pilot sites, and lab schools. Like any and all of these schools and programs, Eagle Rock School and Professional Development Center is taking risks, implementing a number of different reforms to see how they help students learn and sharing the results of these experiments with educators who are trying to figure out a way to help more students learn better.

Not everything about Eagle Rock will match your situation. Eagle Rock is a high school; you may work in an elementary school. Your students may go home (to all kinds of environments) at 3:30; Eagle Rock is a residential school, and students go home infrequently. Reading this book, you will need to decide how what Eagle Rock does can be articulated in your own setting. You may even have to go beyond what Eagle Rock does, get over some of your "yabbuts"—the differences you see between Eagle Rock and the school where you teach—in order to understand the concepts and begin to see a way to implement them yourself. For example, seeing the value of creating a learning community in any situation is the first step in understanding how this concept can be implemented in another setting. The next step is identifying what you have or could have that will help you create a learning community.

Educators who visit the Eagle Rock Professional Development Center, most often in small groups and for at least a day, are immersed in the Eagle Rock experience. After an orientation and a student-led tour, they may accompany specific students to classes and other activities, visit classes that particularly interest them, take part in seminars with students and staff on issues of interest, or view videotapes of student "presentations of learning." At some point in their visit they sit down for a talk with me. After they have asked questions and clarified their understanding of what they have observed, I ask, *So what? What does this have to do with you? What can you do with this idea in your school?* My questions get more specific as they struggle to bridge what they have seen at Eagle Rock with their own situation. Here's a composite debriefing scenario, the first of many stories you'll encounter in this book.

About twenty-five minutes before lunch, the ten teachers who have been visiting from City High School walk into the Professional Development Center reception area. I sit in an armchair in front of the fireplace as, one by one, they are dropped off by the students they have "shadowed." I listen as they say good-bye to their guides and am warmed by how grateful they seem.

When all ten are seated with me around the big flagstone coffee table, I ask them to share their experiences. The two who have gone to the *Write for the Rock* (the school newspaper) class remark how independently the students worked and how seriously they took their editing. The teacher who has observed the Holocaust class isn't able to talk much about the impact the student projects had on her—she is near tears. Two others have observed—no, *participated* in—Hydroponics. They have collected data about the tomato plants that are growing without soil, recorded these observations, and compared current data to previous data. Most important, they have learned how to diagnose the health of the plants and prescribe remedies. They too are amazed at how self-directed the students are. Three others have visited the Pit and Pendulum class, an interactive mathematics project (IMP). They have worked individually with student partners predicting whether or not the arc of a pendulum will touch (and presumably kill) the body of a prisoner. To test their hypotheses, they have helped build several pendulums, varying certain characteristics. The remaining two teachers have shadowed students who are helping build an outdoor amphitheater, a service project that incorporates hands-on mathematics and communication skills. They have helped students stake out the angles of a hexagon using only a scale blueprint that failed to record angles and dimensions. The cement truck is coming this afternoon, and the students were working feverishly to make sure the angles and dimensions they had devised were absolutely correct.

Hoping to push these teachers to the next level of thinking, I ask them to complete this sentence: *I was struck by.* . . . They describe, in particular, how struck they are by how serious Eagle Rock students are about learning and how self-directed they are. I then ask them to think about why this may be so. One answers that it must be because Eagle Rock students are excellent students, unlike City students. I remind her that Eagle Rock students are the ones who sat in the back of other classrooms until they dropped out or got kicked out of school. They are students who have not succeeded in traditional programs, have gotten themselves in trouble, haven't expected to complete their high school education. She shakes her head with some amazement and remarks that they seem like the best City students.

The group ruminates for a while about what conditions at Eagle Rock may allow formerly unsuccessful students to be so successful. They discuss the culture of the school, the wilderness trip, the feeling of community, the emphasis on service learning, and so on. Finally, one teacher ventures that the positive attitudes about learning they have observed may have something to do with curriculum. Another suggests that, in particular, knowing exactly what they need to do helps students be purposeful in learning. A third chimes in that the students see real value in what they are doing. A fourth says that maybe our students know what quality looks like and how to achieve it.

I suggest that our students feel some ownership for curriculum and see that they have power and control over at least some aspects of their learning. Then I return to the comment about curriculum and ask the group to think about how curriculum at City helps students know exactly what they need to do and why. I also ask them to think about how they as teachers can help their students understand what good work looks like. They venture a few ideas and then get discouraged, mostly because they have to cover the district curriculum and state standards. "We're not like you," one of them says. "We can't just make up curriculum. We have to teach required courses."

At this point I prompt them to think about what they could do to make the district curriculum their own. "What if," I ask, "you could customize the curriculum to your school, making sure to cover the district curriculum and be accountable for state standards?" They seem willing to consider this idea with more openness than skepticism.

"Then," says one of the two teachers who attended the service learning class that is building the amphitheater, "we could set up high-interest classes, like building something for the school and learning mathematics at the same time."

"I don't think we could get away with that," says the other. "There's no way we could build an outdoor amphitheater at City."

"Well, it wouldn't have to be an amphitheater," counters the first, "it could be something else entirely," at which point her colleague begins jotting some notes on her pad of paper.

I ask the group to what extent they want students to know the curriculum. "Would it be possible for all students to have a copy of what you expect?"

"It would cost a lot of money," someone says, but the teachers agree that the parent support group could raise the funds.

"Think about what it would mean if students were let in on exactly what they have to know and be able to do to graduate from City," I say.

"You know, we don't even know that ourselves," remarks one teacher. "We just assume that everyone is teaching the district curriculum. And we expect that if you pass all your classes you'll graduate. It might be interesting for us to chart exactly what we do expect students to know and be able to do . . . and share it with each other and see whether students who graduate can really do what we require."

A teacher who has attended the Pit and Pendulum class adds, "We could develop more interdisciplinary units if we knew what we all expected."

"I don't know how we can do this," a man who has participated in Hydroponics worries. "When are we going to find time for curriculum development like this?"

I look around the room for a minute, thinking that the conversation may shut down because of this critical barrier. I'm glad, however, that it hasn't shut down because someone doesn't see the value of our curriculum.

Finally, the other teacher who has participated in Hydroponics says, "The state has some money for technical assistance related to standards. Maybe we can apply for a grant."

The conversation quickly moves on to how City is going to develop its own school-based curriculum that references district standards (that, in turn, reference state standards) and how they are going to make the curriculum accessible to everyone—including students—rather than secret (and probably seldom consulted). Someone suggests that rubrics tied to the content standards would help students understand what quality is. I agree that developing rubrics is the logical second step in making curriculum accessible to students and giving them some power over their learning and that including students in the rubric process is a healthy way to start a conversation about what is "good enough." Then I reluctantly point them toward the cafeteria. It's time for lunch

The group from City spent the night in the guest bunkhouse at Eagle Rock and continued to discuss what they had learned and how they might apply it at their own school, whose students were considered highly "at risk." (I much prefer the phrase "placed at risk," because it takes the onus off the student and puts it on the environment that has affected that student in harmful ways.) The next day they asked the big, hard question: "How can we graduate students according to mastery of the curriculum rather than seat time?" I knew we'd need subsequent visits and broader City faculty involvement to tackle that question, but I was willing.

The point I'm making here is that the learning of this group of teachers was both cognitive and emotional—they were very moved by the successes of the Eagle Rock students, who like their own had struggled so hard and given up. This emotional connection would support them as they tried to make changes at City. Whenever they despaired, they could think back to something an Eagle Rock student said or showed them.

I invite you to visit Eagle Rock in person any time. Just let me know when. In the meantime, you can use the questions at the end of each chapter as your bridge between the Eagle Rock examples I offer and your own situation. These are the questions I might ask of visitors who are exploring curriculum with us at Eagle Rock.

You may want to read all or parts of Chapter 1 to find out more about Eagle Rock School and Professional Development Center. If you're more interested in the concepts of curriculum featured in this book than in our history, please read the sections in Chapter 1 about our culture and our curriculum overview. Those sections will be enough to help you understand Eagle Rock's application of the concepts as you focus on applying them yourself.

Chapter One

About Eagle Rock

Eagle Rock is a high school for students for whom success in traditional schools has been elusive and a professional development center where educators can study the school's methods. The school is year-round and residential, and all students receive full scholarships. The professional development center provides a variety of programs for educators. Both are located in Estes Park, Colorado.

History and Background

In May 1989, the American Honda Motor Company began investigating nontraditional ways to expand on the philanthropic contributions made through their community relations department and the American Honda Foundation. Thomas A. Dean, who holds a doctorate in education and helped design Honda's innovative technical and corporate education programs, and Makoto Itabashi, an engineer, crisscrossed America searching for an appropriate education initiative.

On April 12, 1990, American Honda approved the concept of a professional development school, a school for young people who had not been successful in conventional school settings and needed a fresh start in a new environment. The school would help these students become successful, productive members of society and at the same time further educators' research and professional development. To fund this initiative, the company established a nonprofit corporation, the American Honda Education Corporation (AHEd). This support from within the corporate structure rather than through a foundation is unique in the world of philanthropy and clearly demonstrates a strong level of commitment to social investment. Dean and Itabashi crisscrossed the country again, talking with educators, parents, students, and others who had an interest in restructuring high schools so that they better served young people. They collected recommendations that led to the general framework of the Eagle Rock School and Professional Development Center.

During 1991–92, AHEd hired Robert J. Burkhardt, Jr., Head of School; Sally Duncan Cummings, Director of Operations; John Oubre, Director of Students; Judy Gilbert, Director of Curriculum; and several instructors. It also found 640 acres near Estes Park, Colorado (a small mountain resort town about two hours northwest of Denver and an hour northwest of Boulder, and the gateway to the Rocky Mountain National Park), that had been reserved by the federal government for school use. The school is named after a prominent rock formation adjacent to the property, which resembles an eagle in profile. A governing board composed of Honda employees oversees the school much as a district board oversees a school district. The executive director of the board, Tom Dean, visits Eagle Rock every other week.

In the fall of 1993, the school opened unofficially with sixteen students, two and a half buildings, a set of thematic underpinnings, and a general curricular concept. As the school grew that year, so did its culture, its programs, and its curriculum—and the students participated in the development processes. In the fall of 1994, when the school held its official grand opening, most of the buildings were finished, and the school culture and curriculum had been considerably refined. In the spring of 1995, the first two students graduated. As of August 2001, there are sixty-seven graduates; approximately half of them are enrolled in colleges or universities, the others are working (sometimes to finance higher education), in the armed forces, or in service organizations like the California Conservation Corps or Public Allies. Two Eagle Rock alumni have college degrees; one is now enrolled in a graduate program in social work.

The Professional Development Center hosts as many as two hundred events a year, welcoming as many as two thousand visitors to the facility. These visitors become immersed in the school, learning both cognitively and emotionally what it feels like to be a student at Eagle Rock. They take their learning with them, reforming specific elements of their own environment, restructuring their educational programs. Although not designed to be replicated, Eagle Rock has influenced the design of numerous alternative schools, high school alternative programs, and charter schools. What is most remarkable about the Professional Development Center is how its activities serve Eagle Rock School as a mirror, allowing continuous assessment and evaluation. Visitors, through their comments and questions, keep the school involved in the continual development found in thriving organizations of any kind.

Eagle Rock has grown very quickly. It is a fully accredited school (both with the North Central Accrediting Agency and the Association of Colorado Independent Schools, which is affiliated with the National Association of Independent Schools) with a full complement of students and an expanding group of graduates. The Professional Development Center continues to help any number of professional educators realize their dreams.

The Students

Eagle Rock's students are between the ages of fifteen and twenty-one and have one thing in common: they did not expect to graduate from high school. They have sat in the back of classroom after classroom, disengaged or belligerent. Many have dropped out or been expelled, sometimes from several schools, several times, before coming to Eagle Rock. Apart from that, Eagle Rock students share the diversity found in any American high school. As shown in Figure 1.1, about half the students are male, half female. About half come from Colorado, the other half from elsewhere in the United States. Some of them come from fully functional and caring families; others have been abused, neglected, or abandoned or are the products of messy divorces. Some have turned to drugs or alcohol in their lives; others have not. Some have run away or joined gangs; some have committed petty crimes. A few students initially make a commitment to come to Eagle Rock because they are facing boot camp or jail; most make the commitment without these imposed incentives.

Many Eagle Rock students have been labeled in their previous schools: ADD, ADHD, special education, LD, gifted and talented, dyslexic. Some have not. Some had low skills in reading and writing and mathematics before coming to Eagle Rock. Others were adept students, earning high grades but not sure they were learning anything. Nevertheless, Eagle Rock is a high school, not a therapy or rehabilitation center; students admitted to Eagle Rock must have dealt with their addictions and addressed emotional and psychological issues before enrolling. Once admitted, however, students receive support as they continue to stay sober or nonaddicted or as they continue to work through their issues.

Head of school Robert Burkhardt describes Eagle Rock students this way: "Imagine a continuum. At one end are the students guaranteed from birth a spot at Harvard and probably editorship of the *Law Review*,

Gender	
Males	46
Females	34
Total	80
Racial/Ethnic Composition	
White	44
Latino/Latina	10
Native American	1
Multi-racial	11
Asian	2
African American	12
Geographic Distribution	
Arkansas	1
California	18
Colorado	28
Connecticut	1
Delaware	1
Florida	2
Illinois	1
Maryland	1
Massachusetts	1
Michigan	2
Nevada	1
New Mexico	3
New York	10
Ohio	1
Oregon	3
Texas	3
Virginia	1
Washington	1
Wyoming	1

Figure 1.1   Student Demographics (As of May 2001)

too. At the other end are students guaranteed a bunk at Folsom Prison. If Harvard is 0 and Folsom is 100, our students are between 60 and 80." In part, this profile stems from the presence of the Professional Development Center—educators need to see whether techniques work with the most difficult-to-reach students.

Admissions Process

Eagle Rock admits students between the ages of fifteen and seventeen. There is no cost to students and their families, or to the schools or districts the students come from. In Colorado, students are admitted through districts that have established a partnership with Eagle Rock, agreeing to screen students and take them through the admissions process. (Before Eagle Rock was accredited, these districts also reviewed our graduates to see whether they qualified for a district or high school diploma—they all did.) Out-of-state students are admitted through community groups such as Boys and Girls Clubs; schools and/or districts; or direct contact.

Students are admitted three times a year. They complete applications, including letters in which they and an adult in their lives (students need either a parent or a sponsor to support them actively while they are at Eagle Rock) write about why they think Eagle Rock is the right school for them. There is no waiting list at Eagle Rock; each student's application is considered against all other applications for that admissions date, and students who do not get admitted for one admissions date may reapply for the next. Often, Eagle Rock admissions counselors give students work to do before they reapply: take a class at a community college, get a job, try to give up cigarettes, get counseling, go through a drug or alcohol rehabilitation program, get up before noon. Students sometimes are good applicants, just not quite ready.

Students who fit the profile and seem ready to make a commitment are interviewed in person; those who remain promising candidates for admission are then brought to the school for three days and nights. As prospective students, they are mentored by and live the life of an Eagle Rock student. They do KP (kitchen patrol), go to classes, do service work, sweat through 6 A.M. exercise sessions, and take a hike that previews the wilderness trip. In addition, they meet in small groups and one-to-one with the admissions counselors. In these meetings they are asked if they are prepared to give up their addictions, leave their cars at home, forgo "hanging out," be in residence twenty-four hours a day seven days a week, go to school during the summer, get serious, and give up partying. Prospective students get a chance to live the life of Eagle Rock and decide whether it's right for them— and Eagle Rock students and staff members get a chance to observe students in action and gauge their level of commitment.

Ultimately, admissions decisions come down to four considerations:

1. Has the student enough commitment to—even passion for— change to be admitted to Eagle Rock? (The admissions counselors,

students, and staff can tell if someone else—often Mom, Dad, or another adult—is the one with the commitment.)

2. Does the student really understand what Eagle Rock is—and is not? (Students who think Eagle Rock is a fun summer camp or Club Med of the Rockies are in for a shock.) In other words, does the student see Eagle Rock as a place in which change can happen?

3. How does admitting this student affect desired demographics in terms of race or ethnicity, gender, economics, and geography (i.e., is he or she from an urban, suburban, or rural location? from Colorado or elsewhere?)?

4. What other options does this student have? Eagle Rock is more likely to admit students who have few or no other options than a student who has other resources to tap.

School Culture

The culture at Eagle Rock is essentially that of a community in which everyone has a central role to play to ensure learning. The term *learning community* has become a cliché, but that term, indeed, describes Eagle Rock culture. Four elements in the culture help make Eagle Rock a learning community:

1. Philosophy and beliefs.
2. Structures.
3. Governance.
4. Activities.

Philosophy

Early in the development of Eagle Rock, Tom Dean, Mak Itabashi, and the staff identified critical themes for the school centering around citizenship and individual integrity (see Figure 1.2). The goal of the school was also determined at that point: "To graduate students who have the desire and are prepared to make a difference in the world." During the planning year while the buildings were being erected, the founding group tried to work with the themes as the basis of curriculum. Finding the eight themes unwieldy, they translated them into five expectations (see Figure 1.3). Later, as the school began to consider applications for admission, the eight themes and the five expectations were converted into a set of ten commitments students needed to make in order to enroll (see Figure 1.4). With the exception of commitments 1 and 10,

Individual Integrity
Intellectual discipline
Physical fitness
Spiritual development
Aesthetic expression

Citizenship
Service to others
Cross-cultural understanding
Democratic governance
Environmental stewardship

Figure 1.2   Eight Themes

which capture crucial cultural elements, the commitments bear a direct relationship to the themes and the expectations.

(A word about commitments 1 and 10. Living in respectful harmony with others is critical in any residential setting, especially one bringing together adolescents, especially adolescents whose lives have not been particularly harmonious. And although few adults have a fully developed personal moral and ethical code and fewer live by one, at least consistently, a school that purports to graduate students who will make a difference in the world must at least challenge students to begin to develop such a code. It is work worth doing.)

These themes, expectations, and commitments are captured in the five-element "misequation" that has become the set of principles that governs the school: 8 + 5 = 10. Described as "bad math but good education" by Judy Gilbert, to whom this book is dedicated, this formula lives at Eagle Rock. It is not just a plaque on the wall—indeed, there *isn't* a plaque bearing this formula anywhere in sight. But every student knows the eight themes, five expectations, and ten commitments (which they have pledged to uphold) from the minute they enter Eagle Rock as a student. Staff members know them as well, weaving the

Developing an expanding knowledge base
Communicating effectively
Creating and making healthy life choices
Participating as an engaged global citizen
Providing leadership for justice

Figure 1.3   Five Expectations

Live in respectful harmony with others
Develop mind, body, and spirit
Learn to communicate in speech and writing
Serve the community—Eagle Rock and other broader ones
Become a steward of the planet
Make healthy personal choices
Find and develop the artist inside
Increase capacity to exercise leadership for justice
Practice citizenship and democratic living
Devise an enduring moral and ethical code

Figure 1.4   Ten Commitments

ideas embedded in the principles into learning. (*Hamlet* from the point of view of "developing a personal moral and ethical code" is a rich read!) Head of school Robert Burkhardt challenges students to apply 8 + 5 = 10 during community meetings, especially when he reads a story or news item and demands to know the "8 + 5 = 10" implied in the reading. When a student says, "That's an example of being a steward of the planet," Burkhardt returns, "How so?" and the student must support the answer. A student who has committed one of the non-negotiables (no alcohol, no drugs, no violence, no tobacco, no sexual relations) embedded in the commitments understands the consequences in those terms (i.e., they have broken a commitment to live in respectful harmony or make healthy life choices). Thus, these known and practiced values orient everyone at Eagle Rock toward being part of a learning community.

Structures

A variety of structures also helps. Eagle Rock is intentionally small. At capacity we can take no more than ninety-six students. Like many restructuring schools ("getting small" is one of Ted Sizer's ten common principles), Eagle Rock recognizes the value of smallness and personalization. If you're in a large school, getting small may seem impossible, but many have been able to figure out ways—without significant increases in staff or funding—to break students and staff into small enough groups for personalized learning: schools within a school, houses, families, teams. Some schools even close and then reopen as "pocket" schools rather than the big and impersonal behemoths they were before. Philadelphia's inner city Essential Schools have been broken into charters, each with a specialty, to which students and staff elect to belong.

Twenty-four full-time staff members, ranging from the head of school to the head of maintenance, work with these ninety-six students, twenty-four hours a day, seven days a week, forty-two weeks out of the year.[1] Twelve interns and several undergraduate and graduate practicum teachers also work with students each year. The ratio of staff to students is about the same as that at a traditional high school, if one counts all the kitchen, maintenance, administrative, and support staff. The difference at Eagle Rock is that everyone teaches or works directly with students no matter the job title.

Students and staff (even visitors) can assemble in several purposefully designed "community spaces" at Eagle Rock. An important one is the hearth, around which the morning gathering takes place. Sitting tightly together on the floor, students and staff begin the day as a community. Debbie Meier, former principal of New York City's Central Park East Secondary School, commented in her book *The Power of Their Ideas* (1995) that no staff should be larger than the number that can be seated at the same table. The Eagle Rock staff can sit together (tightly) around a large donut-shaped conference table in the Professional Development Center.

Though there are subgroups among the students (a recent standoff between the Caves, who like meat, and the Veggies, who like vegetarian entrees, proved that), these subgroups change regularly. The smallness of the school eliminates the need students in more populous settings have to identify with a smaller group in order to be known and noticed. And although staff groups form according to primary responsibility (maintenance, administration, instruction, nutrition), staff members come together regularly, teaching and working with students and trying to help them succeed.

Classrooms and seminar rooms feature solid round or donut-shaped tables. Round tables promote community in several ways. First, everyone can see everyone else. Participation in all its forms (an essential aspect of community) is visible to all members of the group. Second, round tables facilitate dialogue and discussion much better than desks in rows. Third, they equalize the group; no one is at the head of the classroom. Fourth, they help everyone in the class take responsibility for one another's learning. Students at Eagle Rock become more than self-directed learners; they also notice when someone else fails to understand, and they work together to help everyone at the table learn. Students, especially new students, sometimes

---

1. Eagle Rock regularly experiments with elements of schooling that might help young people learn better. In September 2000 we changed our schedule. Since the results of the change are not yet evident, references in this book are to the forty-two-week schedule.

complain that there is no "back of the classroom," where they used to hide, but we think that's a benefit!

Governance, Power, and Authority

Everyone at Eagle Rock goes by his or her first name—*everyone*. Although it might seem that this unconventional form of address would breed disrespect, the opposite seems to happen. For all students, but especially for those who have had trouble with authority, using an adult's first name removes a barrier. It levels the playing field rather than suggesting that some are more deserving of a title than others. Also, there are no privileged corner offices with closed doors. All administrator and staff member desks are out in the open. The noise level and commotion are intense sometimes, but we get a much more accurate reading of the pulse of the school than we would if sequestered.

Administrators make final decisions about curriculum, discipline, budget, and other key aspects of the school, but not without considerable input from students and staff. For example, Judy Gilbert, Eagle Rock's first director of curriculum, could have concocted Eagle Rock's curriculum on her own. It certainly would have been a lot more expedient. Instead, she chose to have faculty members develop curriculum and then review and revise it in cross-discipline three-member teams. The resulting document is truly the school's and known well by everyone in the school. Linda Sand Guest, now director of curriculum, has continued these traditions. Each staff member develops a plan for each budget year, forecasts the funds necessary to carry out the plan, and submits the plan and budget to one of the administrators. Final budget decisions are made in conversations between staff members and administrators; items are not slashed behind closed doors.

When a student has violated a nonnegotiable condition, the student comes before the community in a community meeting. Questions and answers clarify for the entire community what has happened, and everyone is invited to send director of students Philbert Smith a recommendation regarding the consequences. Individual opinions from students and staff pour in via e-mailed and handwritten notes, but Philbert often calls a group together to help him arrive at a decision, which is then announced and discussed in another community meeting. Like Judy's process, Philbert's is time consuming and messy but worthwhile in terms of creating community.

Proposal writing is a critical, empowering aspect of community. Eagle Rock runs on proposals. Each member of the community, student or staff, may write a proposal to improve something about the school—use of time, use of space, activities, etc. Staff members are always looking for opportunities for students to become more self-directed, so when a student makes a viable suggestion, the project is almost always given a green light. Proposals have been written—and approved—for a climbing wall, an outdoor volleyball court, a mural in one of the student houses, and similar things that individuals thought would make a difference in the quality of learning at Eagle Rock. The learning and responsibility that characterize proposal writing are important, but the feeling of power within the community is also critical. Students feel they can do something to improve their environment.

Any staff member may submit an agenda item for a staff meeting. Thus, the agenda is formed by the whole school, rather than by the head of school alone. Each staff meeting begins with "one-minute" issues or solutions individuals want to raise or offer. Then, staff members select agenda items they want to discuss (not necessarily their own) until all items are dealt with.

Formal student governance is embodied in Peer Council, a group of students elected by the student body. Problems are referred to the council, and the council decides how to resolve them. Sometimes the problems have to do with student behavior—being late for class, for example—but sometimes they concern aspects of the school that can be improved. In addition, several students are trained in peace mediation and help others negotiate fair settlements. Sometimes, a loose group of students and staff addresses an important issue together (how kitchen patrol can be run more effectively, for example). The group presents issues and solutions to the entire community at a community meeting and then disbands.

Finally, leadership opportunities abound. As the 8 + 5 = 10 precepts suggest, leadership is an important aspect of life at Eagle Rock. Students can belong to Peer Council and informal issues groups; be a peace mediator, KP crew leader, or house leader; and serve on any number of committees (the morning exercise committee, the intramural committee, and the professional development advisory committee are just a few examples).

Activities

The school schedule purposefully sets aside times for meeting as a community. The more informal daily thirty-minute morning gatherings are replaced by an hour-long formal community meeting every Wednesday morning. Every Wednesday evening the whole community gathers again, as a whole community, in gender groups (male students and staff members meeting separately from female students and staff members), or in house groups (students and staff members connected to each dormitory). And, because the school is small and the schedule flexible, an instant community meeting can be called whenever an issue or a need arises.

Morning gathering begins with "a gift to the community." This gift might be a poem, story, or article that a student or staff member shares. It might be a presentation. It might also be a game or a serious discussion of an issue. Gathering continues with announcements that keep us connected, let us know what's going on, and ends with everyone singing. "We rely on an oral tradition," head of school Robert Burkhardt comments, "and that's what keeps us community."

Community meeting includes announcements and singing, but also features greeting one another in thirty different languages, the reading of a poem, and a discussion (often around a story, article, or current event) of the principles and values that govern Eagle Rock. Graduating students present drafts of their moral and ethical codes and ask for feedback. Community meeting might also include the Wonderful Wacky World of Words for Wednesday, a lively vocabulary activity. The librarian shares books new to the library, and the head of school tosses out paperbacks students can keep. ("Anything to get them reading," he says.) Finally, letters from former students, staff members, and interns and friends of Eagle Rock are read aloud to connect us over time.

Gender meetings and house meetings, like gathering, are mostly student led. Gender meetings are an opportunity for students to get together in same-sex groups to discuss issues and build community. Recent women's meetings have featured a member of the community (beginning with the oldest) telling her life story. L'Tanya Perkins, admissions associate, says, "Our students don't get the stories they need, being away from home, and they need stories to learn how to be women." House meetings allow students to solve problems related to living together in a very small dormitory space.

Service activities, in which people unite in doing something greater than they could accomplish as individuals, both within and beyond Eagle Rock boundaries, also promote community. Each student averages five hundred hours of service each year. On-campus service includes KP and a special class in which students tackle an Eagle Rock improvement project. Grafitti and trash are all but nonexistent at Eagle Rock because students and staff members are invested in taking care of where they live and learn. Three times a year students and staff do volunteer work in Estes Park and wider Colorado venues, in an event called EagleServe, which is scheduled for a two-day period before the beginning of a trimester. Finally, some academic classes are built around service. Recently, students designed and built a nature center at a nearby national historic site, along the way learning about animals and plants in the Rocky Mountains.

Rituals and community go hand in hand. When students return from their wilderness trip, they are formally welcomed into the community with a ceremony in which they share skits about their adventure and receive an Eagle Rock shirt. Students are recognized at the weekly community meeting for being "three-P [punctuality, preparedness, and participation] superstars." This award has come to symbolize the real progress a student has made at Eagle Rock. The clapping, especially for students who are receiving it after months or years of avoiding these expectations, is loud, boisterous, and heartily meant. The presentations of learning (POLs) held at the end of every trimester are also rituals of celebration. Other end-of-trimester rituals strengthen community as well; a forty-five-minute slide-and-music show, for example, helps us all recall the events of the trimester and laugh or cry about them again. Even the tongue-in-cheek Eagle Awards promote community.

The School Program

The best way to understand the program at Eagle Rock School is to look at how the school organizes time (see Figure 1.5). The twelve-month school year is divided into three trimesters, each fourteen weeks long. Breaks between trimesters are from two to three weeks for students and one to two weeks for staff members. Each trimester is broken down into two six-week blocks of classes, separated by an "explore" week and followed by a week devoted to student presentations of learning. Each six-week block of classes features three class periods and a fourth "engaged learning" period during which students pursue their own work and staff members are able to meet with students or with one another to develop curriculum, plan classes, or evaluate student work. Some classes are two periods long, in which case students take only two classes during the six-week block. Some classes extend over both blocks and are twelve weeks long.

Eagle Rock admits students three times a year—in September, January, and May. New students have a slightly different schedule than continuing students. They spend the first three weeks of their first trimester getting ready for the required wilderness trip. As part of this preparation, students learn about Eagle Rock, develop group skills, begin to work on their personal issues, learn how to survive in the wilderness, and get themselves in shape through conditioning hikes and bike rides. Then they spend three weeks in the wilderness, hiking and setting up camps each night during the first week, combining their hikes with service projects the second week, and doing a three-day solo and a final service project the third week. All three weeks

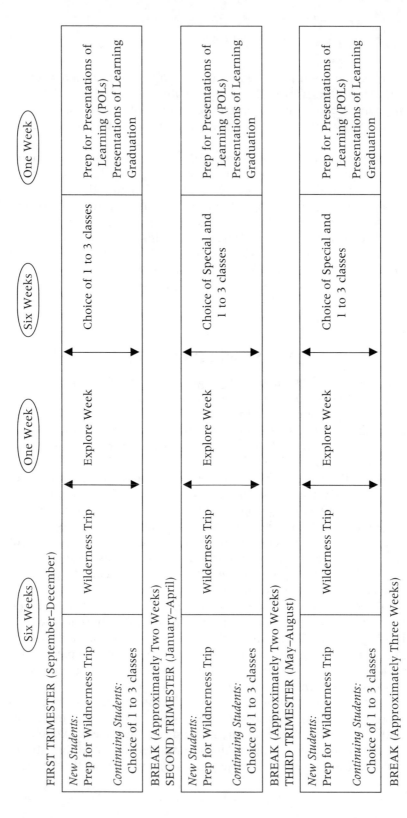

Figure 1.5 Academic Year Calendar

feature some academic learning, usually centered around plants and animals. Students also keep journals during the wilderness trip. They run the last six miles of the trek (minus their sixty-pound packs) onto the Eagle Rock campus, where they are formally welcomed into the community. During the continuing students' explore week, new students debrief their wilderness trip, clean up their equipment and supplies, and prepare to give their first individual presentation of learning (five minutes focused on what they learned academically and personally on the wilderness trip) to the community.

During explore week, students take one class for the entire week, often taught by a visiting artist. Classes range from silversmithing to glassblowing, from taking a bike trip to writing poetry, from a service project in the California wilderness to batik. At the end of explore week, students (individually or as a class) make a "mini" presentation of learning to the community.

Regular presentations of learning are given during the last week of each trimester. These POLs are a half hour in length, fifteen minutes of presentation and fifteen minutes of question-and-answer. The presentations are made to a panel of people from outside Eagle Rock and to members of the community. Students are charged with making a case for themselves as learners—demonstrating that they have grown both academically and personally. They prepare packets for panel members in advance and are given evaluations of these packets, as well as of the POL, by the panel members.

Eagle Rock also graduates students three times a year, with students petitioning to graduate during the trimester before they expect to complete their graduation requirements. If they complete all of their work to mastery level (which we call proficiency), they give an hour-long graduation POL—thirty minutes of presentation and thirty minutes of question-and-answer—to the entire community. They are allowed to select their own panel members. This POL is an incredible rite of passage, well thought out and executed, of very high caliber.

The Daily Schedule

The daily schedule (see Figure 1.6) illustrates how the program is implemented. Students rise early; breakfast KP and/or morning exercise (which may be running the steps on campus, swimming, or aerobics) begins at 6:00. The entire community comes together at gathering on Monday, Tuesday, Thursday, and Friday or at community meeting on Wednesday. Classes are ninety minutes long, with the exception of first period, which is fifteen minutes shorter each day but has an extra session on Wednesday. Students do lunch KP or house (dormitory) cleanup at noon and then go to third period. During fourth

	Monday	Tuesday	Wednesday	Thursday	Friday	Saturday
Time 6:00	KP	KP	KP/Exercise	KP	KP	7:00 KP
6:30–7:00	Exercise	Exercise		Exercise	Exercise	7:30–7:50 Breakfast
7:00–7:20	Breakfast	Breakfast	Breakfast	Breakfast	Breakfast	8:30–9:30 Current Events
8:00–8:20	Gathering	Gathering	8:00–8:50 Community Meeting	Gathering	Gathering	
8:30–9:45	Period 1	Period 1		Period 1	Period 1	9:45–11:30 Saturday Seminars
10:00–11:30	Period 2	Period 2	9:00–10:00 Period 1	Period 2	Period 2	
11:45–12:30	Choir	Choir	10:15–12:30 Staff & Student Meetings	Choir	Choir	11:45–1:30 KP/Hse Cleanup
12:20–2:00	KP	KP		KP	KP	12:15–12:45 Lunch
1:20–2:15	Lunch	Lunch	11:30 KP	Lunch	Lunch	1:00 Activities (Sunday: Brunch KP 9:30 Brunch 10:30–11:00 Dinner KP 4:00 Dinner 5:00–5:30)
1:20–2:15	House Cleanup/ Band	House Cleanup/ Band	12:00–12:30 Lunch	House Cleanup/ Band	House Cleanup/ Band	
2:30–4:00	Period 3	Period 3		Period 3	Period 3	
4:00–5:30	Period 4: Engaged Time/ IS-Interns Planning and Student Meetings	Period 4: Engaged Time/ IS-Interns Planning and Student Meetings	1:30–2:30 Advisories OR 1:30–4:30 Intramurals	Period 4: Engaged Time/ IS-Interns Planning and Student Meetings	Period 4: Engaged Time/ IS-Interns Planning and Student Meetings	
4:30	KP	KP	KP	KP	KP	KP
5:30–6:00	Dinner	Dinner	Dinner	Dinner	Dinner	Dinner
7:00	Activities	Activities	Weds Events	Activities	Activities	Activities
9:00	Quiet Time/ Cleanup	Quiet Time/ Cleanup	Quiet Time/ Cleanup	Quiet Time/ Cleanup	Quiet Time/ Cleanup	10:30 In Houses
9:30	In Houses Curfew	In Houses Curfew	In Houses Curfew	In Houses Curfew	In Houses Curfew	11:00 Wing Curfew
10:00	Wing Curfew	Wing Curfew	Wing Curfew	Wing Curfew	Wing Curfew	

*1:30–2:30 Tuesday—Intern Learning Seminar; 1:30–2:30 alternating Thursdays—IS Meeting

Figure 1.6 Daily Schedule

period, students work on their own projects or meet with individual teachers; staff members attend planning meetings.

The Wednesday schedule is a bit different, with a longer morning meeting and the hour-long first period, followed by time for meetings and individual work. The Wednesday-afternoon advisories are for special activities like goal setting, solving academic problems, selecting classes, preparing the POL packet, rehearsing the POL, reading together, or addressing personal issues. Intramurals are an important part of the program at Eagle Rock, partly because Eagle Rock does not participate in interscholastic sports and partly because the separate dormitories provide a structure in which students can learn both cooperation and competition through sports.

Saturday morning events include a lively current events contest, something like *Jeopardy*. After listening to a National Public Radio news broadcast, reading a newspaper, or watching a news broadcast on television, student houses compete to provide the questions for a variety of answers staff members create based on what has just been listened to, read, or watched. Then, students take a "Saturday seminar," a special class that is often less academic than those offered during the week: they may learn drumming or aikido; they may work on a service project, such as painting murals in a day care center; if nearly ready to graduate, they may focus on writing their major research paper or designing their graduation POL. The rest of the weekend, except for KP responsibilities, is devoted to activities ranging from outdoor sports to concerts and museum trips.

KP and house cleanup are the tip of the iceberg in terms of learning to serve at Eagle Rock. Students may handle logistics at an Estes Park festival or clean out a tin-can dump at a local music camp in order to learn to serve. They also serve to learn through integrated service learning classes, which combine service with an academic area. For example, students learned civics and mathematics while building a playground for the nearby town of Lyons—civics because they interviewed townspeople about how a town works and mathematics because they had to design the playground using mathematical computations and geometry. Other integrated service learning projects have included building a fishing pier for the handicapped on Lake Estes, refinishing a deck on the Chamber of Commerce's visitor center, and remodeling the interior of a sliding-scale medical clinic.

The Professional Development Center

In addition to regularly scheduled tours on Wednesdays and Saturdays, Eagle Rock sponsors a variety of professional development activities, most custom designed. Educators may visit for as little as half a day to glimpse what is happening at Eagle Rock or as many as ten days to plan an alternative school. Sometimes educators hold a retreat at Eagle Rock; sometimes they come to engage in a specific learning experience, such as how to launch POLs in their own setting. Eagle Rock also hosts meetings and workshops, if they are sufficiently related to Eagle Rock's mission. Educators come alone or in homogeneous or heterogeneous groups. Undergraduate and graduate university classes also visit Eagle Rock.

Activities for educators always include time with students during which the students are the teachers. Students at Eagle Rock have very powerful voices and little hesitation in sharing what works (and does not work) at Eagle Rock as well as what worked and did not in their former school experiences. After an orientation and a tour, visitors may shadow students or simply visit a number of classes. Eagle Rock may set up special workshops or seminars related to questions visitors have about restructuring schools. Sometimes Eagle Rock convenes students and staff to hold panel discussions about some topic of interest to visiting educators. When visitors want to learn about service and education, they usually take part in a student service project.

Student contact is critical. Given the profile of Eagle Rock students, many visitors to the Professional Development Center expect to encounter belligerence or indifference and are amazed by what they find instead. They exclaim about the courtesy extended them, the engagement of the students, and the real insights these formerly unsuccessful high school students offer about education. At the very least they say, "Why, these are ordinary students. You could find these students in any high school in America." They are ready to learn from Eagle Rock.

Learning happens when visitors concede their "yabbuts" ("Yabbut, you're in the Rocky Mountains"; "Yabbut, you have Honda's backing") and seriously consider what applies in their own setting. Visitors learn the most when they suspend their judgment and exercise their imagination. Debriefings help. Most educators who visit Eagle Rock take away with them at least one concrete idea, such as using presentations of learning. Many go beyond the concrete to understand the abstract reasons—the relationships, the culture, the program, and the curriculum—why Eagle Rock succeeds with young people who have not met with success before.

The Eagle Rock Professional Development Center also sponsors twelve interns, recent college graduates who work with or are considering working with young people. They intern for a year, receiving a stipend and room and board. Many go on to graduate school in education or a related field or become involved in community service organizations or outdoors programs that work with youth. Quite a few begin careers in traditional or alternative educational settings. Eagle Rock also hosts student teachers and undergraduate and graduate student researchers.

The Curriculum

The Eagle Rock curriculum, like most others, is represented by a curriculum guide. The version referenced in this book is draft 10, but earlier versions exist and later versions will be created. Eagle Rock's curriculum will always be a draft because staff members believe that curriculum needs to change as the needs and experiences of students and teachers change. Version 10 contains the requisite introductory pages and then introduces the individualized learning plan, or ILP (see Figure 1.7, pp. 20–21), the essence of the curriculum. Different from an individualized education plan, or IEP, as used in special education, Eagle Rock's ILP is both the official list of what students need to know and do (and how to document their learning) and our version of a transcript.

What counts at Eagle Rock are the competencies required for graduation. Classes are merely vehicles for helping students achieve the competencies, so we do not keep track of classes on the ILP. (We do, however, keep reports on the competencies students have mastered in each class, so student portfolios do include a record of which classes they've taken.) As you examine the ILP, you'll notice that the competencies or graduation requirements, which relate to academic growth as well as to personal growth, are preceded by a box. Each competency is followed by a list of items preceded by lines. Each of these items, when achieved with a level of mastery we call proficient, documents that a student has learned the content and skills required by the competency. When students have presented documentation at the required level of mastery, they receive a check for it. When each documentation for a graduation requirement has been checked, the appropriate box is darkened. When all boxes are darkened, a student is ready to petition to graduate.

Figure 1.8 (pp. 22–24) shows sample pages from the curriculum guide relative to English. The big-picture items—standards/concepts/goals—are described at the top of the first page. (The letters and numbers in parentheses refer to the Colorado State Reading and Writing Model Content Standards.) On the left below the big-picture items is the list of documentations through which students are expected to demonstrate mastery; this list matches the list on the ILP. On the right, the learning students are expected to demonstrate is made explicit. The

☐ **AIDS Awareness**
  ___ Service Project
  ___ Presentation of learning

☐ **American Government/Civics**
  ___ American Government
    ___ Presentation—close-up (optional)
    ___ Project—national issues
    ___ Project—historical foundations
    ___ Project—laws
    ___ Interview write-up
  ___ Civics
    ___ Project—citizen responsibilities
    ___ Report—citizenship action
    ___ Action plan for change
    ___ Report—public policy action

☐ **American History**
  ___ Project—historical event (2)
  ___ Project—current event (2)
  ___ Project—hypothesis

☐ **Art** (3 of 4 focus areas required)
  ___ Art history portfolio
  ___ Fine arts portfolio
  ___ Crafts portfolio
  ___ Artserve/Eagle Art portfolio

☐ **Environmental Science**
  ___ Local issues
    ___ Composition
    ___ Presentation
  ___ National issues
    ___ Composition
    ___ Presentation
  ___ Global issues
    ___ Composition
    ___ Presentation
  ___ Environmental impact project
  ___ Written reflection

☐ **ERS Orientation**
  ___ Presentation—8 + 5 = 10
  ___ Group-work journal entries
  ___ Service projects
  ___ Wilderness preparedness

☐ **ERS Transition**
  ___ Food service skills
  ___ Information access literacy
  ___ Student success skills

☐ **Food Service**
  ___ Safety sanitation quiz
  ___ Two trimesters crew leader
  ___ Prepared meals—last trimester (2)

☐ **Human Performance**
  ___ Personal health/fitness
    ___ Personal health/fitness plan
    ___ Implementation plan
    ___ Personal health portfolio
    ___ Presentation
  ___ Activities (2 + Aikido)
    ___ Aikido
    ___ Activity Presentations (2)
    ___ Skills evaluation (3)
    ___ Service
  ___ Safety
    ___ Emergency Action
    ___ Performance
    ___ CPR Skills
    ___ First Aid Skills
    ___ Aquatic Skills

☐ **Lifeskills**
  ___ Career Development
    ___ Interest portfolio
    ___ Business letter
    ___ Cover letter
    ___ Résumé
    ___ Job/college interview
    ___ Lifeskills portfolio
    ___ Portfolio of possibilities

☐ **Science**
  ___ Beginning portfolios (2)
  ___ Developing portfolios (2)
  ___ Accomplished portfolios (2)

☐ **Service Learning**
  ___ Portfolio of projects
    ___ Written work—project
    ___ Written work—philosophy
  ___ Legacy project

☐ **Technology**
  ___ 30 WPM keyboarding
  ___ Word processing portfolio
  ___ Multimedia presentation
  ___ Electronic resource portfolio

☐ **Wilderness Trip**
  ___ Journal entries
  ___ Solo "letter to myself"
  ___ Wilderness POL

☐ **World History**
  ___ Project—historical event (2)
  ___ Project—current event (2)
  ___ Project—hypothesis

□ **English**

    Writing

    ____ Essay of explanation

    ____ Essay of explanation in lit class

    ____ Essay of opposing ideas

    ____ Interview

    ____ Review (independent book)

    ____ Review (movie/CD/show/
restaurant)

    ____ Creative writing (lit class if
possible)

    ____ Autobiography (POL packet)

    ____ Major research project

    Literature

    ____ Literature discussion skills

    ____ Participant (4)

    ____ Leader (2)

    Distribution requirements

    ____ Genres (3)

    ____ Time periods (3)

    ____ Cultures (3)

    Independent reading

    ____ 10 books

    ____ Self-description as reader

    Grammer and usage

    ____ Class/test/evidence

□ **Foreign Language**

    (Spanish/French/Other)

    ____ French—basic

    ____ Portfolio Level I

    ____ Portfolio Level II

    ____ Spanish—basic

    ____ Portfolio Level I

    ____ Portfolio Level II

    ____ Spanish for Native Speakers

    ____ Portfolio Level I

    ____ Portfolio Level II

    ____ Other:

□ **Geography**

    ____ Project—physical geography

    ____ Project—own culture

    ____ Project—comparing cultures

□ **Mathematics**

    ____ Beginning portfolios (4)

    ____ Developing portfolios (4)

    ____ Accomplished portfolios (4)

    OR

    ____ Seven (7) accomplished portfolios

□ **Music**

    ____ Project—music history

    ____ Project—music theory

    ____ Presentations (4)

    ____ Performances (band/choir)

    ____ Musical (optional)

□ **Performance**

    ____ Public performances (2)

    ____ Rehearsal periods (2)

□ **Personal Growth**

    ____ Portfolio I

    ____ Portfolio II

    ____ Presentation

□ **Presentations of Learning**

    ER____ ER____

    ER____ ER____

    ER____ ER____

ELECTIVES (optional)

□ _____

□ _____

□ _____

□ _____

□ _____

□ _____

□ _____

□ _____

□ _____

Figure 1.7 Individualized Learning Plan (ILP)

STANDARDS/CONCEPTS/GOALS

- Literature (poetry and prose) is an expression of human experience. (Reading and Writing Model Content Standard 6)
- The ability to discuss responses to a piece of literature with people who hold varying viewpoints is a vital life skill. (RW 6)
- In order to understand what is read, connections must be made between the reading and what the reader already knows. (RW 1)
- Reading, comprehension, and word recognition strategies can be used to understand a variety of materials. (RW 1)
- Writing enhances thinking and understanding. (RWs 2 and 4)
- Growth in reading and writing skills occurs when readers and writers evaluate the quality of their reading and writing and work toward improvement by reading and writing every day. (RWs 1, 3, 4, and 5)
- Information is available from a variety of print, media, and technological sources. (RW 5)
- Writing is a process that includes a series of activities rather than a one-shot-I'm-done effort. These activities include generating ideas, creating a draft, revising the work, editing for clarity, and proofreading for accuracy. (RW 2)
- Each form of writing has its own techniques and requirements. (RW 4)
- Effective decisions regarding word choice, sentence structure, and organization of a written piece are made if the writer has a clearer purpose for the writing and a specific audience in mind. (RW 2)
- Appropriate forms of grammar/usage, mechanics/punctuation, and spelling must be used in formal verbal and written communication. (RW 3)

Documentation (Product)	Learning to Be Demonstrated
WRITING - Essay of explanation - Essay of explanation in literature class - Essay of opposing ideas - Interview - Review of a book read outside of class - Review of a movie, CD, restaurant, or performance - Creative writing - Autobiography (POL packet)	- Ability to explain an issue, concept, or process clearly by supporting oneself with detailed examples - Ability to support a theory about a work of literature through close analysis of the text - Ability to argue both sides of an issue through detailed examples without taking a position - Ability to show confidence and clear communication in a professional setting

Figure 1.8 Sample English Curriculum Guide

Figure 1.8 *continued*

MAJOR RESEARCH PROJECT	**Learning to Be Demonstrated**
LITERATURE • Four (4) discussion rubrics completed at the proficient/exemplary level (see specifications and rubrics) • Two (2) student-led discussion rubrics completed at the proficient/exemplary level • Distribution requirements **INDEPENDENT READING** • A list of ten books read outside of a literature class during the Eagle Rock experience • Self-evaluation as a reader: written reflection of self as an independent reader **GRAMMAR AND USAGE** • Class/test/evidence	• Ability to ask open questions that elicit substantial response • Ability to summarize and highlight a book read independently • Ability to develop one's creative voice in writing by experimenting with sensory details, sound, form, and language and by creating a final piece • Ability to reflect on the events in one's life • Ability to choose a topic derived from a passionate interest, to develop a thesis, and to select information from a minimum of four sources • Ability to discuss and connect to literature in a group setting using effective communication skills • Ability to demonstrate a specialized understanding of a portion of a literary work and ability to lead the class in an in-depth analysis of the piece • Ability to read, understand, and discuss material from three different genres, time periods, and cultures • Ability to motivate oneself to read according to personal interest • Ability to evaluate oneself as a reader in order to plan one's future as a reader • Ability to use language appropriately (to include spelling, punctuation, capitalization) in formal settings

Figure 1.8 *continued*

LITERATURE DISTRIBUTION REQUIREMENTS
(One trimester class may fill one blank in each area)

Genre   *Has read, understood, and discussed
                                   material from three of the following
                                   genres: novel, short story, poetry,
                                   drama, essay.

(Genre and name of class or work studied)

1 _____
2 _____
3 _____

Time Period   *Has read, understood, and discussed
                                   material from three distinct time
                                   periods.

(Genre and name of class or work studied)

1 _____
2 _____
3 _____

Culture   *Has read, understood, and discussed
                                   literature from three distinct cultures.

(Genre and name of class or work studied)

1 _____
2 _____
3 _____

final element in this figure shows the detailed requirements related to the literature distribution documentation. Figures 1.9a and 1.9b (pp. 26–29), also from the curriculum guide, are rubrics or sets of criteria for participating in a discussion (which students must document at a proficiency level four times) and leading a discussion (which they must document twice). All students have the curriculum guide, so everyone knows the requirements (general standards, concepts, and goals and explicit learning elements), how students will demonstrate learning (the documentations), and how good their work must be to achieve mastery (rubrics).

The course proposal form is the template for course design and is directly linked to the ILP and the curriculum guide. It is essentially a backwards-planning device (see Wiggins and McTighe 1988) that requires instructors to begin with an idea for a class, identify graduation requirements and documentations they can help students master through the class, match them with the appropriate Colorado State Model Content Standards and 8 + 5 = 10 precepts, and design assessment criteria. Only when these initial steps have been completed can a teacher plan activities and resources. Figure 1.10 (p. 30) is the proposal form for the course People's History of the United States.

The learning experience record (LER) is equivalent to a report card in other schools, except that it is keyed to the graduation requirements and documentations on the ILP and within the curriculum guide. (Figure 1.11 (p. 31) is an LER for the course ERS Press.) At the end of a course, instructors complete an LER for each student, noting whether he or she has achieved mastery in a documentation required for graduation. If not, the instructor checks "no credit," with the understanding that the student will work on the requirement and documentation in a subsequent class and perhaps achieve mastery then. Some students are close enough to mastery that a little more time, perhaps a little more assistance, is all that is needed to help them achieve mastery; a place has been provided on the LER to indicate this as well.

Unlike Athena, who emerged fully grown from the head of Zeus, this curriculum began as an embryo and is only now a toddler. Each future revision will advance it, we hope, into adolescence, maybe even into full adulthood. It was developed with these key ideas in mind:

1. It should be homegrown—that is, created by the people who use it, but referenced to outside sources such as state standards and reports from national curriculum groups such as the National Council of Teachers of English.

2. It should be constantly revised as staff members and students try it out. What is learned from each trial period should guide each revision.

3. It will never be perfect. The school will have to function with whatever iteration is being tried, even if that iteration is flawed.

Eagle Rock started with a very simple curriculum. Gradually, as staff members and students learned what did and did not work about that curriculum, it has been replaced with more sophisticated versions. Sometimes real breakthroughs in thinking led to the next versions, as when instructors realized that it was not enough just to describe the learning, that they needed to conceptualize some ways students could demonstrate that they had learned, so they began to describe how students could document mastery. The next leap occurred when the instructional staff realized they could help students—and themselves—

Student _____   Class _____   Overall Score _____

Optimally, students would use this evaluation form *at least three times* per course: at the beginning, middle, and end of the course. Final rubric should evaluate the duration of the course period, be arrived at in a discussion involving student and instructor, include written self-evaluation of student's overall participation in the class on reverse side, and be placed by student in his/her literature portfolio.

	1	2	PROFICIENT 3	EXEMPLARY 4
OVERALL DISCUSSION/SOCIAL SKILLS				
Are you able to leave your personal issues with individuals in or out of the classroom at the door?	Never	Sometimes	Usually	Always
Since you have no right to no opinion, do you form and express your opinion about characters and events in the text?	Never/Rarely	Sometimes	Usually	Always
When you express your opinion do you support it by going to the text (GTTT) and pointing out specific evidence?	Never/Rarely	Sometimes	Usually	Always
When you are predisposed to feel bored or negative toward a given text, do you try to move past those feelings in order to read and discuss it?	Never	Sometimes	Usually	Always

SPECIFIC DISCUSSION/SOCIAL SKILLS

Do you ask questions that lead to further discussion?	Never	Maybe once	More than once	Regularly
Do you bring up points that you don't understand well and ask for help from others?	Never	Maybe once	More than once	Regularly
Do you involve others who are not involved in conversation?	Never	Maybe once	More than once	Regularly
Do you add on to what other people are saying ("to piggyback on what so-and-so was saying . . ."; "I agree with what so-and-so is saying, and . . ."; etc . . .)?	Never	Maybe once	More than once	Regularly
Do you disagree with others and how?	Never, or combatively	Maybe once	Yes, appropriately	Appropriately and constructively
Are you an active listener when not speaking?	Never/Rarely	Sometimes	Usually	Always
Do you demonstrate personal involvement with the material?	Never/Rarely	Sometimes	Usually	Always

Figure 1.9a Discussion Skills Evaluation

Student-led Discussion
(at least 30 minutes)

Student _____   Class _____   Overall Score _____

	1	2	PROFICIENT 3	EXEMPLARY 4
Did you focus your session on a theme or issue in the chapter (story/poem/scene/essay)?	Not at all	Some	Mostly	Definitely
DISCUSSION				
Did you involve everyone in the class in each activity	No, only a few people participated	No, only around half the class participated	Yes, nearly everyone participated	Yes, everyone participated
In the discussion portion of your session students supported their statements with details from the text	Never	Once or twice	At least on three occasions	It happened a lot and automatically
The discussion portion of your session digressed from your initial theme/issue	Too much	Sometimes, but without relevance	Sometimes, but with relevance, or Never	Sometimes and very productively
You created discussion by	Talking a lot yourself	Pulling teeth	Asking good questions	Creating an atmosphere in which students naturally wanted to participate

VOCABULARY				
Your session included an activity that investigated the vocabulary of the piece at hand	No	You covered one or two words or expressions	Yes, you found and explored at least three words or expressions	Yes, you ran a coherent activity that explored at least three words or expressions and their relevance to the larger meaning of the text
ACTIVITY				
Your session included a creative, engaging, inter-active activity that got people approaching the text in a different way	No, or There was an activity, but it was not organized or prepared with appropriate materials	There was a planned activity with materials, but it did not really engage the students	There was a planned activity with materials that engaged the students but did not promote more in-depth responses to the text	There was a planned activity with materials that engaged the students and inspired an unusual/deeper response to the text

Figure 1.9b Student-led Discussion

EAGLE ROCK SCHOOL
Course Proposal Form 2000

COURSE TITLE: People's History of the United States   **TRIMESTER:** 24

COURSE DESCRIPTION: **PERIOD:** ○ 01 ○ 02 ◉ 03

This course will look at American history from the Revolution up to and including the Civil War. We will be exploring the birth of our nation from the viewpoint of the people who lived through this tumultuous period. What was it like to be an indentured servant or a slave coming to the New World? What was it like to fight against your neighbors, or even your own family, in the Civil War? These questions and many others will be explored as we follow the trials and tribulations of the fledgling new nation known as the United States.

IS NAME: James ____   **INTERN NAME(S):** ___ Christian ___   **NUMBER OF STUDENTS:** __ 15 __

GRADUATION REQUIREMENTS ADDRESSED:

AmGov	American Government/Civics	Am. Govt. Project—historical
AmHist	American History	Project—historical event
AmHist	American History	Project—current event
AmHist	American history	Project—hypothesis Am History
Eng06	English	Essay of explanation
Eng08	English	Essay of opposing ideas
Eng11	English	Literature discussion leader
Eng10	English	Literature discussion participant
Geog01	Geography	Project—physical geography
Geog02	Geography	Project—own culture

STANDARDS ADDRESSED:
CO State Govt. Standards
1.1–1.5, 2.2, 3.1, 3.3, 5.1–5.4
CO State Civics Standards 1–4
CO State Geography Standards
1.1–1.3, 2.1, 2.3, 3.1, 4.1–4.5, 5.1–5.3, 6.1,6.2

8 + 5 = 10 ADDRESSED
Intellectual Discipline, Expanding
Knowledge Base, Communicating
Effectively, Leadership for Justice,
Engaged Global Citizen

OUTCOMES OR RESULTS OF LEARNING (may be stated as essential questions or problems to be solved or goals to be met):

Students will be able to answer these essential questions:
What was it like to be a "regular" person in America between the start of the Revolutionary War and the end of the Civil War?
What differences are there between what a "regular" person did and what is usually presented in history books?
What is truth in history?

ASSESSMENTS (include those that lead to documentation above) **AND RUBRIC CRITERIA:**
Projects, essay of explanation, essay of opposing ideas: Rubrics that include criteria for describing what the real people were doing, not just what history books say the famous were doing.
Presentations on projects/writing that focus on information/facts/data to back up opinion.
Literature discussion leader and literature discussion participant: Use English discussion rubrics.

SPECIFIC CONCEPTS, GOALS, OR LEARNING TO BE DEMONSTRATED:

Students will demonstrate a solid foundation of the history of the United States
They will understand the global political forces at work behind the American Revolution (i.e., Colonialism, Imperialism, Mercantilism, Absolutism)
They will understand the forces at work and the motivation behind the expansion of the United States through the expedition of Lewis and Clark
They will be able to describe both the common people of the times as well as some of the great leaders in American history
They will kow about the simmering, divisive forces behind the Civil War and its aftermath

MAJOR ACTIVITIES, TASKS:

Reading and discussing Stephen Crane's *Red Badge of Courage*
Reading and discussing excerpts from Howard Zinn's *People's History of the United States*
Reading and discussing excerpts from Stephen Ambrose's *Undaunted Courage: Thomas Jefferson, Meriwether Lewis and the Opening of the American West*
Research and presentations on both Civil War and American Revolution
Exploration of the Lewis and Clark expedition here on the Eagle Rock campus (possible short wilderness component)

RESOURCES/BOOKS/MATERIALS/ACCOMMODATIONS FOR SPECIAL NEEDS:
Stephen Crane's *Red Badge of Courage*
Howard Zinn's *People's History of the United States*
Stephen Ambrose's *Undaunted Courage: Thomas Jefferson, Meriwether Lewis and the Opening of the American West*

Figure 1.10

EAGLE ROCK SCHOOL
Learning Experience Record 2000

INSTRUCTORS: Dave, Diao   **STUDENT NAME:** Student X

COURSE TITLE: ERS Press

COURSE DESCRIPTION:
WANTED—writers, editors, illustrators, researchers, and technicians
The participants in this course will be employees in a book company. We will write as many *nonfiction* books as we can in ten weeks that will be donated to needy elementary schools in Denver. We will research significant individuals, current and historic events, and environmental issues. This research will then be used to write and produce high-quality books. Here is a chance to write books you always wished existed and help teach younger students! No publishing experience necessary, only a commitment to hard work and excellence.

Past book titles include: *Ever Wonder How Motors Work?*, *The Warming Planet*, *"There's Something in my H₂O)!*, *Living with Asthma*, *The Majestic Antler*, *Chiclids: A Disappearing Species*, and *Dave Hoskins: The Man*
Salary: Environmental Science, History, Service, English, and possible advanced Spanish credit
Term of Employment: Ten weeks
Work Hours: 11:00 A.M.–12:20 P.M., 4 days/week + count on putting in some overtime

CREDIT RECORD:
O No credit yet, but student is making progress on the following and is expected to complete this work by:
O No credit
⦿ Credit for learning that is Proficient or Exemplary:

Of these credits, which were offered in the course proposal:

EnvSci01	Environmental Science	Local issues—composition
EnvSci02	Environmental Science	Local issues—presentation
EnvSci03	Environmental Science	National issues—composition
EnvSci04	Environmental Science	National issues—presentation
EnvSci05	Environmental Science	Global issues—composition
EnvSci06	Environmental Science	Global issues—presentation
EnvSci07	Environmental Science	Environmental impact project
Serv01	Service Learning	Written work—project

Student has earned the following credits from "ERS Press":

EnvSci03	Environmental Science	Local issues—composition
EnvSci04	Environmental Science	Local issues—presentation
EnvSci05	Environmental Science	Global issues—composition
EnvSci06	Environmental Science	Global issues—presentation

Instructor Comments:

Student X spent the first few weeks of the course completing a bilingual Spanish/English set of books about coyotes that he started over a year ago. He completed the books and they are currently in use at Cowell Elementary School in Denver.

He spent the remainder of the course working on *Trouble in Dirturtville* (a story of sustainability), an environmental education book for 5th–7th graders. He juxtaposed a fictional story about a town that was faced with the consequences of relying on nonsustainable natural resources with factual information about current natural resource consumption around the world and alternatives for the future. In addition to using photos and charts to enhance the presentation of information, he included original drawings for the fictional story. Although his work rate was inconsistent during the last 6-week block, he did complete this project before the final day of class. His books are being donated to the Center for Discovery Learning, a K–12 charter school in the Jefferson County Public School Distict. Well done, Student X.

Figure 1.11

By graduation, an Eagle Rock student:
  exemplifies and practices 8 + 5 = 10
  understands and appreciates the unity of all knowledge
  is filled with a sense of exploration, intellectual curiosity and wonder
  models the interconnection of individual and community well-being
  is a lifelong learner
  uses reflection as a tool for living
  is a self-directed learner
  solves problems effectively
  thinks critically and imaginatively
  demonstrates literacy across the disciplines
  critiques and refines his/her work independently
  participates productively in group work
  demonstrates effective research skills
  understands and appreciates heritage and culture
  practices effective self-awareness and self-management

Figure 1.12   Curriculum Concepts Students Should Acquire Across
All Disciplines

even more if they were clear about what "counted" in these documentations. So they began to craft (often with the help of students in real classrooms with real student work in front of them) rubrics or sets of criteria for proficiency for each documentation.

Realizing that procedures related to curriculum also needed to be changed, they created a course proposal form to begin the process for each trimester's classes and a learning experience record to end it. They also decided that what they had created should be accessible to everyone. In a related effort, they devised a set of curriculum "big ideas" that crossed over disciplinary boundaries (see Figure 1.12).

So don't be afraid to start small and less than perfect. Trust the people who use the curriculum not only to create it but to revise it. And revise it frequently.

Chapter Two

Curriculum Emanates
from the Culture

It is January 23, about 8:30 A.M., and twenty new students whose first day at Eagle Rock was January 11 drift into Columbine, one of the seminar rooms in the Professional Development Center. Gathering ended early at 8:25, and ERS (for Eagle Rock School) 101 doesn't start until 8:40. But these students come in and sit down around the outside of the large donut-shaped table. Some have a baseball cap on backward; some have one forward with a precise fold in the center of the bill. A few knit caps pulled low hide eyebrows, even eyes. Jean jackets, lumberman jackets, camouflage jackets; jeans or khakis; and heavy hiking boots predominate. Rings and similar "decorations" protrude from pierced eyebrows, noses, lower lips, and chins. Some heads have recently been shaved entirely; others have been shaved to a couple of inches above the ears with curly, wild hair allowed to flourish on top. A few water bottles and coffee cups provide sustenance. Ten minutes before class, these relatively new students greet each other ("How you, man?") and get out pencil and paper, a journal, a book. Some put their heads down; others practice reciting the 8 + 5 = 10 precepts alone and with each other.

Robert Burkhardt, head of school, walks in sporting the school colors—a fleece vest in purple and teal. "Bags off the table, please," and all backpacks find a spot on the floor, so no one can hide behind them. "Cheat sheets away. Take a piece of paper—if you need one—and give me 8 + 5 = 10. We'll do attendance and check-in while you write." He is still standing (and will stand the entire time) while about half the students furiously write what they remember of 8 + 5 = 10.

The other half have already written—perfectly—the eight themes, the five expectations, and the ten commitments that are the E = MC squared of Eagle Rock. They memorize this code of Eagle Rock in order to begin to live it.

Students are beginning to drop the posturing—the clothes, the metal, the facial expressions, the walk—that served them so well in their past lives. Robert begins to take attendance, making eye contact with each student as he calls each name. "So, how are you doing?" "How'd you sleep?" "Are you still glad to be at Eagle Rock?" Catching a pair of straying eyes, he says, "Remember, don't look at another's paper—he or she doesn't know as much as you do. Unless that person is not writing and, therefore, knows a whole lot more than you do." A sense of humor accompanies his every statement, every request, every question, but there is no doubt this class is serious business.

ERS 101 is one of the classes all new students take before they go on their three-week wilderness trip. The class is between two and three weeks long, three or four times a week, and its sole purpose is to acquaint students, at a deep level, with the philosophy and beliefs at Eagle Rock. Students have had several conditioning hikes and instruction in outdoor survival; the upcoming weekend at Balarat, an outdoors camp run by the Denver Public Schools, will be their chance to put it all together for a trial run.

One student calls out, "Hey, Robert, wanna hear a good word for Wednesday? *Ameliorate*, and it means to make better." Robert picks up on this chance to teach: "Your vocabulary is one of the most important determiners of your income." On the board is another of his sayings: "Your mind is like a parachute; it only works while it's open."

A student who is trying to remember just one more commitment calls out, "Hey, I'm having a lot of trouble coming up with these while you all are talking. Can you all be quiet?" Robert says to him, "Keep struggling," and the room gets quieter. There's a moan from another student, "God, I can't think of one more. I've lost it." Another student starts bouncing his feet on the floor, lifting his shoulders and arms to some inner beat. At last, Robert begins taking papers from students. It is clear to everyone that students are expected to commit 8 + 5 = 10 to memory. Each day they're given a chance to perform until they fulfill that expectation. Today, a few writers sigh, "I think I got 'em," and they look forward to the next class when they will join those who have already succeeded. To the others, Robert says, "Look at it this way. You get another chance to study." One says that he got twenty-two and a half of the principles. As he takes the paper Robert says, "That's very good, but it's not 23." The standards are high—all principles committed to memory.

At the board, Robert writes, *We learn* _____. He pauses and looks around to be sure everyone in the circle is with him and asks one student to put away a book so she can focus. "What's this class about? What are you supposed to learn?" The students recall the purposes of the class: to learn about learning and to learn about Eagle Rock—its philosophy, rules, and expectations.

Robert writes *20%* below *We learn* _____ and introduces students to Mr. William Glasser, who "has a bunch of initials after his name, so he probably knows what he's talking about." He continues, "This man Glasser says we learn 20 percent by . . . doing what?" Some students have started taking notes and most students seem to be listening intently. Students call out answers and Robert chooses the correct one—*by reading*—and puts it on the board. "We learn only 20 percent of the material if we just read it," he summarizes. He continues with 30 percent *(just seeing it)* and 50 percent *(both seeing and hearing it)*. "That's the problem with television. Some of you guys think the Simpsons are real." There is some mock shock in the group: "They're not real?"

Back on the topic: "So how many of you would be content with a 50 percent return on your investment?" Students shake their heads or mutter "No way." "How about 70 percent? It's something that happens all the time at Eagle Rock." Students guess, listening to one another, building on one another's answers. Finally someone names one of the five expectations from 8 + 5 = 10, "Communicating effectively," and Robert acknowledges the contribution and its reference. "Yes, discussion with others," he says. "But wait . . . there's more. You can get to an 80 percent learning rate if you . . . ?" Students call out correctly, "Experience it." They've clearly heard about the benefits of experiential education.

"So, let's go to 90 percent," Robert says, and gets out a dollar bill and waves it behind each student as he walks around the outside of the circular table. "If you get paid?" one student guesses. Students call out randomly until, at last, one says, "If you teach it," and that student gets the dollar bill. "I said that," several students call out, but Robert says, "Not spoken with enough confidence. I didn't hear it." Someone says, "Aw, it's only a dollar."

Robert continues: "Glasser says that you retain 90 percent of what you teach to others. That's why you will be teaching your wilderness trip guides 8 + 5 = 10. That's why David [a student] did the gathering today—to teach you what he needs to know when he talks to nearly a thousand people next month."

"But," a student asks, "how can we teach stuff if we don't even know it?" Robert responds, "You prepare to teach. You learn what you need to teach. 'Unprepared minds result in chaos.' That's why I'm the number-one learner here. It's okay. The rest of you can be number-one learners too. We can have as many as we want. Nobody needs to be number two.

"So the next thing we're going to do is to get you awake. We're going out into the reception area and form a circle." He tells Sue to take charge, and the students follow her out. They form a circle, and Sue throws out one ball, which someone catches and throws to someone else. That person in turn throws it to someone else, so that the ball keeps moving. Then Sue throws out a second, third, and fourth ball and there are balls being thrown in every direction. Now and then someone drops a ball, but instead of cussing out that person, the students suggest ideas about how the whole group can get better: "Go slower." "Spread out." "Take a deep breath." "Don't get frustrated." "Be really quiet." "Don't call out the name of the person you're throwing to—just make eye contact." (Robert tells me later that their first few days with this exercise were full of blaming and scorn, even hostility toward one another.) This group is determined to beat the previous new group, which managed eight balls. It becomes absolutely quiet as they concentrate and cooperate. The only sound is a slight exhalation of breath when a difficult catch is made. They get as far as seven balls. The exercise is a good metaphor for how they're going to need to cooperate to succeed on the wilderness trip.

Robert calls a halt to the game and asks the students to go off and rehearse what they are going to teach their wilderness guides (most of the rest of the school community will be there too). "Review what you are going to do. Improve on what you decided last time. I understand that you'll not have a finished product"—he gets in one more guiding aphorism—"because *life* is not a finished product." Four groups of students disperse and then come back to perform for one another.

Robert is the enthusiastic master of ceremonies, introducing first the group that will do the eight themes, then the group that will do the five expectations, then the group that will do the ten commitments, and finally the one that will do the five nonnegotiables. Three of the four performances are pretty ragged. Students manage to introduce themselves (name, age, where they're from) and talk about what they're going to do, but they don't actually do what they're going to do for the whole group.

After each performance, Robert orchestrates a critique. Students clearly have been told another of Eagle Rock's aphorisms, *You have no right to no opinion*, because each person in turn offers a critique rather than saying, "I don't know." The first person to critique the first group says, "That was good," and Robert ups the ante: "Duh? How does that work as a critique?" The next person is much more specific. Robert offers his own critique at the end of the other critiques. He points out that one student was "in the moment" when he mentioned that it is his birthday when he stated his age. Monique has said *like* three or four times, and Robert says, "Monique, you said *ummm, like* like three or like four ummm like times." Monique and others laugh, recognizing their crutches.

The fourth skit, about nonnegotiables, is marvelous and reaps the benefits of the critiques to the other three groups. The group uses a flashback technique—one student says "bing" and another says "flashback," and one by one the rest of the students enact breaking a nonnegotiable rule. They clearly are enjoying themselves and get great laughs. Robert reminds the students to let the laughs roll and to repeat lines that have been laughed over.

The class has been doing things all along to experience the philosophy of the school, and as the session ends one student declares, "And, now, we're going to teach [the precepts] to someone else. I never heard of 8 + 5 = 10 before I came here, but it's pretty cool."

Several key points emerge from this vignette. First, most schools and districts (and a lot of corporations and businesses) assume that if they put a plaque on the wall or a statement in the front of the employee handbook, their vision, principles, or values will be absorbed. However, culture is learned, sometimes naturally, sometimes because it is taught. At Eagle Rock, the culture of the school is directly taught. It is part of curriculum. Robert (or sometimes another staff member) spends two to three weeks, about fifteen hours, teaching the culture of Eagle Rock, represented by the formula 8 + 5 = 10, to new students. Instruction begins with memorization but goes much further. Among the classroom activities that deepen students' understanding of Eagle Rock's culture are:

- Staging a debate about a theme, expectation, or commitment.
- Applying one part of 8 + 5 = 10 to a story, news article, song lyric, movie plot, television show, or cartoon.
- Representing any part of 8 + 5 = 10 through art, music (including rap), poetry, or an original story.

Ultimately, the students teach the meaning of 8 + 5 = 10 to others. If Glasser is right, their understanding, recall, and retention will be much deeper than if they had just read 8 + 5 = 10 on a plaque in the school hallway.

Robert and the rest of the staff reinforce this introduction to the Eagle Rock culture in several ways:

- At gatherings and community meetings, Robert asks students to consider how current events, stories, and poems exemplify 8 + 5 = 10.
- Every Tuesday at gathering (at Eagle Rock, TGIF means Tuesday Gathering Is Fun), a veteran student presents his or her interpretation of one of the twenty-three values of Eagle Rock, often in a creative way.
- Instructors plan to focus on certain themes, expectations, and commitments in the courses they teach, and they often report on the learning experience records (our report cards) that ones students have addressed.
- As part of the requirements for their POLs (presentations of learning) students describe which of the themes, expectations, and commitments they have worked on during the trimester.
- When disciplinary issues arise, 8 + 5 = 10 (especially the commitments) determines how the incident is understood and what consequences result.

Visitors to Eagle Rock are told they can ask any student anything about 8 + 5 = 10, and they do, for the most part receiving accurate responses. Students who have been at Eagle Rock for a while often say that the code is so embedded in their lives they cannot separate it out. They tell of trying to be an environmental steward back home, even picking up trash on the streets of New York City. The precepts in 8 + 5 = 10 are always part of their personal and academic growth and learning. The code has become part of their lives. How's that for learning?

Every student needs to have written down from memory all twenty-three items of the school's code before going on the wilderness trip. Twenty or twenty-one or even twenty-two will not do. Eagle Rock believes that one of the most demeaning and demoralizing things a teacher can do to a student is to release the student from what is expected of others. The expectation needs to be universal, but the time it takes for each student to perform and the support each student is given can—and should—vary. The more schools increase the variables—sometimes with regard to elements of school structure they have previously thought of as absolute, such as time—the more all students can learn. (See Chapter 5 for more about this.)

Robert's statement that he is the number-one learner is intriguing. In a learning community, everyone is a learner. And if we believe what Glasser says about teaching being the highest form of learning, everyone should be a teacher, too. Having students function as if they were teachers is an instructional technique incorporated into Eagle Rock classes in small and large ways. At the very least, students pursuing their own interests in a research project are usually asked to teach what they have learned to others. Sometimes students who have become specialists in a topic ask to teach that topic as a class to others. With the assistance of an instructional specialist (our term for teacher), they do so, developing curriculum, finding or creating resources, helping other students learn, and assessing the work of other students. Matt, a student who won a scholarship to visit Vietnam, devised a course on the country with the social studies instructional specialist, a course that most students praised highly . . . and caused Matt to wipe the sweat from his brows and acknowledge the incredible work teachers do to help students learn. Students teaching one another is important to each student's own learning because, in teaching, one learns. It is also important to the learning of everyone at Eagle Rock and therefore to the culture.

Except for our foreign language competencies, there is only *scope* (our graduation requirements or competencies and documentations), no particular *sequence* of classes in our curriculum. There are no prerequisites, although sometimes there are courses that are more basic than others, and advisers work with students to choose what's appropriate for them. Students do not enroll at Eagle Rock as freshmen, sophomores, juniors, or seniors, and classes are completely heterogeneous, with older and younger students working together on graduation requirements and documentations that are variously harder and easier. Within these heterogeneous classes, students and staff both teach. It's not uncommon for a student looking across our large circular classroom tables to spot another student looking confused and offer to help. It's not uncommon for the teacher to trust students to work with each other to make sense of something. In fact, it's wonderful when a whole class takes responsibility for the learning of everyone in that class. That's part of culture, part of being a community of learners.

How did Robert apply Glasser's formula for learning in this session? First, he was directly teaching about learning. His chart on the board compared the degree and depth of learning possible with several types of learning activities. The learning during this period was mostly at 50 percent—students were hearing Robert say what he was writing on the board. There was some discussion, which brought the learning up to 70 percent. Later the students experienced a group process (the ball-throwing activity) that would be vital to them on the wilderness trip; the learning was now up to 80 percent. And Robert knew they would get to 90 percent when they taught $8 + 5 = 10$ to their wilderness guides.

Teaching about learning is an important aspect of curriculum at Eagle Rock. Educators often assume that students know how to learn when, in fact, they don't. They may never have been taught how to listen for the big ideas or compensate for a learning style that is mostly visual when a teacher is lecturing. They may not be aware of their intelligences (see Gardner 1993) and how they can use the ones they are strong in or develop the intelligences they need for most classroom work. Other Eagle Rock classes besides ERS 101 focus on learning. One—ERS 201—is a transition class for new students when they return from the wilderness trip and enroll in regular classes for the first time. Another, offered periodically, is called Learning with Style.

The class in this vignette was small—twenty students—and the size of the class made personalization possible. Robert was able to check in with each student, find out how each student was doing. He also knew which students had and had not been able to write the themes, expectations, and commitments. The smallness of the class and the donut-shaped table meant there were few discipline problems. As class sizes get larger, discipline problems often require management—not instructional—decisions. Robert had to make few management decisions, because students moved through the tasks easily, even from one setting to another, and worked independently in groups. Things might not have been so easy if the class had thirty-five, thirty, or even twenty-five students. Getting smaller is one of the lessons Eagle Rock passes along to other schools. It's sometimes the first step schools must take to restructure themselves for student learning.

(By the way, Dr. William Glasser is often credited with the description of the power of learning according to percentages for listening, reading, discussion, experiencing, and teaching. Dr. Glasser actually refers to something called the cone of learning devised by Edgar Dale.)

The Culture of a Learning Community

The culture of a school, though somewhat abstract and intangible, influences everything else about it, including curriculum. At its best, culture is a focus, a true compass pointing north, that helps everything else in the school make sense. Even a school that cannot articulate its culture has one, and that unarticulated but operative culture affects everything else about that school. At its worst, the unarticulated culture is an amalgam of attitudes and results in chaotic programs and curriculum.

Culture is the combination of the attitude toward life and learning that drive the school and the mechanisms that emanate from that attitude. The attitude can be detected and described—we say that a school seems "friendly," "tense," "warm," "cold," "caring," "family-like," or "professional." You can often detect a school's attitude the minute you walk through the front door. We at Eagle Rock are often told that our school is a "community," more particularly, a "learning community." Apparently both "community" and "learning" reverberate through the school, whether one "reads the walls" (on which hang newspaper articles, awards, and recognitions) in the reception area of the Professional Development Center, attends classes, or hangs out in the lodge. So, learning community is the attitude part of our culture. The mechanisms that make any school's attitude tangible include its principles, values, and beliefs; structures; governance and decision-making practices; and events. You were introduced to Eagle Rock's mechanisms in the previous chapter.

Creating culture is an intentional activity. It doesn't just happen. It is not a single event, nor is it instantaneous. At first the adults at Eagle Rock instigated the culture, based upon $8 + 5 = 10$. They modeled using the culture, as represented by $8 + 5 = 10$, in every Eagle Rock decision and activity. Within a couple of years, students themselves became the guardians and promoters of culture. Now they watch each incoming class of students with wary eyes. They work with new students who do not understand what it means to live and learn at Eagle Rock. They refer to $8 + 5 = 10$ when a student violates that culture: "How does what you did promote living in respectful harmony with others? I'm afraid to talk to you!" Students initiate community-building activities when they feel something about the culture is slipping.

In 1993, the first sixteen students were asked, "What makes a safe community?" The discussion that ensued from that question constituted the major part of the curriculum for the first several weeks of the school's existence and led to the ten commitments based on the eight themes and five expectations the staff had already devised.

So far, the formula that expresses Eagle Rock's culture has not been changed, but it's not for lack of trying. Robert invites all new students to amend $8 + 5 = 10$ (if only to get the math right!), and several times since 1993 we have, as a community, explored how $8 + 5 = 10$ needs to change. However, we have been unable to add, delete, or substantively change any of the twenty-three principles and values.

What Is a Learning Community?

Wood (1990) distinguishes between an institution and a community: "We take for granted that our schools are communities, when, in fact, they are merely institutions that can become communities only when we work at it." M. Scott Peck (1987) describes typical stages in the development of community: from pseudocommunity, through chaos, into emptiness, and then beyond, into true community. He describes "community by design" (intentional culture) as occurring for the following reasons (p. 84):

1. "Individuals function according to agreed upon laws or rules."
2. "Communication is raised to a high consciousness as individuals struggle to know and understand each other and the rules to live by."
3. "The rules of communication and community-building are directly taught and learned."
4. "Learning can be passive or experiential with the best way of learning the community rules happening experientially."

Driscoll (cited in Caine and Caine 1997, pp. 195–96) suggests that the following attributes can be found in a school community:

1. "A system of values that are shared and commonly understood among the members of the organization."
2. "A common agenda of activities that marks membership in the organization."
3. "Teachers [who] engage in collegial practices . . . [so] that they perceive other teachers as sources of help and support when faced with academic problems. . . . [T]his broadly based connection with other teachers is also manifest in their relation with students."
4. "Parents as members of community."
5. "An assessment of community in smaller units (such as classrooms)."
6. "Respect of teachers, administrators, students and 'classified' staff (such as maintenance personnel) for each other."

Lickona (1991) makes a good case for schools as communities: "To educate people who value community and who see their individuality as developed by rather than threatened by responsibility and commitment to others, we need to provide a positive experience of community as an integral part of schooling" (p. 107).

The word *caring* is often used to describe a community culture (Schaps and Solomon 1990). Lewis, Schaps, and Watson (1996) suggest that these five principles lead to a caring community:

1. "Warm, supportive, stable relationships."
2. "Constructive learning."
3. "An important, challenging curriculum."
4. "Intrinsic motivation."
5. "Attention to social and ethical dimensions of learning."

Deborah Meier, in *The Power of Their Ideas* (1995), suggests that the culture of a high school might best resemble the caring community of a kindergarten class. She acknowledges that most teachers and most schools are caring, but it takes a "structure and style that enables us to show our care effectively" (62). She continues, "If we want children to be caring and compassionate, then we must provide a place for growing up in which effective care is feasible" (63).

Etzioni (1993) pushes community beyond caring to action in his "communitarian" movement, which he describes as "an environmental movement dedicated to the betterment of our moral, social, and political environment" (2). Communitarians, he says, "are dedicated to working with our fellow citizens to bring about the changes in values, habits, and public policies that will allow us to do for society what the environmental movement seeks to do for nature: to safeguard and enhance our future" (3). Schools are but one place where communitarianism can be applied, in particular through character education, service, and moral education.

The word *learning* in front of *community* adds a new ingredient to the mix. A learning community bears all the marks of a community (intention, caring, and action) but has an additional quality—it is dedicated to self-renewal through a continuous learning process. The phrase *learning organization* was invented by the business world and is customarily used to describe corporations, but many aspects of a learning organization cross over into educational communities. Senge (1990, 2000) and Senge et al. (1994) describe learning organizations as those that encourage personal mastery (individual learning), stress the sharing of mental models or assumptions, foster a shared vision, and engage in team learning—all within the discipline of systems thinking. Senge (in O'Neil 1995) also makes the case that "institutions of learning" should become "learning organizations" (20). That they are not is evidenced by the fact that "the whole approach [to schooling] is quite fragmented. Really deep learning is a process that inevitably is driven by the learner, not by someone else."

It's true! Schools, of all places, should be learning organizations, but Isaacson and Bamburg (1992) point out that "it is a stinging experience to read about learning organizations and to realize how few schools and districts fit the definition" (44). They describe how schools would look if they were learning organizations. Personal mastery suggests that adult learning in schools would be valued as highly as student learning; educators would share their mental models about how people learn when making decisions about school life; schools would value team learning; and a truly shared vision would keep the school on course. An understanding of systems thinking would integrate the other four disciplines so that educators would understand some of the mysteries involved in making substantive change.

Calfee and Wadleigh (1992) use *inquiring* instead of *learning* in front of the word *community*. In an article about Project READ, they state, "The Inquiring School arose from the realization that the structures and strategies of critical literacy work equally well in kindergarten or in sixth grade, in peer coaching or at faculty meetings" (28). They talk of the paradigm shift necessary for a school as institution to turn into an inquiring community. "Schools are known for their chaotic agendas, shortage of time, isolation of people, and top-down management. Inquiry, on the other hand, requires a clear focus, a slow pace for reflection, social interactions, and genuine collaboration."

Take all the components of a community, add to them the idea that the community—all of it—should focus on inquiry and learning, as a learning organization does, and you have what Eagle Rock strives to be. Prawat (1992) exquisitely describes what we are trying to do: ". . . in classroom learning communities, individuals engage in animated conversations about important intellectual issues. Ideally, such conversations will occur at the school level as well, involving all teachers and focusing on concerns about curriculum, learning and teaching, alternative approaches to assessment and the like" (13). Because we believe that learning is socially constructed (Vygotsky 1962, 1978; Heath 1983, among others), we like the implications of the designation *learning community*. As Robert says, "I'm the number-one learner here. But that doesn't mean that the rest of you can't be number-one learners too. Any number can play."

Creating a Culturally Embedded Curriculum

Several aspects of a culturally embedded curriculum arise from these ideas about culture, community, and learning or inquiring communities. First, the culture must be articulated. Second, curriculum derives from culture. Third, the curriculum must be manageable for it to be effective within the culture. Fourth, the culture itself is part of the curriculum and must be taught.

Articulating the Culture

You already know how Eagle Rock has articulated culture through 8 + 5 = 10, its set of themes, expectations, and commitments. The important element of our attempt to articulate the culture is that no one person drafted the code with the hope that everybody else would pay attention to it, let alone follow it. Our code was drafted by an entire community, has been taught to all newcomers as they've arrived, is used every day, and is thus deeply embedded. It is open to scrutiny and revision.

Drafting a set of principles or values is the essential first step in the process of creating a culturally embedded curriculum. It is best taken on, as it was at Eagle Rock, with as many members of the community as possible. You'll probably want to include students, parents, business leaders, teachers, administrators. Once the values of the community are clear, endorsed by all, and part of the practice of the school, then curriculum can be built.

Deriving the Curriculum from the Culture

If you look closely at 8 + 5 = 10, you will find that this representation (and determiner) of our culture suggests some curriculum that might not be found in other schools. For example, the themes of *spiritual development, service to others, cross-cultural understanding,* and *environmental stewardship* may be particular to Eagle Rock, as may be the curriculum that emanates from those themes. Similarly, the expectation that students will provide *leadership for justice* may be idiosyncratic to our culture and therefore our curriculum. Several of the commitments may likewise be unusual for most schools but appropriate for Eagle Rock and therefore appropriate for Eagle Rock's curriculum.

Here are some specific examples of how Eagle Rock's curriculum is tied to our culture:

1. The *spiritual development* theme is expressed through the personal growth requirements for graduation.

2. The *service to others* theme is expressed through the service learning requirement. Students complete a portfolio of service learning projects, presenting written work that expresses not only the *what* of the service project but also the *so what* and the *now what.*

3. The *cross-cultural understanding* theme is expressed through the learning outlined for the graduation requirements in foreign language, geography, and world history.

4. The *environmental stewardship* theme is expressed through the environmental science requirement, with learning that addresses local, national, and global issues and documentation that has students design and reflect on an environmental impact project. (We also have "regular" science curriculum requirements.)

Customizing curriculum to the culture of the school does not mean that an outside curriculum (imposed by a district, a state, or the federal government) must be rejected. Indeed, these kinds of standards are a good reference point for a school's curriculum. But that's all they should be. Curriculum imposed from outside needs to be negotiated in each setting. The best response to standards is adaptation, not adoption. (Chapter 5 develops the idea that curriculum should be "standards referenced" rather than "standards based.") This assumption also means that purchased curriculum—textbooks or programs—cannot be expected to work unless the values match the school's stated values, that is, its culture. Schools will either need to customize what they have purchased to make it fit the culture or use it as a reference for their own curriculum. At Eagle Rock, textbooks and programs serve largely as reference points.

A curriculum that speaks directly to the values held by the school is obviously more relevant than a generic curriculum would be. If one of the principles of the school is that students will be *stewards of the environment*, then the curriculum that helps students do that will be an important, even essential, curriculum. Students will have fewer questions about why they are learning environmental science if they know that environmental stewardship is highly valued in their school culture.

A more abstract reason culture and curriculum should be aligned has to do with systems thinking. If a system is working well, all parts of the system are working together, achieving the same end. An educational system is not working well when the plaque on the wall says that students will become good citizens but students are never given the opportunity to learn and practice the habits of good citizenship. A school in which there is no congruence among the various parts, from vision through assessment, suffers from lack of focus. So examine your own culture: what does it tell you about what must be taught at your school?

Making Curriculum Manageable Within the Culture

The curriculum that is derived from—and promotes—the school culture must be manageable by everyone within the learning community: students, parents, teachers, school and district administrators, and all others who come into contact with it. This means that curriculum needs to be understood; it needs to make sense. Students and staff members alike need to know how to navigate it. It needs to be available to all; it needs to be transparent. And, finally, it needs to operate via an easily understandable and executable process.

I've encountered many unmanageable curricula either as a teacher or an administrator. These curricula were unmanageable because they were hard to understand. How did things fit together? What really counted? What was I, a teacher, supposed to do about assessment? To whom did I report how students did? What if they didn't do well? Usually a curriculum like this was bulky, bound in black, and after a while I simply didn't consult it but kept it prominently displayed on my bookshelves, just in case. And then I did my own thing, with less trepidation than I expected, since no one else seemed to be following the published curriculum documents either.

I have also worked in places where the curriculum was a closely guarded secret. Staff members sometimes knew what was expected of students, but students themselves rarely knew. Curriculum was, in fact, quite mysterious. Students went to classes and did the assignments and took the tests but didn't have a sense of what was important, what counted. What did they need to know and be able to do?

The processes of curriculum are indeed very complicated and confusing, especially in light of the standards movement. Students still graduate on the basis of seat time or Carnegie units and passing grades. Their diploma signifies that they have sat in enough classes and done well enough in those classes (anything but an F) to graduate. The system, even though it does not measure learning (see Chapter 5), is clear and straightforward, and that's perhaps why it has hung around so long. But what do you do with a student who has earned all the Carnegie units but has not demonstrated mastery of the standards? What about a student who has demonstrated mastery of the standards (perhaps on a state-administered test) but has not accrued the appropriate number of Carnegie units (perhaps because he or she has flunked or simply not taken the requisite classes)?

An *understandable curriculum* can be written on a single piece of paper. It can be carried around by students and staff members. It can even be miniaturized and put into a pocket.

Eagle Rock's one-page document is called the individualized learning plan (ILP) (see Figure 1.7, pp. 20–21), although all students are held to the same standards or requirements. What varies—is *individualized*— is the way students move differently through the curriculum, taking different courses or learning experiences, to achieve credit. (Chapter 5 discusses this concept in detail.) Eagle Rock students who are approaching graduation usually laminate several copies of their one-page curriculum and carry it around with them, put it into the front of their notebooks, hang it above their beds, and entrust it to their coaches.

It usually takes Eagle Rock students awhile to discover how much sense curriculum makes. They arrive not expecting to see the curriculum. And when we introduce them to the curriculum during their first trimester, they usually don't "get it." They're sure that's not the way things really work. At first, they just go to classes, as they used to, and trust. Only when they've watched a friend work through the process and graduate does a lightbulb go on. "Oh. Do you mean it's not enough for me to just go to classes? I need to learn this stuff and do these documentations? Okay, I get it."

There are twenty-three boxes on the ILP, and they stand for the "big picture" things students should know and be able to do. Having only twenty-three big things, or graduation requirements, seems manageable to most students. Under each box are several documentations they need to produce, at a specified level of mastery, to prove they have learned what they need in order to have gained the big picture. There are a total of 125 documentations, individual pieces of work, and they can sometimes do double duty (for example, a proficient piece of writing about history may count as a documentation for both English and history). When all the documentations are checked off under a graduation requirement, the appropriate box is darkened. When all or almost all of the graduation requirement boxes are darkened, the student is ready to petition to graduate and prepare his or her graduation presentation of learning (POL).

The system is manageable for staff members, too. The anchor is the ILP. It is simultaneously a list of what students should know and be able to do, a reference tool for course planning, and a record of what students have accomplished. I've already discussed it as a list of graduation requirements and documentations that attest to learning. As a reference tool, it helps instructional staff members design courses for each trimester, as they check it to see which graduation requirements students, especially probable graduates, need to work on. With that information, the social studies instructor, for example, can design a new geography class, perhaps working with the art or English instructors to help students work on more than one requirement.

Staff members as a whole consider the proposed course offerings (which they have developed on course proposal forms—see Figure 1.10, p. 30) from the point of view of the ILP as well as other needs. They put together a balanced schedule of high-interest classes that help students work on graduation requirements. Advisers help students select the courses that will let them make progress on their ILP. During these classes, students may work toward proficiency in any number of possible documentations and even negotiate with the instructors to work on other documentations they need. The rubrics for the documentations, of course, help instructors figure out whether students have reached mastery, and they report this information to the registrar on the learning experience record (see Figure 1.11, p. 31), who records the information on the ILP. Thus the ILP achieves its third function—a record of what students have accomplished

The ILP, therefore, holds the entire curriculum process together for both students and staff members. Of course, there are materials that build on this simple one-page curriculum. There is a curriculum guide—available to everyone—that explains what the boxes and the documentations mean, what students should learn and how they should document learning, and how good their work needs to be in order to be declared proficient. But it too is short, less than a hundred pages. Most teachers also share more precise descriptions of portfolio requirements and other rubrics with their students.

The most important aspect of the Eagle Rock curriculum is that it makes sense of standards, both the Colorado Model Content Standards and those proposed by professional organizations. It incorporates them right into the requirements—the big-picture items, the learning, and the documentations. So students graduate based on having met standards and proved their learning rather than on having accumulated an arbitrary number of Carnegie units.

Many Eagle Rock students felt powerless in their old schools. Someone else was deciding what they should learn and be able to do but wasn't telling them what it was! Here's what Kate, an Eagle Rock graduate, says about her former school:

> The reason I took accelerated classes is that I couldn't stand the crap in regular classes and the teachers yelling "Shut up!" and the kids not engaged at all. At least that didn't happen in accelerated classes. Even though I thought the kids were ridiculous putting such effort into what I thought was ridiculous to put effort into, there wasn't the control issue. There were other issues, though. I remember my physics class. I'd been getting by without notes. I sat behind a kid who went to the Naval Academy [after graduation], and in front of a kid known as a genius; I'd sit while they took notes, copy notes from one of them, and ace the tests. Maybe I absorbed something in copying the notes, but I always headed the curve when the teacher passed out grades. I thought it was really funny . . . but sad . . . so I went to the guidance counselor to change my schedule. I told her I wanted to drop this class. She just didn't get it at all. I kept telling her, "I don't know anything in that class. I'm good at repeating things. I just don't know anything." As a result of dropping that class I was ineligible for track, but I didn't care about that anymore. Competition was not important to me.
>
> So, basically, school was a joke. I just thought it was a complete waste of time. The diploma was a joke. I had no idea of what I'd like to do with my life, no direction; I just wanted to get the heck out of there. My problem was that the curriculum and graduation requirements were crystal clear—I had to take these classes—but they were not worth doing. Classes and grades. Who cares? It was just jumping through hoops. I didn't see the point. I wanted to learn something worthwhile.

Kate was not sure that what she was doing mattered. Going to classes and doing homework were a joke. A diploma was meaningless.

Knowing the curriculum gives students power. Most of our students may have been rebels in their former lives, but almost universally they appreciate the power and control they have over their learning at Eagle Rock. They like knowing exactly what they need to know and be able to do. They like choosing classes that will help them learn. They like knowing how they'll document their learning. They like knowing how good their documentation needs to be. They like deciding when they are ready to graduate.

You may have "rebels" like Eagle Rock students in your school, too, perhaps many of them, who would like to have more power and control over their learning. It's safe to say that most students would like to have more power and control over their learning. Why not share with them what you expect them to know and be able to do? They may even have some ideas about improving the list of required knowledge and skills. Learning is one of the most personal activities we engage in as humans, but schools usually take away power and control over this most personal activity. One way to give it back is to make expectations transparent and clear to all students.

Teaching the Culture Directly

Visions, mission statements, principles, values, or beliefs that reside only on a plaque or in a faculty or student handbook are unlikely to be actualized. We are what we do. Our walk must align with our talk. We cannot assume that just because we have stated what we believe somewhere, students and staff will know and understand this, much less shape their school lives accordingly. One way to make sure that the culture of a school lives is to teach that culture directly, as Robert is doing in the vignette at the beginning of this chapter. In Robert's class, the culture of the school is the curriculum.

We know we have succeeded as a community in bringing the culture to life when we hear a student give as a reason for signing up for a particular course, "Well, I just want to *expand my knowledge.*" Or when a student picks up a discarded candy wrapper along Dry Gulch Road because he wants to be a *steward of the planet.* Or when a student writes a proposal for some change in the way Eagle Rock is run because she wants to *practice citizenship and democratic living.* These students are living the culture. Their curriculum is the culture of the school, and the culture of the school is the curriculum.

Problems and Solutions

Any process has its problems. Here are some of the problems we've faced with our curriculum, along with our solutions.

Problem. Some students still have difficulty believing our system. Some of them just go to class and do nothing, expecting that attendance is enough. While it's good to have them going to classes (something they may not have done before attending Eagle Rock), it's not enough. We have to work to help them see that the ILP is their key to graduation. Sometimes we have to go beyond friendly reminders and gentle nudges to get them to begin working on documentations.

Solution. Advisers are sometimes the best people to help new students adjust to a new system, especially when students sign up for courses. Even more helpful, however, are prospective graduates who haul around laminated versions of their ILPs and constantly check to see whether the registrar has recorded their latest accomplishments. Pairing a new student with a veteran often brings about the understanding that the new student needs in order to succeed.

Problem. Our transcripts are sometimes a mystery to the schools to which our students transfer. We have had to create a parallel transcript translating our documentations and graduation requirements into credit hours or Carnegie units. The parallel transcript works well for graduates but less well for students who enroll in other high schools after being at Eagle Rock. For example, a graduate gets one credit (one full year of class attendance and a passing grade) in American history if she or he has completed all the documentations in American history. But if a student has done only four of the five documentations in American History when she transfers to another high school, we cannot give her the entire Carnegie unit; try explaining eight tenths of a credit to a high school counselor!

Solution. Usually this dilemma is solved through one or two phone conversations between our registrar and the counselor at the transfer school. Eventually we hope we'll no longer need a parallel transcript.

Problem. Colleges and universities are mainly interested in SAT or ACT scores and grade point averages. At Eagle Rock a student who achieves proficiency on a documentation does so at the equivalent of an A (or perhaps a B+) level. Because they don't graduate until they have mastered the curriculum, the GPA for our graduates is usually 4.0.

Solution. Many colleges and universities (including state institutions) have special admissions categories for students from alternative programs. They are interested in portfolios, including digital portfolios, and willing to look at competency-based transcripts. Especially in standards-based states, institutions of higher education are interested in students who have demonstrated their mastery of standards. We encourage our graduates to highlight that aspect of their learning when applying to Colorado colleges and universities. Sometimes, however, scholarship-awarding agencies are as confused about our system as the high schools to which our students transfer. Again, patient explanations do the trick.

Problem. Students like grades even if they haven't been particularly successful in school in the past. It's not enough to know that they've achieved mastery or proficiency on a documentation—they want that concrete sign of how well they did in the class.

Solution. This is usually a short-lived problem. As soon as students see that the ILP and the documentations they master are the basis for their graduation, they lose interest in grades. Nevertheless, we write notes on their learning experience records telling them how well they did.

Problem. Since students don't always achieve mastery on the documentations they work on in a class, they don't always get credit. They need to take another class—or the same class offered later—in order to continue working on those documentations. Sometimes a student may take three different science classes and not get credit for their science portfolio until the third class.

Solution. It's hard to explain this phenomenon to parents and others (including high school counselors). And it causes us to walk a fine line between putting on the pressure and letting students take the time they need to achieve mastery. If a student consistently (for two trimesters, for example) earns no credit in any classes, we generally begin to work more intensively with that student, having him choose a coach and attend weekly meetings with the director of curriculum and the director of students. Sometimes we even put a student who has consistently not gotten any credit on some kind of academic probation, perhaps sending her home for a few weeks while she renews her commitment to learning at Eagle Rock.

Problem. Planning is sometimes difficult, for both students and staff members. Students planning to graduate need to know that the classes or other learning experiences they'll need to achieve the documentations they still lack will be offered when they need them. Staff members like to repeat some classes, but they also like to create new classes, often in response to student interests.

Solution. Solutions are in the works. The director of curriculum has devised a "year-in-advance planner" whereby staff members commit not to the exact classes they'll teach but to the graduation requirements and documentations they'll address each trimester. There's also a "graduation planner" that advisers use to help students decide what to take each trimester in order to move toward graduation.

Problem. Students do not realize they can achieve more than one documentation in a course. They are content checking off one documentation per class when they could be checking off several. Then they look at how slowly their ILP boxes are being filled in and get discouraged; they'll never graduate!

Solution. Again, this problem is usually short-lived. As soon as newer students realize a class can be used to fulfill several documentations, they change their approach. Eventually, they begin to take advantage of the system and negotiate extra documentations that fit.

Problem. The learning experience records are more ambitious than most report cards. Completing an LER is not just a matter of marking a grade. Instructors put considerable time into each LER.

Solution. This problem probably shouldn't be solved! The LER goes home to parents in lieu of grades. It needs to communicate a great deal. It's worthwhile to capture in depth how a student did in a class. Many instructors set aside some time during a class period to work with students on the LER, incorporating students' opinions into the comments section.

Questions to Consider

1. Has the culture of your school been expressed in writing? by whom? How well known is it? Are these principles known at a deep level? How well are they practiced?

2. What is contained in the student handbook? the faculty guide? the statements of vision, mission, and goals? faculty meeting minutes? the school's newsletter? communications with parents? news articles about the school? How is culture represented in these artifacts? What are the consistencies? What are the disjunctions? How does what is said in these artifacts fit with or contradict the culture as you've defined it? What assumptions do these artifacts make about students? about teachers? about parents and community members? about relationships? about power and authority? about learning and curriculum?

3. Can you say something succinct about your current culture?

4. What is contained in your curriculum book(s)? your transcript forms? the state standards you are responsible for? course syllabi? How well is your curriculum customized to your culture? How understandable is your current curriculum? In what ways is it coherent? in what ways is it not? What parts make sense? What do these artifacts say about how transparent your curriculum is? What do they say about the process? Is it direct and straightforward? Does it make sense?

5. What can you do to make culture more powerful in your school? What can you change about how it is represented? about who is/was involved in the creation of it? about structures (size of school, size of groups, use of time, use of money, use of space)? about governance (who makes decisions, how meetings work, how power is distributed among students and staff)? about events that promote your culture?

6. To what extent do you directly teach your school culture? How could you do so more effectively?

7. How can you change curriculum so that it is more representative of culture? If you were to create curriculum from scratch, what elements of culture would you have to be absolutely sure would appear in that curriculum? How can you be sure that those elements appear in your current curriculum?

8. To what extent is your curriculum imposed from outside your school (state standards, for example)? How well does the imposed curriculum fit your school's unique culture? How can you embed required curriculum into your own curriculum in such a way that the uniqueness of your curriculum is preserved?

9. In terms of manageability of your current curriculum, what works? What does not?

10. How understandable is your curriculum to students and their families? to staff and administrators? to the outside community? How can you make it more understandable?

11. How transparent is your curriculum? Who has copies of your curriculum? students? staff? families? people outside your school? Do they understand how to use it?

12. How effective is the curriculum process? Does it work and make sense for all involved (including students and their families, staff members, and people outside your school)? How can you make it more effective?

13. Does the curriculum process ensure that culture is part of course development, instruction, assessment, and reporting?

14. What difficulties can you see in tying curriculum more closely to culture? To what extent will your school community support a more powerful and "live" culture? To what extent will they support a curriculum customized to your culture? To what extent will they want a more manageable and transparent curriculum that enhances culture?

15. How can you overcome barriers? Are there people who want to keep the system the way it is? Are there requirements that appear to block a curriculum related to culture?

16. What, if anything, about Eagle Rock's curriculum and culture could you adopt wholesale? What would have to be modified? In what areas are you going to have to design something more suitable for your own school?

17. How can you communicate with various constituencies—the school board, other schools, the community, business leaders, parents—about what you are doing?

18. What objections will these constituencies raise? How can you respond to their objections? In what ways might they support your ideas?

19. What will be the repercussions if your school changes how it thinks about culture and curriculum, but no other school in your district does so?

20. If you are in a high school, what relationships do you need to establish with nearby colleges and universities so that they understand your new curriculum? Would a parallel transcript (one that reports according to Carnegie units) be a good temporary or permanent solution?

21. What role can students play in your process of converting from your current system to a different system?

22. How will you know that the new system works, both in terms of short-term and long-term learning benefits? What data can you collect? How can you share these data with your constituencies?

23. What kind of professional development is needed to bring about these changes? What kind of ongoing support will teachers and administrators need?

Chapter Three

Curriculum Includes Instruction and Assessment

I

"There's so much in my head. I ran out of time. I could have written more." Ian and the other enrollees in Touch the Future are debriefing their experience serving as environmental education teachers and counselors for inner-city fifth graders. Here's what Ian had to say:

> Balarat was absolutely amazing. I really was loathe to leave the kids, and even a day later pangs of *sehnsucht* (German word—means "longing") frolic in my stomach. I remember my apprehension as the bus rounded the corner and came to rest in front of Moe, Ashanti, and me. I nearly tucked tail and ran up the trail, and as the kids filed off the bus I bit my lip a little. All for nothing. The anxiety quickly wore off, and I became increasingly comfortable with the students. The first thing we did was take the kids toward Pond Camp to eat a snack and use the restrooms. I mingled with the boys and quickly discovered that this was an energetic group, albeit with potential to cause trouble, but well-behaved nonetheless. Eventually the girls returned from their break and sat near the boys. The three of us stood back and took in the sight before us—each surely wondering what the next couple days would yield. Fun. That pretty much sums it up. We split the sixteen students before us into three random groups, and each Eagle Rock student took one group. I had a chipper crew of five students—two boys and three girls—and we adopted the team name "The Ticks." Zach, Daniel, Kristi, Estrella, and Sarah. All of them absolutely amazing people in their own right.
>
> After the kids were all refreshed and filled with a snack, the moment that had Moe, Ashanti, and me so fraught with suspense and worry arrived—it was time to begin the montane ecology hike. My

group was extremely observant and respectful, and though a lot of information was thrown at them, they seemed to retain a vast amount. I often used the things we learned as "passwords"—for instance, in order to head down to dinner, I would have each student tell me one thing they learned. Everyone was able to come up with some bit of the day's learning each time I asked, and my heart swelled with pride whenever one of them said, "Hey, Skittles (the nickname they gave me), is that a Douglas fir?" or identified some Balarat flora. I will forever associate the ponderosa with Sarah. She had considerable trouble remembering the word, and I frequently pointed at a pine and said, "Name that tree!" I even went so far as to wear my house intramural shirt (which says *Ponderosa*) for her. Eventually, she was able to remember it and smiled shyly whenever I asked her.

Later in the evening . . . we all headed up to Mystery Wall for what was called a "night hike." Well, the hike was great. I took Daniel aside, and he pointed out Vega to me in the northeastern sky, and he asked me just what a star was. After a short astronomy lesson, he went back to the group with a smile on his face and some facts in his brain.

Unfortunately, the trip down wasn't so uneventful. My group took off at a running pace, with me straggling behind, and somewhere along the way Sarah took a tumble. She was a little distraught and cried periodically, but eventually she cheered up, which really helped the evening. I learned an important lesson about kids that night—how *tough* they are! I saw lots of kids take falls or somehow manage to injure themselves but get up and walk away. Amazing!

The second day was even better. We did the morning exercise, a hike to the large pond, and ate a wonderful breakfast of pancakes and sausage. The zipline that day was the highlight of the trip for many of these youngsters, and I watched as one elated student after another came flying across the gully. Even Sarah, with her sore hip and dented confidence, made it across.

That afternoon, I took my group to the Duvall Mine. While Zach and Daniel headed to try their luck at panning, the girls followed me into the mine drift. Once inside and seated on the benches within, we discussed how the mine was created, how gold was found and removed, what it is like to be a miner, and the risks involved. When I later read some of the kids' journals, I found that the mine, with its horrible reality of possible death, made a big impact. . . .

That very night, after a lengthy montane ecology lesson, everyone participated in a solo walk. I sat high and hidden on some boulders along the selected route and reprimanded a few runners along the way who intended to catch up with a friend in front of them. . . .

The third day was great. I ran the "pond life" activity and walked along the bank as the anxious youngsters tried their luck at bug catching and identification. It was a hit. Even the kids who were reluctant to look at or handle the creatures participated. Two days earlier, on the first hike, the kids had given the pond the moniker

"Dead Bird Pond" for the carcass discovered floating near the bank. Two days later, the swallow corpse was recovered and laid out in the sun to dry. Kids are great.

Touch the Future has proven so effective in helping students learn that the class is offered twice a year. On the surface, it is an environmental science class. Students study and learn the ecology of the Estes Park area—montane (the biogeographic term for upland slopes below the timberline) ecology—in order to teach it to younger, inner-city children who are bused to Eagle Rock for daylong experiences in the mountains. Sometimes, Touch the Future students also serve as volunteer "counselors" at a camp south of Eagle Rock called Balarat where students in the Denver Public Schools come for overnights and extended field trips.

Underneath this obvious *curriculum* lie two other curricula. First, Touch the Future students learn adventure games and activities in order to work with younger people. The third curriculum is subtler and more exciting: Eagle Rock students learn how to be teachers. One goal of Touch the Future and, indeed, Eagle Rock itself is that our graduates seriously consider teaching as a career.

Instruction and *assessment* are a little less easy to define. Before the younger students arrive (and before Eagle Rockers go to Balarat), the Eagle Rock students learn the environmental science curriculum by pretending they are second, third, or fifth graders. Imagining they are the inner-city youngsters who come to Eagle Rock or Balarat knowing nothing, they walk the area and make a list of the questions they have. Getting their questions answered is the instructional methodology, and they do it in a variety of ways: they ask the instructors; they look up material in reference works and on the Internet; they visit local museums; they ask experts, such as Forest Service personnel. Then they share these answers with one another, half the class playing inquisitive youngsters and the other half playing the "counselors." They also rehearse the adventure games. These rehearsals can be considered an aspect of instruction or a kind of formative (as opposed to summative) assessment.

The instruction that the Eagle Rock students give the elementary students is yet another layer of their own instruction, but it can also be considered summative assessment: how effective are they at it? Priya, the intern in the Touch the Future class, wrote this about Ian:

Ian really impressed me during this trip. The [Eagle Rock] students expressed fears that Ian was going to be just like the fifth graders and run all over the place being hyper. I had some of that concern as well. [But] Ian was mature, responsible, caring, gentle, and added a perfect balance of fun and safety. He talked to the students with respect and with a calm voice. He loved talking and joking around with them, letting them call him Skittles, but also really did them a service with his vast knowledge of ecology and science. His confidence in these areas was definitely a plus. I never once saw the hyperactivity that Ian displays at Eagle Rock from time to time as cause for concern for the kids' safety at Balarat. I saw Ian joining right along with the kids during their games instead of hanging back and observing, but he would not be overly controlling or dictating. He would let them try something first before giving them advice or suggestions. Ian had a challenging group when doing the wall, but he was safety-conscious, calm, and encouraging.

Ian's self-evaluation of his Balarat experience is another form of summative assessment.

II

All About Alice is an IMP (Interactive Mathematics Project) mathematics class that explores exponents using Alice's growing and shrinking experiences in *Alice's Adventures in Wonderland*. Katy, an intern working with math instructional specialist Jason, is in charge today. She says, "Get out your homework. Andy, did you do it? Nezzi?" It is clear that Andy, who was absent the day before, has not done his homework, so Katy instructs Josh and Nezzi, who are working with Andy in a small team, to get him up-to-date.

Josh complains, "I'm really spacy, Katy; I forgot how to explain the logarithm."

Katy replies, "This is the perfect opportunity for you to figure it out, Josh, and Nezzi is there if you need help." She moves away to check on other groups of students.

Nezzi and Josh take different approaches to helping Andy—and themselves—figure out this difficult concept. Josh tries to describe the problem by referring to the original premise about Alice, "You already know how tall she is now, but you don't know how tall she was originally. You don't know what it took to get from her original height to her present height." Meanwhile, Nezzi goes to the board and writes a number; Katy consults with him quietly, and he erases the number and rewrites it with a flourish. Katy says to Nezzi, "You're awesome. I thought you said this was hard for you. Show Andy what a log is and what it means."

Josh and Nezzi begin with a log 10. Josh explains to Andy why the number 10 is special and why it makes the answer two digits and why 100 makes it three digits. Andy is confused and Josh says, "I'm a bad explainer." Katy, overhearing him, responds, "Your knowledge is no use in your head. If you have it all in your head—like Einstein with his theories—it would be of no use. The power to be able to explain is really, really important. You've got to put it out there!" Josh, ever a joker, moans, "You mean the knowledge in my head isn't useful?" Katy and he laugh.

Katy begins again with Andy, beckoning Josh and Nezzi to listen in, "What do you understand about logarithms?" Andy just shakes his head, but Josh says, "It's kind of like square root. Something by something equals twenty-five. What does? You take five times five and that's it. Logs are the same thing." That seems to be enough to get them started again.

Nezzi goes to the board, saying as he writes, "I know the first one. In the book, between what two whole numbers does log 10 of 162 come? What exponent? What two exponents are whole numbers? Ten to the second power would be one hundred and ten to the third power would be one thousand. So the answer is two [100] and three [1000]. One hundred and sixty-two is between those—ten to the second power, or a hundred, and ten to the third power, or a thousand."

Katy, overhearing this, says, "Do you agree with that?"

Understanding, Josh and Andy say, "Yeah."

Katy pushes them, "How about the next one?"

Josh goes to the board now and writes another problem, and Katy leaves once more to check on other groups working through whether or not they agree on the homework problems. The other groups, too, are arguing and proving, often going to the board to make their calculations, sometimes erasing and trying again as the groups struggle to reach consensus on right answers.

Josh poses the next problem, taking over Katy's role. He explains the answer, "It's because she's shrinking." They go to the next problem, alternately jumping up and down to work at the board in front of them. At various points, they ask questions like this one from Andy, "Do you agree? You seem to be agreeing." Enthusiasm is high as they discover the secrets to this system. They move to the last problem and then Nezzi says, "I'm going to make this one of the chapters in my portfolio. I get it."

The course description for All About Alice, the first six weeks of ER 21, reads: "Alice (from *Alice's Adventures in Wonderland*) doubles her height if she eats the 'magic cake' and shrinks if she drinks the 'magic drink.' This IMP unit explores exponents through this story." Students can work toward their graduation requirements in mathematics by developing a portfolio in this class.

The *curriculum* is clearly mathematics, specifically exponents. Several *instructional techniques* are employed: learning by teaching other students; using language (articulating, explaining, justifying) to understand mathematics; achieving right answers through consensus; using logic and common sense as a check on the mathematics of a problem.

Formative assessment may occur in relation to the instructional techniques described above: when they have helped other students learn, when they have been able to use language to explain the mathematics of a problem, when they have achieved consensus, and when they have checked their mathematics answers against logic and common sense. The summative assessments are the portfolios they put together, chapter by chapter. The portfolio includes a table of contents, three skills chapters, two problem-solving chapters, assessments, and a self-evaluation. Here are the instructions students receive for completing a mathematics portfolio:

- *Table of contents.* It's difficult to locate all the materials in a portfolio. For our reading convenience, we require that you type a table of contents that allows the reader to find your specific chapters, pieces of evidence, problems of the week (POWs), assessments, and self-evaluation. Tabs, page numbers, and other locators are helpful.

- *Skill chapters (3).* Every chapter of your portfolio should address an area in which you made learning gains. Each chapter consists of a cover letter, followed by evidence that you have leaned it (usually three pieces of your best work). Your cover letter should identify and describe the concept, skill, or understanding you claim to have learned, refer to each piece of evidence, and specifically explain how the attached work shows evidence of your claim.

- *Problem-solving chapters (2).* Problem-solving chapters consist of a POW or other open-ended problem. Thoroughly describe the processes you used to solve the problem, even those that did not work, and defend your solution. Present each chapter in standard form: problem statement, processes, solution, extension (make up a similar problem or develop the problem), and evaluation (did you consider the problem educationally worthwhile? what did you learn from it? how would you change it to make it better? did you enjoy working on the problem? what was the level of difficulty?).

- *Assessments.* The instructor(s) will assign assessments that relate to the concepts and skills you claim to have learned in class. Include these in your portfolio.

- *Self-evaluation.* Write about your personal development during this unit. Make specific references to work you have included in the portfolio. Also answer the following questions: What worked and what could have been improved in the class or learning experience? What specific and measurable goals will you establish for yourself on the basis of the work you did to produce this portfolio?

The rubric that students and instructors use to evaluate the portfolios describes performance according to three benchmarks: beginning, developing, and accomplished. We encourage students to work toward accomplished portfolios. The following requirements must be met for a portfolio to be designated accomplished:

- *Organization.* All sections of the portfolio can be accurately located through a table of contents and other organizers (tabs, for example).

- *Skill chapter cover letters.* Cover letters specifically describe the student's claim to knowledge. Work supporting the claim is directly referenced. Summary shows the ability to move from particulars to general models.

- *Skill chapter evidence.* Work supports the claim. Choice and application of procedures demonstrates an understanding of specific mathematical demands of the task. Strategy chosen leads to a conclusion that is logically supported by evidence.

- *Problem chapters.* Restatement and processes are rated accomplished according to separate POW rubrics. Clear description of mathematical relevance is included. Reflection describes specific evidence of growth.

- *Assessments.* Solutions to problems are clearly presented. Work process leads directly to solutions. New skills are actively applied to the solutions.

- *Self-evaluation.* Reflection leads to clear future goals that are specific and measurable. Evaluative statements are substantiated with references to specific work.

III

Students are reflecting on their experiences in the Holocaust class.

Reggie: So far, we've learned about guys who were very important in the Holocaust. I did my presentation on Joseph Mengele, a very mean guy. I found it very disturbing, but I did it anyway. Now we're here, and we're talking about the resistance, and Patrick and I are doing a project. We're doing the camp— Auschwitz—and the Warsaw Ghetto.

Patrick: I know a whole lot about this era, but I've learned so much more in three hours of watching the movie about gypsies. We just really go through everything in such detail to know why certain things happened. I've learned so much. I did my research on Albert Spier, a confidant of Hitler's.

Gen: I did my presentation on Martin Borman, a personal secretary to Hitler. We've been reading *Maus I* and *Maus II*. We finished *Night*, by Elie Weisel.

We've been getting into individual cases, too. Especially the Jewish children, their final fate. We've been looking into resistance, even German people who helped out Jews. It started off with bread by the fence and then more serious things like hiding them in houses and putting their own lives on the line.

Will: My first presentation was on Anne Frank, and I found out all kinds of stuff. The Nazi governor of Poland was known as the Nazi Butcher. I'm looking at the resistance in the ghettos and the uprising in them, mostly Krakow and Warsaw Ghetto. When we started class I didn't even know what the Holocaust was.

Patrick: We had before and after quotes from Hans Frank when he was a maniacal Nazi—he wanted to get rid of all the Jews wherever he saw or found them. Afterward, when he was traveling, he said something like Germany would never get rid of the guilt from what they did. He said, "I hope God will take me. A thousand years will pass, and the guilt of Germany will not be erased."

Whitney: The first week we did our profiles, like what the Jews had to go through. Our background and names. Skull measurements. Eugenics. We measured the size and shape of our noses and ears. Eye color and shape. We did racial profiles for everyone in class. We did side profiles. It became really clear who would live and who would die. Only one of us would have lived. We also played a game called Gestapo. We were given life cards and family, pride, house, religion, home, and community cards. Oh, also civil liberties. We had to put something down that we were willing to give up or risk. We listened to a real scenario in chronological order. If the situation applied to something we'd given up, we would lose.

Will: Die.

Gen: When Will was almost out of life, people donated. We got to know what people experienced in the Holocaust. This gave us a chance to act as a community. We could bargain: "I'm down to one life." Ruffy says, "Take one of mine. I've got seven prides."

Reggie: This game helped us see what the people went through. At first, life was still pretty regular, then things started piling up and the events were more severe.

Patrick: I died—the only one—but I felt like I'd really won because I never had to give away religion, but I died with it.

Sophia: I had one life left and would have died, too. Patrick and I watched a movie last weekend about the gypsies and the Romance culture. It symbolizes so much about people and how they bring about what they hate and fear. The gypsies originated in India and came by caravan to Europe, so they brought traces of lots of cultures. People thought they were from a very foreign culture. They stayed in Eastern Europe mostly, but after about thirty years, people started to hate and fear them because they had misconceptions— gypsies were so secretive. They turned their misconceptions into the descriptions of gypsies we have now—they are thieves and promiscuous. As they traveled, they were not allowed to do anything because they were always on other people's lands. I had no idea that gypsies were persecuted the whole time, like the Jews were. They sold kids into slavery. They had to steal because they couldn't have jobs, couldn't even get drinking water.

Patrick: Yeah, that's right. When they couldn't support themselves, people had a right to kick over their pots of boiling water and food.

Gen: It was a race of people spread out all over the world. They had no single nationality and language and dialects. There were five million kids in the Holocaust, and there have been no reparations or apologies. They're still fighting to get a public apology.

Patrick: Their experience throughout history has been very similar to the Jews'. They have been singled out since the Middle Ages, and then the Nazis singled them out.

James (the instructor): I found a quote in a book about rescuers. Check this out. It tells the story of common individuals who took on the job of rescuing Jews because it was the right thing to do. Anti-Semitism was deeply ingrained in European culture. Who knows who Martin Luther is? (*Several hands go up, and James gets a right answer.*) Yes, he was a man of religion, and he started the Protestant Reformation. He says about Jews that there is no enemy more cruel than a true Jew. In 1543. Synagogues were set on fire. Spread over with dirt so no one could see a cinder or stone. So, Hitler was drawing upon something deeply rooted.

Reggie: So Luther was a Nazi.

James: No, but Nazism didn't just fall out of the sky. It was built on a tradition of European culture. And it continues.

Gen: The neo-Nazis.

Patrick: They have sites on the Internet. I don't see how people can watch this happen and do nothing.

Ruffy: The Nazis are all about white culture. There were people in a town—La Cambon—who were Protestant and they saved all these Jews. Klaus Barbe was head of the fourth division of the Gestapo in Lyons, France. He was called the Butcher of Lyons. He killed and tortured Jean Moulin, one of the leaders of the French resistance.

Whitney: What's the matter with Jehovah's Witnesses?

Gen: They were seen as antisocial people, outcasts, and deviants because of what they believed. They were outside German society.

James: A stain on German culture.

Reggie: Do you think since Hitler's grandmother was a Jew, she was rounded up?

Patrick: She died before that happened, didn't she? And his mother died when he was thirteen. It's really weird, his Jewish background.

Like Touch the Future, The Holocaust: Theory and Practice of Hell has had such an impact on students that it has been offered more than once and will likely be offered regularly. The course description is:

The years 1939–1945 saw the world descend into the madness of world war and the genocide of millions. This interdisciplinary social studies/ literature/humanities class will take a hard look at what happened under the Nazis and why—and at the same time try to make some sense of it. The shock waves of the Holocaust continue to affect us profoundly. Please join us for a thoughtful and important learning experience. The course will involve a substantial literature component.

Students are offered chances to work on requirements in *world history* (possible documentations: oral/written report on a historical event; oral/written report on a current event), *geography* (possible documentations: project that traces/examines one's own culture over time; project that compares cultures), *American history* (possible documentations: oral/written report on a historical event; oral/written report on a current event; oral/written report on an hypothesis regarding American history), *technology* (possible documentation: multimedia presentation), and *English* (possible documentations: essay of explanation, essay of opposing ideas, interview, review of literature).

The *curriculum* is to learn the history of World War II, the Holocaust, and precipitating events and understand what happened on a personal level.

Instructional techniques include:

1. Profiling themselves as if they are in Germany/other occupied countries.
2. Playing the Gestapo game to experience what happens when they give up or hang onto their own values.
3. Researching and sharing information about a person who played a part in the Holocaust (pair or group activity).
4. Researching and sharing information about resistance to the Nazis (pair or group activity).
5. Reading several books about the Holocaust (individual activity, with whole-class or small-group discussion).
6. Watching movies about the Holocaust (individual/pair activity, with whole-class or small-group discussion).

Some of the instructional activities lend themselves to assessment products like a report on an individual who played a part in the Holocaust or an oral presentation on some aspect of the resistance. In order for these reports (oral and/or written) to be submitted as a final assessment to earn credit in world history, geography, American history, technology, or English, students have to revise and refine their work according to a rubric for a final product.

IV

Nezzi and Spencer are the discussion leaders for today's Read On, Write On class. The novel the class has read is *Catcher in the Rye*. A little background here. Celeste, the instructor, has distributed two kinds of discussion rubrics. One focuses on what individual students do during a discussion, the other on what students do as discussion leaders (see Figure 1.9, pp. 26–27). Among the Eagle Rock requirements for graduation are demonstrated competency in the ability to participate in a discussion of literature as well as demonstrated competency in the ability to lead a discussion of literature. Students complete a rubric on themselves as discussion participants and on one another—or themselves— as discussion leaders. Chief among the requirements for both rubrics is GTTT— pronounced "git"—which means that the discussant or leader needs to Go To The Text for specific evidence to support a point. The discussion leader also needs to pay attention to these criteria:

- The discussion should be thirty minutes or more in length.
- It should focus on a theme or issue in the chapter/story/poem/ scene/essay.
- It should involve everyone in the class or group.
- The leader should limit digressions.
- The leader should talk little but instead draw others out.
- The discussion should include an activity that is creative, engaging, and interactive, inspiring an unusual/deeper response to the text, perhaps through an investigation of the vocabulary of the piece.

Both Nezzi and Spencer are relatively new to Eagle Rock, and neither has led a discussion of literature before; in fact, neither has read a whole work like a novel before. Both have been recommended for this class—and have chosen it—because they need to focus on and practice reading.

Nezzi has decided on a typical approach. He moves to the whiteboard on one wall of the room (there is no real "front of the room" in these seminar-style classrooms in which students and instructors sit around a donut-shaped table), erases what's there and writes, "Is Holden mentally unstable or is he a normal sixteen-year-old kide?" He sits down at the round table until Will whispers to him, whereupon he gets up and erases the *e* after kid. "Okay, first we're going to have thirty minutes of silence." After the laughs die down, he says, "Just joshing."

One person at a time volunteers an opinion about whether Holden is mentally unstable or normal for a teenager. Everyone in the classroom speaks at least once. At one point, Nezzi volunteers, "I think he's mentally unstable too, and I think our proof from the book will show that. I'll read one part." He tells the others which page he is reading from, waits while they find that page, then reads the passage. Then he continues, "He said he was walking down the street and he was really tripping out, hallucinating, even though he was not on drugs. I think that's part of a mental problem. So, maybe he is mentally unstable. Here's another proof." He directs the students to another page. "Look at his family, a middle-class family, and he has very low self-esteem and that's what got him to being mentally unstable. He's always stressing out. He thinks people are phony and tries to act like an adult. He lies."

Celeste asks, "Do you think his trying to act like an adult makes him unstable?"

Nezzi and Celeste have a conversation about that point, and several other students offer their opinion about this aspect of Holden's "craziness." Going with the flow of the conversation, Nezzi then poses a question to the group, "Have any of you guys ever had any experiences like Holden and did you think it was normal or not?"

Ben says, "Yes, about a half hour ago."

Not knowing whether Ben is joking, Nezzi rephrases the question: "Like, have you ever been in that position, gone through the problems, experienced something like that?"

Will asks, "That would make me mentally ill."

Nezzi replies, "Unstable maybe."

The students do not seem to be able to draw from their experiences a connection to Holden Caulfield. When Celeste says that Holden may be perfectly normal, Nezzi tries one more time, "I guess in a way he could be normal, but I don't know. He just doesn't seem pretty normal to me. Like seeing myself going through those problems, when I was fourteen, fifteen, or sixteen, it didn't seem normal to me. He has a family he can go back to, a pretty wealthy family, and putting myself in his shoes, when I was going through problems like that, I didn't feel normal like that. I cried, grabbed my hair, told lies. Made people think I'm a really good kid!" (The last is said with a trace of sarcasm.)

Then Nezzi moves on to another topic. "What about his relationship with women?" The students stay with that for a while, but then they wander back into immaturity being the problem, not mental instability. The thirty minutes are up, and Celeste asks Nezzi to use the rubric to reflect on his first try as a leader.

Nezzi thinks a moment and then says, "I talked too much."

Several other students bob their heads in agreement. One says, "But you got us to go to the text."

Nezzi adds, "I think we answered my question okay, and we got some agreement."

Celeste asks, "Did everyone participate?"

Nezzi looks around the room, "Not everyone."

"How could you get everyone involved?" Celeste continues.

Nezzi doesn't answer because he is looking at the rubric. "I didn't have an activity," he says. It's apparent he's heard Celeste's question, however, because he adds, "I could have had an activity that everyone would do first, like write their ideas."

Ben volunteers, "I think it went pretty well. I tried saving you a time or two when you were lost. Something he could have changed is maybe asking more questions directly to a person, and that would have saved you."

Celeste says, "It's obvious that you really read deeply; you didn't just read words but absorbed what was happening. Being in that [discussion leader] seat is hard. You did a great job citing from the text and a nice job of relating one theme or concept to another. I like how you talked about your own point of view and related some of your own experiences. You slowed down about halfway through and didn't really have a structure to go from. Next time, concentrate on a structure, some specific questions. Lay out your instruction a little better, a little more organized. Maybe we could work together on that." She asks the students to complete evaluation sheets on Nezzi as a discussion leader and on themselves as participants.

It's Spencer's turn. He goes to the board and erases what Nezzi has written earlier. He puts up a chart:

Holden	or	Holden
chicken****		nerd
yellow		dork
scaredy cat		immature

He asks two students to join him, drawing out chairs for them, one on either side. He sets the scene: "So you guys are in the computer room. Do computer things." They mime appropriately. He says to one, "You see this CD case, someone else's CD case, and you get this idea that you can pick it up and go through it and listen to some CDs you like. So you do it." Spencer nudges one of the students, who puts a CD in the boombox he has with him; it's rap but played at an abnormally low volume that allows Spencer to be heard. "You know whoever owns the CD case and all the CDs in it is not here so you decide to take the CD, just the one CD, out. You put the CD case down and start to leave." He addresses the other student, "You are in the room but you didn't see anything. Then the person who owns the CD case and the CDs comes in and says that the case is open and there's a CD missing." Spencer says these words with expression.

Now he ties the scenario to *Catcher in the Rye*. "Do you remember when someone took something of Holden's? His baseball glove in

Chapter 4; it was in his drawer in his closet. Holden knew when it was gone and didn't do anything about it. The longer he waited, the harder it was to do anything about it. He doesn't ask this guy for his glove back." Then he makes it personal. "First period, this is what happened to me, and I was in the exact same situation as Holden. My CDs were taken, but I didn't go up to the person and demand them back. I didn't go to anyone else. Then I thought I could just ask them if they have my CD, but if they stole purposefully, they're gonna say no. So I said, 'How long are you planning to borrow my CD for?' The person said, 'What CD?' 'The one you got from me in the Learning Resource Center.' 'Oh, that one, I'll get it back to you at lunch.' So I made it seem like I knew they had my CD. I got my CD back at lunch. I could have blamed this person and gotten into a fight. I wasn't chickenshit about it, was I? So, what do you think Holden could have done about his glove?"

Spencer, who has learned from Nezzi's discussion, calls on several students. He summarizes what's been said occasionally and queries what someone means: "So you think he automatically thought he'd get into a fight?" Several times he comes back to his own situation. "He could have made it seem as if he'd approved its being borrowed and expected it to be returned. There are other ways he could have done it, too." Students go back and forth, sometimes talking about what Holden could have done, sometimes talking about what Spencer did, and sometimes talking about what they would have done. As they debate these actions, they are both relating the book to themselves and considering Holden's character deeply.

Then Spencer directs them to the board and asks what each of the words means. Students offer stereotypes: "A nerd has glasses, looks weird, acts weird." Spencer drives deeper. "What do you mean by weird? What does a nerd actually do?" As students talk, he expands the chart on the board with their descriptions of each word. He prompts them: "Anything else?" They add terms like *ditz* and *jock* and *valley people*. Then he poses the key question, "So, what do you think Holden is?" Students choose various words and support their choices with expressions such as, "Like it said in the book."

The time is up, and Celeste asks Spencer what he thought of his discussion.

He replies, "I really like how I started off with the scene."

Another student says, "It was good that you related it to you."

Spencer continues, "I didn't GTTT."

"Right," Celeste says, "but you did start off strong with the scenario, and you didn't give them any choice about participating. Your reference to Chapter 4 was very good, and you connected it to your scenario. I got a little lost in the stereotypes you put on the board. I see you were having us define who Holden is, and you finally brought us around to him as coward. Good job of pulling people in. Good job for doing your first one."

Will says, "We need more people like you. If only we had a whole classroom full of you." He doesn't say it sarcastically, and no one laughs. The students complete their rubrics and turn them in.

Read On, Write On is an intensive class in reading and writing. We highly recommend that students take this class if they've had difficulties with reading or writing in the past. At first, few students took us up on the recommendation, but the class has sharpened its focus and gotten a good reputation. Now many students take it and benefit from it.

The *curriculum* in this class is the novel *Catcher in the Rye*. Underlying that curriculum—which is essentially reading the book—are two other curricula: reading to understand and leading and participating in a discussion. The story becomes the vehicle for the other two curricula. (And there is even a third curriculum related to student confidence: we want students to believe they are capable of reading and understanding text.)

Instructional techniques focus on leading and participating in a discussion. The students taking the course experience a whole lot of "firsts." For many, just reading a whole novel is a first; for all of them, being expected to do certain things as a participant in a discussion is a first. But the biggest "first" is leading a discussion of a book. That's what a teacher does!

Assessment happens at the end of each discussion, when the student assesses orally how he or she did as a discussion leader and the other students and the teacher contribute their ideas. Finally, the discussion leader, in writing, applies a rubric to his or her handling of the discussion, and all the other students apply the same rubric to the discussion leader's performance and another one to themselves as a discussion participant. The discussion leader rubrics are collected and recorded by the instructor and then given to the discussion leader for his or her portfolio. The discussion participant rubrics are also collected and recorded and then given back to each participant.

Separating CIA to Get At Coherence

In real teaching and learning, it isn't always easy to separate curriculum, instruction, and assessment. Sometimes curriculum is many layered and can be confused with instruction. Or what may seem to be instruction can also be assessment (formative assessment in particular). In the four vignettes in this chapter, curriculum, instruction, and assessment sometimes are so interwoven it's hard to tell which is which—they become a single entity, CIA.

The organic nature of CIA makes it hard to dissect teaching and learning, but it's good that these elements are so interwoven. What's important about curriculum, instruction, and assessment is that they fit one another. The most obvious example I can think of to illustrate the *lack of fit* is my own experience as a seventh grader in Miss Teller's English class. Monday through Thursday we worked in a grammar workbook, identifying parts of speech, learning punctuation rules, and correcting examples of poor usage. Friday we applied what we'd learned. We were given a topic at the beginning of class; then, using our pens and a fresh piece of blue-lined notebook paper, we wrote about that topic in order to illustrate our understanding of the grammar and usage we had learned during the week. We did no prewriting; we wrote only one draft; we were using pen and could not erase anything or cross something out. We turned our compositions in at the end of the period Friday and got them back on Monday with grammar and usage problems circled in red and a score of X/Y, the X portion for grammar and usage and the Y portion for content (which, if my memory serves, we never discussed).

If Miss Teller's goal was to make us good writers, her *curriculum* would have had to have been the steps of the writing process (steps which in 1958 she may not have known). Her *instruction* would have been related to those steps. She might have led us in whole-class brainstorming. She could have had us form peer revision groups. She might have had individual conferences with us about our later drafts. She might have had us use a rubric to make final corrections. *Assessment* would have been evidence of the process (a collection of papers showing brainstorming or prewriting through editing the final draft) as well as an evaluation of the final product against a stated rubric.

If her goal was to have us know rules of grammar and usage, her instruction on Monday through Thursday was probably appropriate. However, on Friday, she should have given us a test that mirrored the exercises she had us work through on Monday through Thursday.

It isn't particularly important to distinguish what is curriculum, what instruction, and what assessment. In this book, I often use the term *curriculum* when I am actually describing *instruction* or *assessment*. In those contexts, curriculum encompasses instruction and assessment as well. However, it is very important to look at the congruency of curriculum, instruction, and assessment. In that context, distinguishing them is appropriate. Miss Teller's curriculum and instruction and assessment were not congruent. Depending on her goal (which I could not discern), either her curriculum or her instruction and assessment did not fit.

Why should there be a fit? Why is congruency important? Congruency focuses the entire classroom on expected learning. Let's look at some standard definitions of curriculum, instruction, and assessment:

- Curriculum: what students are to learn.

- Instruction: how students will learn the curriculum.

- Assessment: how we (educators, parents, students) know the curriculum has been learned.

The assumption is that instruction and assessment derive from curriculum. That is not always the case. Some teachers are "activity experts." They may have a title or general concept for a unit floating around somewhere, but they really just assemble a number of activities that are fun, exciting, and engaging. They then fling these activities at their students in the hope that something will "take." Assessment usually comes near the end of the unit when these teachers reflect on the activities students have done and devise a test or other assessment that they hope will measure what they hope the students may have learned. This is sometimes referred to as a scattershot approach.

At Eagle Rock, we prefer what some have called *backwards planning*. Educators involved in the Coalition of Essential Schools were instrumental in describing this process and urging its adoption in order to make the learning process coherent. In particular, Grant Wiggins, now a private consultant with his own firm (the Center on Learning, Assessment, and School Structure, or CLASS), has described and taught backwards planning in a series of books and workshops on curriculum design (Wiggins 1998; Wiggins and McTighe 1998).

At Eagle Rock, we make the idea tangible via a course proposal form. In order to propose classes for consideration, instructors and their interns begin with an idea for a great course (which they later develop in a section of the form called *course description*). Then they begin at the end, selecting the graduation requirements the class will address and focusing on the documentations that students may be able to work toward. For example, the Holocaust class offered students the chance to work on *world history* (documentations: oral/written report on a historical event; oral/written report on a current event), *geography* (documentations: project that traces/examines one's own culture over time; project that compares cultures), *American history* (documentations: oral/written report on a historical event; oral/written report on a current event; oral/written report on a hypothesis regarding American history), *technology* (documentation: multimedia presentation), and *English* (documentations: essay of explanation, essay of opposing ideas, interview, review of literature). The instructor, James, and the intern, Josh, also selected some Colorado State Model Content Standards that could be worked on in the course and some of our own 8 + 5 = 10 precepts that students could address.

Knowing these outcomes, James and Josh then reframed them as either an essential question or a problem to be solved. The overarching essential question was, "What does the Holocaust have to do with me, an Eagle Rock student?" It was a big question, with room for each student to answer it individually and personally. It related to all the outcomes, including 8 + 5 = 10, because most students chose to look at the Holocaust through the lens of themselves as leaders for justice. (For more information about essential questions, see Wiggins 1989.)

Next, James and Josh identified specific assessments that would let them know that students had mastered the documentations, which required that they consider specific rubrics (even though they did not always go on to develop each rubric). They had to think about what mastery of a documentation would look like in order to be sure to offer students opportunities to learn how to do what would be required. Thus, if students wanted to work on a project based on a hypothesis (American history), they knew they would need to offer students a chance to understand what a hypothesis is.

Their next step was to break down the outcomes into some specific concepts, goals, or learning to be demonstrated, such as learning what a hypothesis is. Only then did they think of the major activities or tasks that would help students learn what they needed to know in order to achieve the outcomes. (Think how different this is from beginning with activities, hoping that if you choose enough fun, exciting, and engaging ones students will somehow learn what they need to know and be able to do what they are supposed to do. The latter is a very fingers-crossed endeavor.)

Finally, after conceptualizing the activities and tasks, they looked for resources, books, and materials and began to think about how they would accommodate special needs. The form completed, they turned it in and, as part of a group of instructors and interns working with the director of curriculum, considered it and all other course proposal forms for the next six-week block or the next trimester.

The process may seem arduous and time-consuming. It is. However, going through it helps to make sure that the class accomplishes its goals. Curriculum should be purposeful, not just hopeful. When a course's tasks and events relate directly to why they are being done, these purposes are also reference points for any additional activities or tasks that come up serendipitously. This process makes learning coherent, so that what students are supposed to be learning (curriculum) is congruent with how they are taught (instruction) and how their learning is measured (assessment).

More on Curriculum

Should there be an entire course on the Holocaust? What about World War I, the events leading up to World War II, the rest of World War II, the other twentieth-century military engagements? Isn't this specific concentration a bit shortsighted? We don't think so. Less really is more (McDonald 1996; Cushman 1994). Here's how it works. Imagine a line representing all there is to know about twentieth-century conflict, with a segment of that line representing the Holocaust:

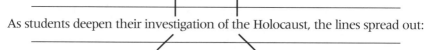

As students deepen their investigation of the Holocaust, the lines spread out:

They discover that the Holocaust was related to other events in World War II and that World War II was connected to World War I. Often this happens individually. One student may learn more about World War I than other students as she explores the root causes of the Holocaust, but because students present their learning to one another, each learns something about what all the others know. The material covered by the class as a whole broadens because each member of it has gone deeply into one aspect.

I call this the "Franco-Prussian War problem." Very few of us are likely to remember details about the Franco-Prussian War (or any other war throughout history, except the most recent or the one that involved us personally). Will we suffer from not knowing about the Franco-Prussian War? On a quiz show we might, but in real life, suffering from that missing piece of knowledge is unlikely. On the other hand, should we know about war? Yes, of course. Knowing about war—any war—may guard against our repeating our past and that, after all, is one of the reasons we study history.

Another argument in favor of less is more is that what there is to know multiplies itself every few months. How can we possibly come to know it all? and remember it? and use it? Learning one representative thing *deeply* seems a sound response to that dilemma—unless, as I said, you're planning to be on a quiz show!

More on Instruction

Eagle Rock students are also teachers. They teach their classmates (the All About Alice class, the Holocaust class, the *Catcher in the Rye* class) and they teach others (Touch the Future). This instructional technique is purposeful. The person who learns the most—and who learns best—is the person who must teach someone else. Teachers who lecture learn the most as they prepare their notes. They really know their subject. So we ask students to teach what they are learning.

Do they know how to teach? It's surprising what they as learners have come to understand about how to help others learn. When educators visit Eagle Rock, they are often surprised at the insights our students have about good teaching. And sometimes—as in Touch the Future—they are taught effective instructional strategies directly and given the opportunity to use them.

What if they teach something wrong? What if they have the wrong facts? Sometimes the consensus method used in All About Alice works. Other students do not agree with what has been taught, so the whole group returns to the learning task. Sometimes logic, common sense, and reasonableness alert the group to a problem. Sometimes the instructor or intern steps in and asks the student who is teaching to re-check some facts or get more information. Seldom does a wayward "fact" remain unchallenged and uncorrected. We do not believe we are turning out students who carry around misinformation.

Students teaching sometimes looks like what we know as teaching. Other times, it looks like presenting. However, when students present their learning, we encourage them to make their presentation a learning experience for other students by having the other students participate in the presentation or asking them to do something with what they have heard and seen.

Students are also learners in other ways. Even if they are not teaching, they are learning by researching, asking questions, experimenting, and actively engaging in what they are supposed to learn. If the teacher has all the knowledge, has organized it to make it understandable to students, and dispenses it to students, the real learner is probably the teacher. This does not mean that instructors and interns never lecture at Eagle Rock; indeed, lecture is sometimes the most efficient way to get sufficient information out to students to allow them to take off on their own as learners. We ask this question to keep us mindful of the need for students to be the main learners: "Who is doing the learning work here?" If the answer is the students, we are on the right track.

More on Assessment

Of all the components of learning, assessment is perhaps the most inseparable from instruction at Eagle Rock. The reports students do on individuals associated with the Holocaust are part of instruction (students doing research) but are also an assessment. Are they learning what they are supposed to be learning? Are they understanding? Are they helping others understand? Assessment is ongoing at Eagle Rock, a regular—often daily but at least weekly—event in every class rather than a one-time-only opportunity at the end of a course.

Assessment is also closely tied to curriculum and instruction through its form. Although Eagle Rock students sometimes are given quizzes and tests, assessment is more likely to fit the deeper requirements we have for student learning—understanding, analyzing, evaluating, personalizing, interpreting. In order to know whether students are engaging in these higher-order thinking skills, we need assessments that measure them. The methodolgies most likely to help us do so are presentations, documentations, teaching experiences, portfolios, dramatizations, original art, technological media, and writing in various genres.

Even though we prefer these forms of assessment to tests and quizzes, students entering and graduating from Eagle Rock take a norm-referenced standardized test. For 90 percent of our students, the scores on this norm-referenced standardized test when they graduate are dramatically higher than when they come to us. Although there are numerous explanations for this, it does allow us to be confident that our higher-order assessments do not make it impossible for our students to perform on multiple-choice tests. Nevertheless, even if we did not have test-score data to reassure us, we are not likely to use assessments that are incongruent with the curriculum we want students to learn and the ways we help them learn it. Curriculum, instruction, and assessment should be one—CIA.

Questions to Consider

1. Examine your curriculum guide, a set of course descriptions, some communications to parents or your board of education about what students learn in your school. How do you express curriculum? What are students supposed to know and be able to do? Watch students learning in one of your classrooms. How would you describe typical instructional techniques at your school? What do they do to learn? Look at some representative class assessments. How do you assess student learning in your classes? How do you know they have learned?

2. How coherent are curriculum, instruction, and assessment in the same learning experience? To find out, set up a chart with four columns:

Curriculum   Instruction   Assessment   Comments

In the first three columns briefly describe your artifacts for each component of learning. What do these artifacts say about your beliefs about learning? What assumptions are you making? In the fourth column, reflect on how congruent or incongruent you see the three components of learning as being. How well did they fit with and complement one another? Do you have enough data about curriculum, instruction, and assessment to be able to measure the congruency? How can you gather more data? Will learning improve if curriculum, instruction, and assessment are congruent? How could you change one or more of the components to make them more congruent?

3. Are there some areas in which it is more or less important to have fit among curriculum, instruction, and assessment?

4. Are there some teachers in your building who might not see the point of having congruency among curriculum, instruction, and assessment? Does CIA need to be a schoolwide consideration . . . or can it be addressed teacher by teacher?

5. Do teachers in your school use backwards planning to design units or classes? If few use it, how could you help them learn about it? Do you think they would see improvement in learning if they used backwards planning? How would you and they know if learning improved?

6. Does your school currently have a less-is-more approach to curriculum? If not, what might be the barriers to taking such an approach? How could you overcome those barriers? How might your board of education and parents react? How could you help them to see the positive effect of less is more? Would some teachers be unwilling to give up curriculum coverage for curriculum depth? What would convince them to take that step? Would there be protests from students? How could they be convinced?

7. How might you use state standards and district curriculum to help you take a less-is-more approach?

8. To what extent are the teachers in your school the real learners? To what extent are the students the learners? What would have to change so that students were usually the real learners?

9. Are students ever the teachers in your school? Could they be teachers of one another as well as themselves? What would need to happen to afford your students the opportunity to teach themselves to learn and to teach others?

10. What would happen if fewer tests and quizzes were given at your school and more documentations of learning (presentations, demonstrations, artwork, writing, computer presentations, etc.) were used? How do you think your students would do on multiple-choice tests, especially norm-referenced, standardized tests? what type of action research project could you establish to find out?

Chapter Four

Curriculum Is
Learner Centered

Loula is nineteen and has been a student at Eagle Rock since she was sixteen and a half. She grew up in the North African country of Eritrea, from which she and her family tried to escape, once unsuccessfully and ultimately successfully, during the slaughter of her people by the Ethiopians. She watched as members of her family and other families were imprisoned and killed. She spent one week imprisoned herself, scheduled for execution. At last, she came to the United States and lived in Oakland, California, too old to attend classes with children at her learning level. Harassed by her classmates and unable to speak English, she had a hard time learning what she calls "the basic stuff."

Loula is giving her tenth presentation of learning. She stands with some confidence in front of her panel and her audience. In addition to one Eagle Rock staff member, the panel comprises an off-campus educator, a local holder of public office, and an owner of a local business. In the audience are other Eagle Rock students and staff members and her sister Haimanot. The panel has been briefed: a POL is not about getting credit for classes. It is a time for the student to reflect on learning—to pause to make sense of learning, connect current learning to past learning, and project future learning goals.

Loula is well prepared. She has hung posters on portable dividers. She has brought in a couple of plants (for decoration?). She has placed stacks of papers on the floor in a line in front of the portable dividers. She is dressed up for the occasion in a long, light blue flowered dress, a blue sweater (even though it is August, it is chilly in the Rocky Mountains), and white platform shoes.

She announces the theme of her POL: knowledge and power. She elaborates: "Knowledge is power to me. To me, when I think of knowledge I think of what I can learn from a book, experience, technology, or religion." She points to examples of each on one of her posters, a collage representing these sources of knowledge. "Here is a father teaching a boy how to do something. Here is another picture—the boy is able to do what he was taught. Here is a picture of a man who is hungry. He has had the experience of being hungry and so he is going to go home and understand what happens to people who are hungry." Then she becomes specific: "For me, I have to experience things to know them. I have to do something." She moves on to another, similar collage, saying, "And the other thing is power. Once you have knowledge, you have power." The examples she offers are of a marriage in which both partners have knowledge and therefore power, and a mother who must teach her children so they will have power. She smiles and says, "For me to be knowledgeable and to have power is to strip my mask off and see clearly."

Loula is animated and personable, often smiling at her audience, using no notes or note cards, and moving comfortably around the space. She elaborates on her knowledge and power theme, weaving in one of the expectations that are part of 8 + 5 = 10: "When you have knowledge you can communicate effectively and show people what you know, especially when there are different opinions involved. You must share knowledge."

After this energetic introduction, Loula says, "The first thing that I'm going to talk about is *Huckleberry Finn*. In class, we focused on censorship, whether books should be banned or not, especially this one. Some people think it is racist and some people think that the grammar is not good enough. However, for me, this book was really important. I could find meaning in it. I don't like to read books just to find out what's going on; I like to find meaning. This book had a real moral value to me." Loula describes the relationship between Huck and Jim and how they learned things about each other, smiling as she reiterates her theme of knowledge. She says that what Huck and Jim experienced went far beyond the things they had been told about white people and black people. "This book showed me how people could be so narrow-minded because they didn't have experiences." She describes how Huck's prejudices changed because of a number of experiences with Jim along the Mississippi. She summarizes: "If we could teach students [the way Huck learned] instead of the way most students are forced to learn in school, we would learn a lot."

Next, Loula describes some class activities, emphasizing that each student had to teach a chapter or two to the rest of the class. She describes the two papers she wrote on themes she found important to her. "I wrote one that talked about the misconception of Jim." She reads portions of her papers to the panel and passes them around. Her papers reveal some strong feelings and cite passages from the novel to support her opinions. She summarizes her learning experience: "This was much more than reading a book. It made me think about life, my life. It also made me think about reading, how you should not just read a book and put it away but you should analyze it."

She bends over and picks up a notebook from among the papers on the floor. Bringing the notebook to the panel she says proudly, "Now I want you to see some other learning I did. For this math portfolio, I got [a rating of] "accomplished" the minute I got it in." She brags, "My problems of the week are sixteen pages, and I'm really proud of that, and I put a lot of effort into them. It's easy to get [a] "beginning" [rating], but I think I might as well go all the way." Then Loula steps up to a whiteboard, telling the panel that she is going to teach them something "really quick." She says, "I know how to do algebra and all that stuff, but I didn't know how to do the easy stuff, like fractions. When I came to the United States I hadn't done that stuff. I knew how to do the math, but I didn't understand it. I didn't see the picture." She writes a problem on the board, one involving dividing fractions. "I knew how to do this. I knew how to find a common denominator and all that, but I wanted to see how that works. So I just started to draw a picture. I knew what the answer would be, but what would it look like?" She shows how she thought through the problem by drawing circles. She makes a mistake and laughs softly as she corrects it and explains how that was the way she used to think, before she had pictures in her mind. She translates her learning about division of fractions into multiplication of fractions and makes clear to the panel and audience that she now understands what before she only "knew."

The student timekeeper signals to Loula that she is nearly out of time, so Loula changes subjects quickly. "Now for my personal growth." She moves to her right to stand next to one of the plants she hung from the portable divider. "It was really hard this trimester. It's been really difficult. I've been bitter, and I really have a lot of problems inside me right now, and I've been trying to deal with them. I want to share with you guys how to grow plants, and how plants and humans are similar." The plants are not just homey decorations.

Loula then reads aloud from a paper she wrote in her hydroponics class. She compares plants needing the sun to humans needing love to survive in this world. "We need nurturing in the form of people caring for us, just like plants need fertilizers. And, you know plants always have weeds growing around them. That also happens to us. I want to be able to take the weeds out of my life, because I have a lot of them growing around me right now. I can't learn when I'm being choked by the weeds." She talks about one thing that is helping her cope—"spiritual email from my 'mom' Belle. She's a coach, working with me every day, sending me stuff, helping me raise up and up." She mentions other people in the community who help her, like Audrey, the registrar, who just lets her sit down to talk.

She finishes her POL by pointing to another poster on the portable dividers, this time one of a lantern: "Right here, my light, is that I want to be able to come out of my darkness; I want to be able to light up. I'm really scared to move on in my life right now." She talks about a tutor from the town who is working with her on the possibility of college. Loula is clear that she wants to go, but she is scared, as well. "[Going to college] means a lot to me because it's the thing I'm scared of most."

If you visit Eagle Rock when students are giving presentations of learning (POLs), you are invited to participate in a briefing and a debriefing. During the briefing, you hear how POLs are designed and for what purposes. During the debriefing, you share with other panelists and audience members what you observed. Debriefings often start with the prompt *I was struck by . . .* , which allows panel members and others to describe their impressions, negative and positive. As you read about Loula's POL, you may have been struck by a number of things.

For example, did you take note of the purpose of POLs? They are about making sense of learning, something much more important than getting credit. Some visitors, seeing that the Eagle Rock schedule reserves a whole week for POLs, wonder if that's not an awful waste of learning time. I tell them that it is during this week that the most and best learning goes on, as students process their past thirteen weeks of learning, connect it to previous learning, project it into future learning (application), and reflect on, interpret, and analyze it. That's powerful education!

A POL lasts a full thirty minutes (sixty minutes if it is a graduation POL). For some brand-new students, hardly able to look an adult in the eye when they arrive much less present themselves as learners, the thirty-minute POLs seem impossible. But they rise to the occasion. And they are provided plenty of practice in presenting themselves. Before they leave for the wilderness trip, these new students work in small groups to be able to teach 8 + 5 = 10 to their wilderness guides. When they return from the trip, they give a solo five-minute presentation before the immediate community. In the classes they take during the second six weeks of the trimester, they make frequent solo presentations to their classmates. The expectation is never lowered, but a series of increasingly more challenging practice opportunities makes it possible for them to achieve the expectation. Learning is a process.

We look at POLs as a representation of a student's academic and personal development. We do not expect a first-timer's POL to be as sophisticated and introspective as a graduate's, but we expect quite a lot of a graduation POL. We keep running records of POLs on videotape so we (and the students) can examine and compare early and later POLs to determine growth. Learning is developmental.

POLs are individualized. Within some boundaries (they need to include academic growth, personal growth, and 8 + 5 = 10), students may do whatever they want. Each POL is custom crafted and unique. Members of small communities pay attention to one another, however, and any POL innovation is bound to appear in other POLs the next trimester. This copycatting has a benefit: instructors and administrators don't have to do much talking about quality and raising standards. Quality ratchets up by itself because students see what other students have done successfully and craft their next POLs similarly. Learning is personal and social.

Were you surprised that Loula has so much insight into her own learning? She is very clear about the purposes of learning and how she learns best, particularly her need to make pictures in order to understand something. Community life at Eagle Rock is all about learning. Learning is a frequent topic of conversation, formally in gatherings, community meetings, and classes, informally in conversations students have with adults and their peers. Adults share with students their own learning processes and have conversations with other adults about learning. Learning about learning is as important as learning.

Asking students to talk about both academic and personal growth in their POLs is a deliberate choice. Loula makes clear that her academic and personal growth are linked. At an age when most children would be learning to read and write (in their own and other languages), Loula was focused on basic survival. When she was finally able to start school in the United States, she couldn't learn "the basic stuff"—partly because she had to learn English first, but also because her classmates harassed her. Her thwarted emotional growth stalled her academic growth. She continues to have emotional problems. Who wouldn't? Some of her instructors believe Loula suffers from post-traumatic stress syndrome and are helping her learn about and deal with that disorder. Learning is about the whole person. Loula graduated in August 1999, six months after her younger sister Haimanot did, spent one year at a small college, took a year off, and is back in college.

Why Learner Centered?

The question visitors often ask when visiting Eagle Rock is, *Why learner centered?* This question often implies a second: *Why not student centered?* A third question, deeply embedded in experience and not politically correct, usually remains unasked: *Why not teacher centered?* That last answer is easy: our curriculum is about how students learn, not about how teachers teach. Old-timers at Eagle Rock remember when the curriculum they were taught (or taught themselves in their first days as teachers) was centered around how teachers teach—composing syllabi, providing content outlines for lectures, using textbook chapters to cover the material, assigning end-of-chapter questions for homework, and assessing learning with tests. A popular saying illustrates one manifestation of the teacher-centered curriculum: *I taught them. I don't know why they did not learn.*

Teachers back then did too much of the learning work. The real learning work in a school needs to be done by students. Eleanor Duckworth's elegant book *The Having of Wonderful Ideas and Other Essays on Teaching and Learning* (1987) describes students as learners. In her many examples she explores the learning that her graduate students do—both learning about teaching and learning about themselves as learners of subjects outside teaching. In her chapter Teaching as Research, she presents two aspects of learning: (1) engaging with phenomena and (2) having the students explain. As she develops her thesis through descriptions of her students studying the moon, she remarks, "This is quite a new and difficult experience for people whose idea of teaching is to do the explaining" (124). Later in the chapter, she zeros in on the teacher's practice of explaining, exhorting her teacher learners to practice "teaching by listening rather than by explaining" (129). "[I]t is the students who make sense of all this. It could not be otherwise. And they make sense by trying out their own ideas, by explaining what they think and why, and seeing how this holds up in other people's eyes, in their own eyes, and in the light of the phenomena they are trying to understand" (130). She adds, "First, in trying to make their thoughts clear for other people, students achieve greater clarity for themselves. Much of the learning is in the explaining. (Why should the teacher monopolize occasions for trying to make herself clear?)"

The answer to *Why not student centered?* is subtler. The following statements help distinguish between a student-centered and a learner-centered approach:

1. Learner centered allows for *the whole person,* not just the academic or student side of the person.

2. Learner centered implies a *process* related to how people learn, not a state of being.

3. Learner centered *equalizes* the inhabitants of the classroom and the school building.

4. Learner centered allows the *adult to be a learner,* along with the younger people in a school.

The Whole Person

It may be quibbling, but *student centered* implies that only the academic side of a learner is being considered. *Learner centered* allows the whole person as a learner to be considered—the cognitive, emotional, and social aspects—all of which are important in learning. Our work on the whole learner is informed by the work on emotions and the brain summarized by Daniel Goleman (1998) and the work done on character development and moral education by Thomas Lickona (1991).

Loula recently took a class called Chick Lit, which focuses on literature by and about women. The day I visit, students have read "I Stand Here Ironing," by Tillie Olson, and they have responded to it with writing of their own. Ashanti has written:

> I was [one] of four other kids. My mom had kids with three different guys. Both husbands died on her, so I grew up without a father like Emily. And with a mother who wasn't really around like I wanted her to be. She provided a house, clothes and food. And, yah, she loved me, but I didn't see it in her. I didn't feel it. And I felt like what ever I did wasn't good enough. My mother always told me that I was her most beautiful child ever, like Emily's mother told her. I was never sent to a home. But a lot of my time I thought one of those places would have been best for me. It was hard for me to open up my heart and self to my mother. My mother regrets everything she ever did wrong to me, but she can't change the past.

She reads her piece matter of factly, even dismissively. A student new to Eagle Rock, she does not expect much response, but she gets it. Loula tells why she likes it and relates Ashanti's experience to her own background. Jena chimes in with a similar experience. Loula gives sage advice: "Never give up on your mom, never. She may not have seemed to be there for you, but she was—in her own way." Students around the table waggle their hands in agreement (the deaf signal for applause). Danielle asks Ashanti how old her mom is and nods at the response: "My mom is the same as yours. It's best when I'm here away from her. When I go home, it's not good. The patterns repeat themselves." Loula says, "We think our parents should be perfect—that's what we expect. I predict that your mom will look at you someday and apologize." Danielle disagrees, "You don't know Ashanti's mom."

Ashanti comes back in with, "You don't know how pissed I am about her." It is quiet for a moment, and then Ashanti continues, "But maybe everything my mom put me through has made me strong. Maybe I'm the parent." The conversation about Ashanti's paper has gone on for about seven minutes. Amanda, the intern leading the class, quietly brings it back to the story with a direct question to Ashanti, one that piques her interest: "So, who do you relate to, the mother or the daughter?" Ashanti eagerly describes how she relates to both the mother and the daughter, and then the rest of the students have twenty more minutes of animated discussion about the book and their personal lives. Several times they come back to Ashanti's writing or their own to say, "It's just like that" or "See, that happened to me, too." Reacting emotionally to the story they have read helps them understand it cognitively.

Think how differently this class would have played out if Amanda had asked the students to analyze some aspect of the story (plot, character, symbols, theme), told Ashanti she had not fulfilled the assignment when she responded personally as she did, or stopped the other students from offering empathy and advice.

Why do we value the personal at Eagle Rock? For a couple of good reasons.

First, personal issues are very much on students' minds. Most students at Eagle Rock are emotionally troubled, but all young people deal with emotional issues that sometimes cloud their learning processes. Before they arrive, Eagle Rock students must address the addictions they've used to protect them from the emotional problems they need to confront. Once admitted to Eagle Rock, students begin to sort through their emotional issues and learn how to address them. Sometimes they don't earn much credit for the first one or two trimesters with us because they are working on their personal growth. We have learned to be patient. Once they have acknowledged these personal issues—if not solved them—the academic growth that has so long eluded them occurs. The reading and writing problems, the mathematics frustrations, the opaqueness of social studies and science, all lessen, and students can learn. To ignore personal issues and emotional responses is to ignore so much of what being adolescent means.

Second, cognitive processes are fueled by emotional responses. In other words, students learn better when they have an emotional tie to what they are learning. A good example is Antoinette's response to a class on the Holocaust. Antoinette wrote:

> Another class that I took was the Holocaust. When I came to Eagle Rock, I had no clue what the Holocaust was, not one clue. I never knew that millions of people died just because of who they were. I never realized during World War II that ovens were burning innocent

men, women, babies, and kids. Who would have known that ovens were no longer made to cook food but to burn flesh? While taking other classes, I understood more about the past, but I never learned anything that leads us towards making our lives better. But with this class, I have been questioning myself: What if this happens again? Why is hate so strong in our eyes? When will we learn? When we can no longer count the bodies that lie before us? I never knew this thing before, but now it's my job to make sure that people know.

Many schools are afraid to design and implement a personal development curriculum (Eagle Rock's catchall term for emotional growth, social skills, leadership, and character development). That fear is justified but must be overcome if students, who cannot be parsed into their academic, emotional, and social selves for educational purposes, are to learn. Many schools realize that stated or not, they have a personal growth curriculum. Many decide that it's better to bring that curriculum out into the open, examine it, and decide whether it represents what the community expects of the school. Most schools make the examination of the personal values they want to teach a community event, one in which parents, the churches, and civic organizations play a large part. The Baltimore County School District bases its character development curriculum on the Constitution of the United States and the Bill of Rights. Few object to teaching what's in those two documents, and each year each school community in the district selects something from these documents on which to focus.

Eagle Rock's graduation requirements include personal growth related to character development and leadership. Although the curriculum related to that requirement is infused throughout each day through gatherings and community meetings, individual and group interactions, and special events such as gender meetings, it is best expressed through two graduation activities. Students who have petitioned to graduate from Eagle Rock put together a portfolio filled with items that attest to their personal growth, which is then presented to a panel of their choice. Chapter 7 discusses personal growth POLs in detail.

In one of CJ's POL packets he described his struggle with alcoholism (he began to drink at the age of five) and how he put up walls so he wouldn't get hurt. Then he wrote, "While I was at Eagle Rock the same thing happened. I was a rock with my feelings. I did not share what was really going on with me. While I was stuffing my feelings and not letting anyone know what was going on with me, I was not getting any work done in any of my classes. I was at Eagle Rock for nine months and didn't hardly get any credit. I think part of the reason was that I wasn't dealing with my emotions. . . . My self-destruction interfered with my ability to think straight and stay focused on my studies."

And, yes, we have not allowed students to graduate if they have not achieved as much in their personal growth as they need to. Sometimes the decision is mutual—the student knows that he or she is not ready to graduate. Sometimes the student has denied the real situation and needs both to overcome the denial and to move on.

The Learning Processes

When learning was seen as one-dimensional, focused around IQ, and education consisted of getting students to produce the right answer, learning was mostly a single process. Using the term *learner centered* instead of *student centered* helps us focus on the *processes* of learning. At Eagle Rock students, as individual as each one is, *find their own particular pathway through the curriculum*. That's why our transcript is called an individualized learning plan. It's not that we change expectations for each student but that each student works his or her way through the curriculum differently, taking this or that six-week class to learn about something while another student takes some other course to learn about the same thing. A student can pursue an interest in civil rights both while learning history and while writing an essay of opposing ideas. Within a few boundaries, *students* choose the ways they will learn content.

Our students not only *choose specific ways to go about learning what they need to learn* (listening to tapes, reading books, interviewing people), but also *represent what they learn in different ways* (a video, an essay, a model, a dramatization). They work together, informally and formally, teaching and helping one another learn.

Most new students don't trust that Eagle Rock is a place of *emotional safety* until they have been here awhile and have learned that no one laughs when someone makes a mistake. They also have to learn that the most respectful thing we can do is hold them to *high expectations* rather than excuse them from learning. They learn that we mean what we say when we require something and that we'll offer them sufficient scaffolding—cognitive as well as emotional—so that they can achieve our expectations.

Finally, students are given *regular chances* (once a trimester) *to process their learning* and identify themselves as learners through presentations of learning. POLs are a time for students to step back, reflect, and consider themselves as learners. (This long view is complemented in the classroom by a wide variety of other assessments, mostly documentations—exhibits and demonstrations, for example—but also tests and quizzes.) These presentations of learning are individualized—students find a variety of ways to express themselves, sometimes visually through paintings or sculpture, sometimes dramatically through skits, monologues, or dramatizations, sometimes kinetically through dance. Students write about their learning processes in the packets they prepare for the panel members who will observe and critique their POLs. What they write about themselves in these packets reveals the different pathways they have taken as learners. Let's look at a few examples.

Donnie wrote: "One of the best places to grow as a person at Eagle Rock is in classes. I have known this for some time, so this trimester I decided to take full advantage of this fact. In my class called Let the Games Begin our goal was to learn the history of the Olympics and at the end of the class design and implement our own Eagle Rock Olympics. In this class, I found myself not challenged by the curriculum. In the past I had looked at this and decided I was lucky because I got to coast through a class. In this situation, however, I decided that I was going to make challenges for myself." Working with his instructors (a regular instructor and an intern), Donnie planned his own pathway through the curriculum. At the end of the class, he said, "It would have been easy to not do anything, and doing nothing where no one would notice has been typical of myself in the past. Throughout this course I challenged myself in ways far outside of my comfort zone and, despite that discomfort, I was successful."

Courtney chose her pathway through a class called Mysteries of Humanity Uncovered, a mathematics and social studies course team-taught by instructors in both areas. She wrote in her packet, "The class started with math mysteries such as pi. A couple of weeks into the course we expressed things that we were interested in, then we did intensive research on that subject. My interest from the beginning was on fractals, the infinite pattern. My research was like a fractal in a way, branching off in many directions, mostly tangents of math. This was one of my favorite classes because of my enthusiasm, independence, and motivation."

Darby wrote, "The new knowledge that I have acquired has started the momentum of my learning capabilities. Now that I have officially allowed myself to expand my knowledge base, I expect for its velocity (speed with direction = graduation!) to continue accelerating. Too bad my physics class doesn't have a formula to teach that calculation! I am even beginning to enjoy these calculations. In [Mysteries of Humanity Uncovered] I took on an independent study of the golden ratio and the golden rectangle. Whoa, this is some seriously insane math! I *think* I still have a dislike for math, but I am going to admit that it did feel extremely gratifying to get my hands dirty in confusion and then wash them off with my own understanding, simply by persevering."

Danielle found her way through a class called Toxic Sludge and You: "Toxic Sludge and You was an environmental science and a regular science class, focusing on pollution here in Colorado and in our home towns. This class was exciting. We went on a field trip every week that had everything to do with the subject we were dealing with in the class. I worked hard in this class, and I pulled a lot of work out of it. It was easier for me to work with a partner in trying to get the work done, and that was okay with the instructors. At the end of the class, David and I had to give a presentation on the top polluters in our home towns. The presentation turned out beautifully. David and I teamed up and finished all our work at about the same time, and we received the most credit out of all the people in the class."

David wrote: "My other class, Toxic Sludge and You, was one of my all-time favorite classes since I have been here at Eagle Rock. This class was . . . basically an original class, which means it was the first time at Eagle Rock to have the class. The class focus was on pollution and the many different aspects of pollution in the United States. The class got a chance to go to Rocky Flats to learn about how they are working themselves out of their jobs by cleaning up after the mess they made. They were releasing plutonium into the ground regardless of the hazardous level. So the class got a chance to see a plant reinforce itself and take responsibility for their fault. The class learned about other aspects of the role of a hazardous waste cleaner, the role of the Environmental Protection Agency, and the role of clients that have to clean up after their mess. I liked this class because we got to learn about what we were interested in; we had guidelines but we didn't have to do the same thing. Learning is fun when you get to learn about what you're interested in. I learned and was so interested about environmental pollution that I have changed my major research paper to environmental racism. I was previously doing a paper on the stock market, but this class influenced me and caught my interest so I decided to change my major research project."

Stephanie wrote a prose poem called "Testimony: Tasting Heaven." Her opening paragraph is quite dramatic: "Time is settling and collecting like pooling blood, like smoke from the fury of love. I'm hiding from the minutes, losing my sanity as they pass. I've lost my heart in the turmoil. I've lost my face in the crowd. I'm praying for an awakening. I'm praying for a taste of heaven."

Elizabeth began her autobiography with a poem:

Learning never stops.
Just when I think it's all over and I can sit down and catch my breath,
life pulls the rug
out

from under me.
There I am, in the middle of the air, grabbing frantically in all
directions for a handhold. But what better thing to do than
stop. Take a breath and
enjoy
my moment of clarity
split second
when everything is
possible.

She went on: "I don't understand very much about life. After all, I have
only been here eighteen years. Not so long, you might say. But I can
see a little. All of what I know I turn over and over in my head, polishing and sanding off the excess until I have tiny gleaming bits of
truth. I take these pieces and throw them down in front of me, hoping that they lead my way." Then she shared four pieces of truth with
her readers.

Ariann's entire autobiography was a poem, "Swimming Inside My
Thick Skull." One section used her swimming class as a metaphor:

I'm doing more than getting my feet wet this trimester.
I put my body in and my head under.
I learned to tread water for at least
Ten minutes
Of my time taken out to discuss past issues
I've never dealt with before I came here.
Do more than keep your head above water.
Get somewhere!

Thanks to cognitive psychologists, brain researchers, and construct-
ivists, we know so much more about the processes of learning now. What
brain researchers have discovered about how the brain works correlates
highly with what cognitive psychologists have theorized about cognition.
And the constructivist theory of learning complements these discoveries
and theories. At Eagle Rock our reference points have been Howard
Gardner, Renate and Geoffrey Caine, and Jacqueline Grennon and Martin
G. Brooks. The implications for instruction embedded in their theories
have led us to consider multiple intelligences, learning styles, and brain-
based learning, among other things. We ensure that our students can
make choices in their learning, not only about how to learn but also about
how to demonstrate that they have learned.

Equality in the Classroom

Curriculum that is learner centered provides students some power
and control over their learning. Caine and Caine (1991) warn that
"teachers must not overspecify what students are exposed to. Because

what teachers emphasize shapes what students are permitted to grasp, excessive control may actually inhibit learning" (123). Curriculum must be stated in broad enough terms that each learner can find his or her own pathway through it. It must provide a multitude of ways for students to learn what they have chosen to learn within the curriculum expectations. For example, Rachel researched her interest in firefighting by enlisting as a volunteer firefighter; she wrote poetry about a firefighting experience she had; she researched the growth of a forest for a science credit; and in another science class she investigated the chemical properties of various firefighting techniques.

Finally, curriculum must allow students to document learning in a way that is important to them. In a Touch the Future class, David designed a nature center to show what he had learned. Joe edited a videotape of the class events into a training manual for future enrollees.

Many students at Eagle Rock have previously attended schools in which the key aspects of learning seemed to be a closely held secret. They have had to ask, "Will this be on the test?" They have not known what is important and what is peripheral; as a result they are not good note takers, and they don't know what to study. They are wary when they are told to "make it as long as it needs to be." In "Secure Tests, Insecure Test Takers" Grant Wiggins (1990) speculates that students who don't feel they have power over their learning often "turn off" about learning, drop out or sit in the back of the classroom, passive rather than active learners.

In addition to providing students more power and control over their own learning through curriculum, instruction, and assessment, Eagle Rock equalizes power relationships in more concrete ways. Eagle Rock students relish the symbolism of round tables—there's no front of the classroom where a person with power and authority over learning resides; there's no back of the classroom in which to hide from learning. Everyone sits at the table together, everyone goes by first names. In discussions, students make comments to and ask questions of one another rather than with just the teacher. Sometimes another student, not the teacher, explains something.

Even more important, students are often teachers in their classrooms—sharing research, giving presentations, making demonstrations, exhibiting their knowledge. It's true that students learn more when they have to teach it (we all do), but it's also true that students sometimes learn better from other students. The expectation that all students will teach helps equalize the power in the classroom.

Everyone Is a Learner

Student centered implies that there are students whose job it is to learn and teachers whose job it is to teach. Being *learner centered* suggests that we all can be learners, that, in fact, it is our job to learn. It's good for students to perceive their teachers as learners, within and outside the classroom.

Teacher learning is usually thought of as professional development, often listening to a motivational speaker or attending a formal workshop. This may have value in the moment but it seldom produces lasting or substantive improvement. Pundits call this "drive by" professional development. "The sage on the stage" departs and what he or she has said has little relevance to the complex tasks of teaching and learning.

A better way to think about teacher learning is to look at it as embedded in the teaching process. It is learning that arises out of the daily life of teachers and students. Sometimes it takes the form of action research wherein the teacher, sometimes with a colleague, poses questions about what is happening in the classroom or school: *What happens when . . . ? Why does . . . happen? What difference would it make if . . . ?* Research requires careful observation of the learning environment.

Sometimes the best teacher learning happens when teachers develop curriculum, design courses, or evaluate student work. For some teachers, real learning happens when they put together a portfolio for certification or a performance evaluation or simply their own benefit. More collaborative and formal learning opportunities embedded in teaching and learning include the tuning protocol (Easton 1999) and its variations, study groups (organized around a reading, theme or issue), peer coaching, networking, teaming, mentoring, and needs assessment or data collection.

Another form of professional development we use at Eagle Rock is to let our students be our teachers. We learn from them whenever we observe them closely and ask them direct questions: *How do you know this? How did you learn this? What will help you learn this? How can we design this learning experience so that all of you can learn? What gets in your way when you are trying to learn this?* Their answers help us design a course or a rubric. Students and teachers can be learners together. Problems that affect both students and staff members are solved more effectively when everyone works on them together.

Questions to Consider

1. Would most people in your school describe it as teacher centered, student centered, or learner centered? What is teacher centered at your school? What is student centered? What is learner centered?

2. How is being teacher, student, or learner centered reflected in your curriculum guide, teaching units, requirements (required books, required courses, required assignments), assessments, professional development experiences? What does each artifact say about being or not being learner centered?

3. Where do you have evidence of powerful learning? What are the common characteristics of the experiences that produce powerful learning?

4. What does the role of practice look like in your school? Is it meaningless? meaningful?

5. Do you have mechanisms in place that equalize learning for everyone? What additional mechanisms could you employ?

6. To what extent is your conversation at school (student to student, student to teacher, teacher to student, teacher to teacher) about learning? What would we hear in the halls, in an assembly, in the teachers lounge?

7. In what ways are adults learners in your school?

8. What kinds of professional development do you provide? Is it the type that trusts the school experience and begins with it? In what ways is professional development embedded in the real issues of teaching and learning in your school?

9. When are students the teachers in your school?

10. What is your approach to the whole student? Do you ignore personal growth? Do you consider it individually but, to be safe, not make your considerations overt? Do you address personal growth overtly, involving the whole school community in the effort? What expectations do you have for students' personal growth at your school?

11. Are there a variety of ways that students can work their way through your curriculum? Can they choose their passions in each subject? Can they connect what they are learning in each subject, so that it makes sense to them? Are there a variety of ways students can learn in your school?

12. Are there a variety of ways students can be assessed on their learning in your school?

13. How does the whole system focus on learning?

14. Who is the head learner at your school?

15. How can your school be more learner centered? Which of these ways could be most easily implemented and would have the greatest effect?

Chapter Five

Curriculum Is
Competency Based

Here is a section from the autobiographical essay Jeremy included in his graduation presentation of learning packet:

> I do not remember much about my life before Eagle Rock. I remember sitting in front of a record player listening to the Jackson 5, and all those good memories, but I do not remember the times I was hurting myself. For a couple of years, all I did was drink, get high, smoke, and ditch school. When I did go to school, I would show up around my last period or only to meet some friends. I remember my mother asking me if I planned to drop out of school when I was old enough. My answer was, "Yes, and get my G.E D." All of the time I was out getting high, fighting and not going to school, I was building a police record. A large amount of my early teenage years were spent in jail. I even did time in Santa Fe, New Mexico [Jeremy grew up in Denver]. Eventually a magistrate saw that the way to change me was not through being in a lockdown facility, but through counseling and one-on-one attention. Magistrate "N" ordered me to attend a drug and alcohol rehabilitation center that also dealt with anger management—that is what I needed. This is where my strengths were brought out and my leadership skills were sharpened. When I completed that program, the director told me about Eagle Rock and what a great place it would be for me. So, I applied and was accepted.

It is August 1999, and Jeremy is delivering his graduation POL. Talia, a classmate, is introducing his panel from the stage of the Human Performance Center (our name for the gym). Jeremy's "set" (from right to left from the viewpoint of the audience) includes a display board with the sayings "How Do I Become Better by Not Doing Good Work?" and "What Does It Help to Do Good?"; a whiteboard; a display board with brightly painted trees (apple trees?) in front of which is a ladder; a model building with the label "Highland Folk School" on it; another display board with what looks like a bus, labeled "Montgomery," on it and a row of chairs in front of it; and a final display board with a set of dramatic red and black symbols.

Finally Talia introduces Jeremy, telling us that this is his sixth and final POL. Jeremy swaggers down the aisle that halves the audience of about three hundred people, swinging a cane and wearing a brown fedora, a beige formal shirt, a beige sweater vest, and brown pants; his shoes are brown and white oxfords, and he sports a goatee that tapers at the end to a few long hairs.

Gesturing to someone in the audience, he says, "Can I talk to you, sir?" A man in a white shirt stands up and comes forward, his back to the audience. He is the head of school, Robert Burkhardt. Jeremy and Robert confer, the microphone attached to Jeremy's sweater picking up their words. "I've been here for a while, and I've done a lot here." Robert looks exasperated, his eyes directed toward the ceiling, not looking at Jeremy, his hands clasped, his mouth tight. Then they face each other. "I've done very well. I want to be out of here." Jeremy's goatee bobs.

"You want to be out of the family?" Robert asks. "The Godfather wants to know why you deserve it." There is laughter as the audience realizes the premise of the POL.

"I've worked hard; I've worked hard for the last two and a half years."

"Talk is cheap," replies the Godfather harshly. "You're going to have to prove it." He turns, walks away, and sits down.

Jeremy immediately says, "I guess I'll start with math." He walks to the whiteboard. "I'd like to tell you about my independent math study. I had four developing math portfolios and one accomplished math portfolio. [Eagle Rock requires portfolios as documentation of mathematics learning. Portfolios are accepted at three levels: beginning, developing, and accomplished. Students need a certain number of each category, but they can continue to work on beginning and developing portfolios, if they want, to make them accomplished and therefore reduce the total number of portfolios.] I could have settled on doing developing, but I went for a higher goal, accomplished. In the full six weeks of the class, I got them done in four weeks. I did what was needed to make all five accomplished. It was a lot of hard work, a lot of questioning, a lot of mistakes, corrections. One of the things I learned in the independent study is always to set my goals higher.

"I was in a math class called All About Alice to prove to myself that I could understand math. That's the ultimate task—proving it to yourself—and then you explain it to others so they can learn and understand how to do it. Here's an example of what I needed to prove to myself. I'm going to go through why any number to the 0 power is 1." He is at the whiteboard now, writing on it. "So, we'll start with 2 to the third power. The way it works is that this is your base number; this is your exponent. The way I see it is that there are this many numbers—one, two, three—of 2 and then you multiply them together." He demonstrates, linking the first two 2s and getting 4 and then linking the third 2 and getting 8. "Now we're going to go back, why 2 to the 0 is 1. You take this number 8 and reverse the procedure, dividing instead of multiplying." He divides 8 by 2 and then by 2 again. "Divide instead of multiply. Go back one more time and it's 1.

"Fine. That didn't mean anything to me, so I had to go back to the structure of the class—its meaning." He explains that the premise of the class is that Alice changes size as she drinks various potions, sometimes losing and sometimes gaining height. "Say Alice is five feet tall." He writes 5 on the board. "When she eats a piece of cake she'll double in height." He writes 5 × 2. "Let's say she eats three pieces of cake, so we have 2 to the third [power]. We'll put the 3 as the exponent. We just proved 2 to the third was 8, so 5 × 8 = 40." He writes this. "So remember that this," he says, pointing to the exponent, "is how many pieces of cake she ate. And 5 is how tall she is. So 5 × 2 is how she doubles each time she eats cake. But if she doesn't eat *any* cake, then she stays the same. Five feet. So 2 to 0 (no cake) = 1 and she stays five feet. You understand?"

He speaks clearly, personally, with gestures, turning to his audience several times, checking for their understanding. He smiles. He had to make his own meaning of the formula, the story rather than just the numbers. "That's what I had to do with all the mathematics portfolios I brought to an accomplished level; I had to find the meaning. The numbers were not enough." He goes over to a table and holds up his thick portfolios: "Each of the portfolios I've done—this one, this one, this one, this one, and this one—they're pretty thick. A lot of good math in these. They're accomplished." He steps to the podium and says, "It took a lot of self-discipline to have the *intellectual* discipline to do the portfolios this way." He points to the math on the whiteboard.

Then he points to the display board with sayings on it. "A few questions started coming to my mind, like *What does it help* not *to do good? How do I become better by* not *doing work?* So I sat down, didn't do any work, and started thinking about it. I couldn't come up with an answer. Then I came up with an opposite question, *What does it help to do good?* And the answer came easily—it came quickly, I mean. To do good, it helps to have good follow-through, and good follow-through helps with good responsibility. You get self-gratification. So while I was doing math," he points to his portfolios, "I learned about other subjects

. . . and life." He points to the sayings. Then he sighs, "Sir, am I ready to go?" He rubs his hands together in expectation.

Robert gets up ponderously, in the manner of Marlon Brando as the Godfather. He shrugs his shoulders to the audience, palms up. "It's not just about math. Is this all you've done? This? This is the learning?" He shrugs again and waves his hand in dismissal. There is gentle laughter from the audience.

"Okay, okay," Jeremy says. "I'll teach you something! I'll teach you about some things I learned about the fifties." He picks up his cane and moves to his left. He explains how the whole school studied the 1950s together to get ready to put on *Grease* in August. "So the first period was broken up into different sections—pop culture, advancements, social issues in the world—and the last two weeks we chose a specific area, a class you'd make for yourself. I chose We Shall Overcome, a class on the civil rights era and the blacks in the South fighting for their rights. So we discussed people like Malcolm X and Martin Luther King and the Montgomery bus boycott and all the events leading up to it."

Several students come forward and take seats as if they're on a bus. "One day Rosa Parks sits on a bus after a long day of work." He sits down in a chair on the "bus." "Her feet are tired, or so she says, and the bus driver yells out. . . ." Someone from the audience yells, "Hey, colored, move on back." "Rosa Parks moved enough to let the man next to her get out of the way." The students move around. "She knew that it was time, that this had to come to an end. She knew segregation had to come to an end. That's how we always heard the story. How we were taught the story. You've got to look before that, however, at least a year. See, I think that Rosa Parks planned the sit-down. It was a plan. Here's why." The other students have left the stage now, and Jeremy is teaching the audience.

"First reason—and the most convincing reason for me—is that she worked for the local NAACP. For the local NAACP! She was the head secretary for the NAACP. She was already involved in the civil rights movement. She wasn't just an ordinary person; she was already planning that this would come to an end. Six weeks before she sat down, she went to the Highland Folk School." He gestures to his display. "This place recruited people they thought would be good civil rights leaders. Taught them civil disobedience and peaceful means of change. She went there six weeks before she decided not to stand up on that bus. That's two reasons. The third reason, the same NAACP she worked for had tried to start the same bus boycott twice before but was unsuccessful because the first girl, a girl named Claudia Colvin, sat down on the bus, and the bus driver allowed more whites to come onto the bus and called 'Negroes move back,' but she didn't want to, so she didn't.

She sat there; they called the police on her; the police asked her to stand up, and they picked her up and carried her to the station and booked her. The NAACP jumped on that—this was their chance—let's start the boycott. But Claudia got pregnant about a month later, and she lost credibility. To start this movement and everything else to come after it, you have to have everything else perfect, but she got pregnant. Couldn't deal with her, so the boycott quit.

"Another time, another woman did it but, for some reason, she lost credibility. So Rosa Parks was a secretary at the NAACP, went to the Highland Folk School, was already involved in civil rights, wanted change. . . ." He moves back over to the "bus" chairs and sits down again as Rosa Parks. "That day she sits on the bus—feet probably were tired—bus driver calls out 'Coloreds move back,' and she probably thought right then, 'I think it's time. Today's the day.' I think that's how it happened.

"But doing all this I started to think, 'Where were the Hispanics? Where were they? Were there any?' Of course, but never in the history books; I could never find anything out about them at that time. And that's when I began. . . ." He reaches behind the podium and brings out a dramatic red-and-black poster of an eagle, wings spread. He holds it up and shakes it and students call from the audience, "Viva La Raza!" They applaud and clap in unison. Jeremy steps forward and addresses his grandmother, who is in the audience. "So, Grandma, tell the absolute first thing, first thing, the absolute first thing that comes to your mind about Hispanic civil rights." She replies, "Cesar Chavez." "Good." Then he points to another family member in the audience, "Give me some other names." She is unable to do so. He addresses a panel member. "Tim, tell me, where did civil rights happen?" Tim answers, "The South." "See," Jeremy says, "other than an educated, very brown, very smart woman," pointing to his grandmother, "we don't know about more than blacks in the South. Yes, that's huge, a huge part of American history, and I think what they did is help all others get their rights, but you don't hear about Cesar Chavez; you don't hear about his story to get people rights. Blacks, Latinos, Asians, Mexicans. Everybody.

"So we need to recognize that in the fifties, Cesar Chavez did a boycott of grapes. He asked people not to buy grapes without a union sticker on them. Let me tell you why. When he was a young boy, he owned land—I think in Arizona—about eighty acres. A company came to him and said, 'You have a Spanish land grant. That doesn't mean anything anymore, so what we're going to do is buy forty acres of that and give you a land grant for the rest of it.' Chavez said that was okay, better than all the legal stuff. The deal started to go through, but he found out that the land he had coming to him wasn't worth anything, so he went to a lawyer to get the land grant land. 'Can you help me out?' The lawyer said yes and lent him the money and said, 'Just pay for the land and then pay me back.' Everything was fine until he couldn't start making payments, so the lawyer took the land back and sold it to the company that had originally screwed him in the first place. They lost all the land. The whole family—about seven of them—had to move to California and all the boys started picking. Picked fruit all his life, even quit eighth grade so he could pick for his family. And when his father got sick and died, his mother wanted to replace him in the fields, but Chavez said no and that he would work more. So he kept picking. He went to work and came home and started picking again."

Jeremy, a large wicker basket in hand, climbs the ladder in front of the painted apple trees. "He knew what it was like to be mistreated on the farms. In some places the farm owners would make the pickers buy a cup, a little one to get water. They would make them buy a new cup each time they needed water, a new one. They'd take the old one and throw it away." Jeremy is "picking" fruit preset on top of the display screen. "In some cases, the farm owners would not provide the baskets. They would tell the farm workers that in about three days of picking they would be able to pay off a basket. They 'sold' them these baskets and so they would work as hard as possible, filling the baskets. At the end of the third day they would be told they were fired before they could turn in their last basket. The farmers got their baskets back and repeated the scam." Jeremy has gotten off the ladder and presented the basket to a panel member as if he were a picker about to be fired. "'Is it my basket now?' 'You're fired. It's our basket.' So Cesar Chavez knew what that was about. He knew that it was wrong. So, what he did is go from farm to farm telling people that it was wrong. 'Let's strike; we can change.' But they said, 'No, I don't want to lose my job. Can't afford it.'

"Finally, he got a start in one place; people were willing to strike for higher pay, and Cesar Chavez wanted them to fight for a recognized union, like the United Farm Workers, which is what he was. And so they started striking and they got the higher pay but they wanted to quit. They didn't get the recognized union—heartbreaking. Another time came around and they struck for higher pay, a recognized union, and benefits. They got higher pay but nothing else. He was heartbroken again, but he had it in his heart that what he was doing was right and he could not quit until success happened. Another strike came around, and this time he went around to about sixty different farms altogether and all of them—or most of them—decided to strike, so he went and he joined up with another union that was mostly Filipino and some Hispanics and whites and blacks. This time they struck for higher pay, better living conditions, a recognized union, no poisonous pesticides on the grapes they were picking, and so they struck for about three to four weeks, and farms began to lose money. So one of the farms flew a plane over the striking workers and sprayed pesticide on them, and the boycott against grapes was ruined. They struck again, but the farms brought in strikebreakers who pushed aside the strikers. The farm owners called the police, who pushed the workers aside as well, beating them down, just like the beatings you see on the newsreels from the fifties. The workers knew that what they were fighting for was right, even though they might not see the day that it came true. So finally one of the companies gave in, and then the others. Things haven't been perfect since then, but it has gotten better." He checks his notes at the podium. "So one thing that came to me is that the best way to do anything is with all your strength and all your will and to fight and fight and fight until you have nothing left except your will to get to your goal. Something as serious as that especially." An exhalation. "So, is this enough? Or do I need more?"

The Godfather stands up, faces the audience, shrugs and raises his shoulders and arms, hands with their palms up. "So, you think it's that easy. What have you done to change the world?"

"You're right," Jeremy says. "One thing Cesar Chavez said, and I think it's especially relevant to this school, is, 'The end of any education should be service to others.'" He has gone behind the podium and brought out two poster boards with this quote spread across them. He repeats the quote with vehemence. Then he says, "You know it; give to others. Service is something I've done plenty of here. Well over fifteen-hundred hours, not because I've been in trouble, like other places require, but because I find it self-gratifying, instant gratification. I've cleaned rivers in Estes, torn down this little structure—a whole house—so it could be rebuilt. I've painted, taken care of children. I've recycled. It can be as small as seeing someone struggling to carry something and offering to help. Something as easy as that—it's nothing to do."

He is given a signal from the timekeeper and knows he needs to move on. "At college I will be a Bonner Scholar [Jeremy was accepted to Marysville College on a full scholarship]. What this means is that I do at least ten hours of service weekly and they give me my money for college. Not a bad deal! What I'm going to try to do with that is teach tolerance. Tennessee, where I'm going to college, home of the Klan! Eighteen sixty-five, that was the start of the Klan there. Like Philbert [the director of students] says, there's some places still fighting the Civil War. I'm going to a place that's right in the center of that, rural Tennessee. Course there will be racism."

He checks his notes and follows up on his transition, moving to the last display board, covered with a bright poster of a cross on fire with symbols around it. "In 1865, six men from Tennessee started a group not much different from a fraternity—based on fun and pranks. The members were quite racist because they were all former Confederate soldiers, but the organization wasn't racist . . . yet. The group grew within a year because they did a different thing—it was fun and none of the members showed their faces in public. They put on hats, funny faces on the front of their masks, long robes, and they went around saying they were ghosts that had died in battle. And they'd go to a black person's home and they'd say, 'I haven't had a drink since I died,' and they'd start chugging the water down, one gallon, two gallons, three, four, five, and it would go down a tube into a container. So in doing this, there was a conscious and unconscious purpose. One, it scared the black families with their superstitions. And, I think it was an unconscious attempt to take back the South. So, in about a year, the Klan grew into every single state that was part of the Confederacy, and people started to do things in the name of it, like burning and killing.

"By 1867, Reconstruction had started. Most of the whites down there thought it was the way of the North, giving blacks superiority. It was the big, radical Republicans' way of punishing the South. So the six men from Tennessee called a meeting and asked, 'What are we going to do about Reconstruction?' Their enemies: the North, the carpetbaggers who mostly came from the North to take advantage of the South, the blacks. Nathan Bedford Forest. I just give you that name, Nathan Forest. Remember that name. So we have carpetbaggers who are trying to show people their rights, blacks who are taking on their rights as human beings. But here's what blacks heard, 'Here's your voting card, don't vote again. Tell all your people or they'll be killed.' Of course, people have the right to live, to do what's right. It's in the human soul to do what's right. So the blacks kept doing what was right, voting and being in political parties. And they kept dying. Mostly being killed, followed by warnings.

"This history has continued, from 1865 to now, 1999, in one form or another. The Aryan Nation, New World Order, World Christian Trade, National Alliance, Eastside Boys, neo-Nazis, all the skinheads. To this day! So, I know that's my mission. It's to step up and to teach tolerance. And do it in a peaceful way. Not, 'You're a Klan member, you're a racist, go to jail.' Say something with a hug, 'I love you.' I don't know how to do it," he shrugs and smiles slightly. "I want to do it. So, learn about the Klan, about Forest. Some of you think I take it too hard—and in some ways I do. I need to know it; I need to know the enemy within. What's ironic is," he points to the Montgomery sign, "1865 to 1964, ninety-nine years later, it repeated itself, and the Klan during both times and in between was very prominent. So this is one thing I'm very passionate about."

Jeremy moves to conclude his POL. "Another passion is sign language. I'm going to college to study sign language, and it's one of those things that's hard to explain. It's something I have to do. I love sign language and I like the Delphonics. You're going to laugh at my cheesy song, but it's wonderful. So, I'm going to sign to you this song. I'm a little jittery, so I might mess up. But here goes." The tape is slow to play so Jeremy does a vaudeville jig, then refers people to the words and music he has put below each chair. The song begins, "I love you so. . . ." There is applause when the sentimental song finishes, and he returns to the podium, grins and steps out again, "So. So, have I proven it yet? Have I done enough?"

Robert rises. "The Godfather wants to know. Has anything you've ever done made your life better?"

Jeremy wheels around, his back to the audience, and spreads his arms to encompass the entire set for his POL. The applause peaks with a standing ovation before the Godfather can make his pronouncement: "The Godfather says it's good, you can move on."

Students take special pleasure in designing their graduation POL. These become very personal expressions of their growth, both personal and academic. Some, like Jeremy's, have a dramatic structure that knits together what they have done. Some focus on a theme to give unity to their presentation. Others use a student's main interest, such as music or athletics, to bring in whatever else they want to present. Eric, for example, used his love of basketball as his organizing device. He had the audience sit in the bleachers rather than in seats on the floor, and he came out dressed for a game. And a game he delivered, complete with time periods, a scoreboard that lit up each time he "scored," music, and an announcer.

The POL packets can be similarly personalized. Standard components must be included, but the packet might be designed as a newspaper, a basketball program (that was Eric's), a set of drawings, a long poem, or a musical composition. The required components in all packets are:

- A letter to the panelists thanking them for participating on the panel and highlighting the learning during the trimester.

- An autobiography. The first trimester this is a full autobiography leading up to entering Eagle Rock. Thereafter, it focuses on growth and changes since coming to Eagle Rock.

- A résumé, updated each trimester.

- A cumulative list of learning experiences (classes and other experiences), service projects, books read, and ambassador and extra-curricular activities.
- A chart depicting *I used to be . . . but now I am. . . .*
- Their personal, moral, and ethical code.

Students are not required to present on everything they've done. We generally require that they discuss both academic growth and personal growth. Within academic growth, we expect them to discuss briefly a wide range of subjects, focusing in depth on one or two. But Jeremy did not talk of science, art, human performance (physical education), music, or English, at least not directly. His passions—from teaching himself the meaning of mathematics to civil rights to La Raza to signing—were intense and took up the entire presentation of learning. His personal growth was expressed through the quotes that meant something to him and his goals in life. Based on everything at our disposal (including his completed ILP) we felt confident that he had mastered everything we required for graduation. He was able to concentrate on things that were important to him and that were representative of the quality of his work, overall. This former gang member discovered signing and made it into a work of art. He had developed his logical thinking through mathematical concepts. He had developed a philosophy toward life. He had found a passion in human rights and a mission in terms of serving others through teaching tolerance. He was able to make himself clear and understood. He was a fine dramatist. Can we ask more of our graduates?

We think it's very important for students to be able to present themselves well, whether it's to an audience of peers, staff, and family members or in an interview with a prospective employer or in a doctoral defense. We try to stage these presentations so that students do them for longer periods of time and for increasingly higher stakes as they progress through Eagle Rock. Here's the typical order of presentations a student might make:

- Five-minute group presentation on $8 + 5 = 10$ for the Eagle Rock community before leaving for the wilderness trip.
- Five-minute individual presentation on the wilderness trip for the Eagle Rock community after returning from the wilderness trip.
- Class presentations.
- First fifteen-minute end-of-trimester presentation of learning, followed by fifteen minutes of questions and answers, in front of an outside panel and the Eagle Rock community.
- Subsequent end-of-trimester POLs.
- Hosting visitors one-on-one.

- Speaking to visitors on campus.
- Making presentations at conferences, workshops, and seminars.
- Thirty-minute graduation presentation of learning, followed by thirty minutes of questions and answers, in front of an outside panel and the Eagle Rock community.

We don't have speech classes at Eagle Rock. However, most of our graduating students speak quite well in public, and I often take students with me to speak at conferences. How do they learn to speak publicly? As in so many other things, the learning is experiential. Even brand new students make public presentations. They don't speak as clearly as they will later. Their presentations either ramble on too long or are much too short. They usually haven't included audiovisual aids. Their insights may seem superficial. But the simple fact that they are addressing, in public, adults they don't know is remarkable. Many of them demonstrate a spectacular inability to raise their eyes to adults or do more than mumble or hide beneath shaggy hair or baseball cap bills when they first arrive. But they are asked to do many, many informal presentations as well as formal POLs before they graduate. They get feedback from peers and staff whenever they give a presentation. We videotape each POL so they—and we—can remark on their growing skill and presence as speakers.

While we do not have a specific agenda for student activism, we are clear that we want students to see a role for themselves in terms of leadership for justice, one of the principles listed in our code of 8 + 5 = 10. We do not want them learning about history and government and civics dispassionately; we want them to see their role in what happens in their own neighborhood, city, state, country, world, and universe. Therefore, our history classes are more likely to be organized around a pivotal event such as the civil rights movement or the Holocaust than around consecutive time periods or specific countries. Perhaps we sacrifice something in not having sophomore-year world history from the beginning to the present or junior-year American history from pre–Revolutionary War to the millennium. But I believe we gain something in terms of both retention and application. Students remember what they've learned in terms of history, and they find their place in history-in-the-making.

Seat Time Versus Documentation of Learning

The most important words uttered during Jeremy's graduation POL were, "You're going to have to prove it." They point up an important element of Eagle Rock. From the beginning, we were convinced that we did not want to graduate students based on credit hours or Carnegie units. We are not alone in this belief. The Coalition of Essential Schools, founded by Ted Sizer, holds as one of its ten common principles that students will graduate according to documented learning rather than seat time.

What's the matter with seat time? First, let's make clear what is meant by seat time. Seat time—together with grades—is the measuring stick by which most American high schools determine that a student is ready to graduate. Most American high schools require that a student have a certain number of years in each subject and a passing grade each year in order to graduate. Four years of English, four years of social studies, four years of science, three years of mathematics, two years of physical education. Each full year equals a whole credit or a Carnegie unit. Four years of English with a passing grade each year means four credits or Carnegie units. Most states require between 22 and 24 credits, most in the basic subjects, with the rest earned in electives such as art, music, drama, woodshop, and computer technology.

What do students know and what can they do when they've completed those years and earned those credits? The answer varies because the curriculum varies. Sometimes it comes from a textbook. Sometimes it is established by the district. Sometimes it is based on state or national standards. Sometimes it is created by teachers working by themselves or with department colleagues. It is hard to look at any graduate who has had four years of English and understand exactly what that graduate knows and is able to do in comparison with any other graduate who has had four years of English. And grades are notoriously nonstandard across the country as well. The quality of work required to earn an A in one school may very well not be the quality of work required to get an A in another school. The same holds true for the other "passing" grades.

Is sitting in class for the requisite years and "passing" enough for today's graduates? The lowest passing grade in most schools is a D, and a D usually means that the student has not put forth much effort or achieved much. Perhaps the student has not even learned much. Is that good enough? The bottom line is, what does the diploma mean? How are people—parents, business leaders, colleges, the students themselves—to understand it? Can we be content giving a diploma to students whose knowledge and skill vary considerably both in terms of "what" and "how well"? Are we acting with integrity when we do so? Is it sufficient to graduate students on the basis of uncertain learning and low grades?

Graduating According to Documented Learning

Eagle Rock's individualized learning plan (see Figure 1.7, pp. 20–21) is an excellent tool for documenting competency. It indicates general areas in which competency is required and specifies the work students must produce to a level of mastery. Sometimes the documentation specifies just a format, such as a math portfolio. Other times, the documentation specifies both a format and a content subdivision (a project on national issues in American government, for example). However, in no case does a documentation specify what topic a student will pursue; a math portfolio can focus on statistics or on exponents. The national issues project can focus on the environment or civil rights. We believe in leaving the documentations as open as possible so that students can pursue their own interests. (That means we don't guarantee coverage of the entire curriculum. See Chapter 3 for more on curriculum coverage.)

Types of documentation vary. Here is a list of the some of the types we've used at Eagle Rock:

- Portfolios: beginning, developing, accomplished; working portfolios; a portfolio of possibilities (career options, for example); a reading or writing portfolio.

- Oral documentations: presentations, gathering recitations, dramatizations, skits, monologues, scenarios, interviews, panel presentations.

- Written documentations: research papers, reports, compositions, poems, dramatizations, action plans, statements of purpose, summaries.

- Combined oral and written documentations: projects, demonstrations, videotapes, multimedia presentations, critiques/defenses, reviews of performance, self-assessments, reflections; reading and speaking a foreign language.

- Other: finished artworks (visual, dramatic, musical), sketchbooks, journals, test results; others' assessments of performance, work habits, or attitudes; evidence of skills (checklists); letters or notes from adults or peers verifying learning; exemplary records of something over time; use of a planner or organizational device; sign-off sheets or calendar records; physical demonstrations of skills; performance scores over time.

Documentations are required in more than academic classes. Students need to achieve documentations in ERS orientation (learning about Eagle Rock, including what 8 + 5 = 10 really means, usually in a class called ER101), ERS transition (learning how to succeed at ERS, usually in a class called ER201), food service, life skills, personal growth, and the wilderness trip.

Specifically, our system of documentation works like this. Schoolwide, instructors and interns plan classes keeping in mind both a graduation requirement (American history, for example) and a number of documentations that students might create (a project on a historical event or a project on a hypothesis). As much as possible, instructors and interns in one subject area work with instructors and interns in other subject areas to create interdisciplinary classes (see Chapter 9), so that a student in a class on American history might also work toward documentation in English by writing an essay of explanation or in environmental science by doing a composition and presentation on local issues or in geography by doing a project comparing cultures. Instructors and interns complete a course proposal form (see Figure 1.10, p. 30) for each course.

The entire faculty, led by the director of curriculum, reviews the course proposal forms and puts together a class schedule for each trimester. Students, with the help of their advisers and their ILPs, select the courses they need to take to achieve requirements for graduation. Although the enrollees in a class do things together, ultimately each student selects the documentations he or she will work on, based on preference as well as the status of his or her ILP—what's needed, what's already been accomplished.

The work of assessing all these documentations is eased somewhat by the rubrics created for each documentation. Some are generic, some are specific to the documentation—the product or outcome. These are generally available, not only to instructors and interns but to the students. Sometimes they are created within a class, with the whole class speculating on what would be a quality product or performance—a worthwhile activity, by the way, even if it doesn't lead to a rubric. Sometimes rubrics are revised by a class or by an individual student and instructor to fit a variation the student is proposing. Sometimes instructors ask for help from other instructors when assessing something outside their area of expertise.

Trust is at work here. We ask instructors and interns to step out of their subject specialties quite a bit at Eagle Rock, to be generalists more often than specialists. When James, the social studies teacher, offers students a chance to create an art portfolio in his Holocaust class, Mary, the art teacher, needs to trust that her rubric for an art portfolio is sufficient for helping him evaluate those portfolios. She also needs to trust James to do a fair evaluation. James needs to trust that Mary's rubric will, in fact, help him perform that evaluation.

Students have as many chances as they need to bring their documentations up to a proficient rating, the level of mastery we require. A student's learning experience record (LER) (see Figure 1.11, p. 31) for a class provides for three possible "grades": no credit yet (the student is making progress on the documentation and is expected to complete the work); no credit (the student will take another class in that subject area and work on documentation from another angle); credit for learning that is proficient or exemplary (the student has mastered some aspect of the subject area through a documentation of learning). These forms—one for each student in each class each trimester—and accompanying materials if necessary (a completed rubric, for example) are submitted to our registrar, who records proficient performances on each student's ILP by checking off the relevant documentations. When all documentations are checked, the registrar darkens the box for the related graduation requirement. All LERs, whether indicating mastery or that more time and work are necessary, are put into each student's cumulative portfolio.

Calibration is an important aspect of this process. For the whole process of documentation to work well, instructors and interns—and students—should gather regularly to work with sample documentations and rubrics until they all are able to agree with some degree of reliability whether or not each piece is proficient. Then they can apply the rubrics to other documentations with reasonable confidence.

A tuning protocol (see Easton 1999) is another process that helps with calibration. In this process, a group works collaboratively to fine-tune a documentation rating. An instructor brings to the group a piece of student work, a portfolio perhaps. After the instructor has presented the context for this piece to the group along with two or three questions about it, the group asks clarifying questions of the instructor. Following that, everyone writes answers to the instructor's questions. Then, while the instructor who brought in the work takes notes, everyone else evaluates the student work and discusses the questions the instructor posed. The instructor then reacts to what he or she has heard while the group is silent. Finally, there is a general debriefing discussion. This process works largely because it does not descend into offense–defense, and because working together prompts a deeper investigation.

Presentations of Learning (POLs)

POLs, such as Jeremy's graduate POL, are above and beyond regular documentation. They are not about getting credit in classes; however, they do serve, in a very public way, to help students and staff reflect on the quality of learning at Eagle Rock. Students think back about their whole trimester, connect it to previous trimesters, and project goals for future trimesters. Staff members learn how students have benefited from their classes. It is a time for synthesis, reflection, interpretation, and analysis—in short an *integration* of learning.

POLs take place during the last week of each trimester. Students prepare their packets (contents are described on page 102–03) several weeks prior to POL week and mail them to their panel members. During the weekend before POL week and on that Monday, students prepare and rehearse their POLs. Tuesday, Wednesday, and sometimes Thursday (depending on the number of students scheduled), we have four simultaneous morning and afternoon POL sessions, each session consisting of four POLs. With sixteen POLs per session, we can accommodate ninety-six POLs in that three-day period—and our maximum number of students is ninety-six.

Each POL is a half hour long, fifteen minutes for the presentation and fifteen minutes for panel member and audience questions. There are ten minutes between POLs for the panel to finish up their evaluation and for student helpers to change the set. We are strict about keeping time, because people need to move from one location to another to catch particular POLs.

Every student has a role. The four most important people at any given time are those presenting. The rest of the student body is on hand to support them as greeters, in-room hosts, water providers, videographers, timekeepers, presentation assistants, evaluators, and audience members. An Eagle Rock staff member is assigned to each POL room, facilitating transitions from presentation to question session and back again, contributing questions if there is a lull. Other Eagle Rock community members—staff, family, friends, visitors—are also in the audience.

A panel is composed of at least three people from outside Eagle Rock. These may be people from the town of Estes Park or nearby cities—or even from out-of-state. They may be educators or lawyers, mayors or DARE officers, real estate agents or booksellers. It is important to have a wide variety of people on the panel and in the audience. Panel members, who usually know only what they read in the student's POL packet, ask objective questions and bring an outside perspective to the issue of quality. Their questions help students know whether or not what they've learned and how they have presented it apply in the outside world. After the panel members ask questions, members of the audience ask questions. If a student has tried to "put something over" on an unsuspecting panel member—which rarely happens—another student or a staff member will usually ask just the right question to bring the attempted deception to light. These questions from members of the Eagle Rock community are usually more intimate and often have to do with personal growth. Whatever their source, these questions keep students on their toes.

Panel members receive a half-hour orientation before each four-presentation session. During the orientation, they are introduced to a rubric whose directions begin with the words *Make this rubric your own.* It is essentially a Likert Scale with categories that can be rated using the numbers 1 through 6, but we emphasize that students prefer written comments over the numbers and encourage panel members to use the considerable white space provided for comments and tell them they can ignore the ratings entirely if they'd like. We encourage panel members to make their rubrics messy—to cross out what doesn't apply, to draw arrows, to circle items, etc. The rubric categories and descriptors are:

Academic Growth

Content and Range

- Academic learning is discussed in depth.
- Academic growth and personal growth are woven together in an integrated presentation.
- An extensive range of academic experiences is presented.
- Academic experiences are connected in some way.

Documentation of Learning

- Learning is clearly and compellingly documented through relevant examples, demonstrations, exhibitions, projects, diagrams, charts, etc.

Application

- Application of learning is elaborated on by references to past or future learning and by specific examples and references to other learning situations. Significance of learning is addressed.

Personal Growth

Content

- Identification and understanding of personal growth are well articulated, elaborated on, and documented.

Application

- Reflection is evident in identification of goals. Specific information is provided on how the learner has used or plans to use learning in other areas.

Presentation Style

8 + 5 = 10

- Relationship of 8 + 5 = 10 is creatively woven into the entire presentation.
- Vocabulary of 8 + 5 = 10 is used.

Materials

- Materials are creative, organized, correct, and used effectively.

Delivery

- This is a polished presentation in every way; it is within the time limit; presenter is poised and at ease in front of the audience.

Organization

- Sections are organized in a logical, cohesive, even creative way; ideas are related to one another; there may be a theme.
- Introduction and conclusion are powerful and effective.
- The presenter clearly has the audience's need to understand in mind and helps by providing an organizing device or structure.

Q & A

- The presenter listens well to questions, answers fully, and checks answers.

In addition to jotting down comments and perhaps circling a number from 1 to 6 for each descriptor, panel members are asked to provide a holistic total score, a gut level response to the whole presentation, one that does not necessarily "add up" from the circled numbers. In our orientation, we also make clear that we do not expect everyone's numbers will agree—they haven't received any training that would promote consistency.

At the end of each session, the panel and audience members convene for a debriefing that, first, asks them to share what they observed in their separate "snapshots" of the school and then asks them to suggest improvements to the process.

All in all, our system of graduating students according to documented competencies ensures that we (along with parents, business leaders, colleges, and the students) know what a student knows and is able to do—and how well. The Eagle Rock diploma is meaningful. It has integrity. And it represents the belief that sitting in a class for a certain period of time and earning a passing grade (at least a D) shortchanges both students and society.

Varying the Conditions for Learning in a Mastery System

Whether you are operating according to a competency-based system, as Eagle Rock does, or according to a standards-based system, as many states, districts, and schools across the country do, you need to consider how to vary the conditions for learning. Here's why.

Achievement used to be a variable. Students performed well or poorly. They earned (or were awarded) grades—A for superior performance, B for better-than-average performance, C for average performance, D for below-average performance, and F for insufficient performance. All but F counted in terms of passing from one grade to another or graduating from high school. Although high achievement, represented through GPA or class rank, was desirable, any performance short of failure was sufficient.

With achievement a variable, factors such as time and place, curriculum, learning style, and assessment techniques could all be absolutes. Students learned in school. Nine months was judged adequate for deciding whether students were ready to pass from grade to grade. In some areas achievement might be an A, in others a C or a D, but being in a grade for nine months and receiving passing grades got a student into the next grade. Being in high school four years and passing all courses resulted in a walk across the stage and a diploma. For the most part, school could be finished in twelve years. Curriculum in high schools especially meant taking all required classes, often in a prescribed sequence, and choosing an elective or two. Whole-class learning methods were sufficient. All students took the same tests. (I am intentionally painting these absolutes with a broad brush. Of course, caring teachers in supportive schools figured out how to make time, place, curriculum, style of learning, and assessment techniques fit individual learners.)

But things are changing. In this age of standards, all students are to be held to the same expectations. Achievement is an absolute, not a variable. The refrain is usually, "All students can learn." Embedded in that refrain are the standards developed by a state or district: "All students can achieve these standards." The underlying meaning is that all students must demonstrate at least a certain level of achievement in order to pass from grade to grade and eventually clutch a diploma signifying graduation.

At Eagle Rock, time, space, curriculum, style of learning, and assessment are variables so that achievement (in the form of our graduation requirements, or competencies) can be absolute. Our refrain is, "All students can achieve the standards *if* time, space, curriculum, learning style, and assessment techniques are variables." Every student can learn if the learning experience is tailored to the needs of that student.

High Expectations and Standards

In "The Authentic Standards Movement and Its Evil Twin," Scott Thompson (2001) distinguishes between two approaches to standards.

The first "aims to hold high expectations and provide high levels of support for all students, teachers, and educational leaders" (p. 358). The second is tied to high-stakes, standardized tests. The first aims for equity, and the second aims for separation or sorting. Eagle Rock's focus is on high expectations and support.

The least respectful action Eagle Rock faculty can take with regard to Eagle Rock students is to excuse them from learning. Lowering an expectation, making an exception, says to students that adults don't believe they can learn, and, guess what, often they don't. Eagle Rock graduate Talia said it well, "Holding me to high expectations made me believe in myself. I was worthwhile. I knew you'd help me, but I also knew I'd have to perform. And I did." *All* Eagle Rock students—even those who have not been in school for a couple of years, have been labeled special ed or learning disabled, or have used drugs heavily—must meet our standards in order to graduate. We do, of course, provide strong scaffolds and make sure everything else in the equation is variable.

Schools throughout the country have no trouble setting high expectations—they need only consult the state standards, district adoptions or adaptations of these standards, and the national subject-matter recommendations. However, as Chapter 2 makes clear, I would much rather each school develop its own standards. If district or state standards are being required of a school, I believe the school community must first decide what it expects of students and then fit the district or state standards into the picture. Beginning with the standards may lock schools into a standard-a-day mentality in which expectations are not personalized to the school (and, therefore, not likely to be personalized for individual learners). Equally important is the way the standards are stated. A standard should be kept as general as possible in order to allow individual teachers and individual students to find their way into it and express their knowledge of it.

Let me give you an example of how Eagle Rock goes about the process and how we express our standards. We start out with what we believe. In our 8 + 5 = 10 precepts, we refer to environmental stewardship (a theme), participating as an engaged global citizen (an expectation), and becoming a steward of the planet (a commitment). Based on that premise, environmental science is important for our students to know. In Colorado, the fifth standard for science is expressed as students knowing "the relationship among science, technology, and human activity and understanding connections among scientific disciplines." We build this standard into our environmental science curriculum by focusing on a global environmental issue. Students become an expert on one issue and propose and present a plan to solve the problem. In doing so, they express an understanding of how science, technology, and human behavior have affected the world. They write a composition and deliver a presentation that express their learning. Although the composition and presentation can take a number of forms, the rubric includes whether or not students have addressed some understanding of the interrelationships and connections. Although students select their own pressing global problem, they work toward the standard—within a general expectation related to a global environmental problem, students meet a specific state standard.

It strikes me as odd that even though content standards were the bandwagon of the eighties and nineties and are still big news this decade, they are seldom brought up when making promotion decisions. We run a dual system. We require standards but still promote and graduate students according to seat time and grades. It is very possible for a student to graduate on the basis of attendance and grades without having achieved the standards. It is also very possible for a student to have achieved the standards—and demonstrated competency—but not have the grades and attendance to graduate.

It's not that I want a single test of standards to determine whether or not a student is ready to move from grade to grade or graduate from high school, not at all. In some cases, state tests purport to measure standards, but they are merely a proxy for real documentation of learning. Administered randomly in terms of subjects, items, and students, they may at best give the state a snapshot of to what degree standards have been achieved—and that's all they should be used for. They are unsatisfactory—even dangerous—if used to determine promotion for a school, a classroom, or an individual student.

How can schools and districts climb aboard the standards bandwagon and use documentation of standards achievement as a way to graduate students? Well, what if a school or district said, "We're going to graduate students according to the state standards *as they are embedded in our curriculum.* We'll document that our students have learned and can demonstrate what the standards require. We'll have proof that our graduates have mastered the state's standards. Our students, their parents, and other community members will be able to tell us whether we're doing a good job. But if you're worried, come in once in a while and sample for yourselves how well our students are doing."

Time for Learning

Students entering Eagle Rock do not enter as freshmen, sophomores, juniors, or seniors, designations related to an expectation that it takes four years to graduate from high school. Students enter as part of a cohort group; the first group was ER (Eagle Rock) 1 and we're now up to ER 25. They graduate when they are ready.

At first, some students proceed very slowly through the competencies, often concentrating on the growth that comes from dealing with personal issues that have blocked their learning for so long. However, as these issues are raised and addressed, students begin to focus on academic learning. They enroll—much as college students do—in six-week classes that will help them achieve documentations in the competencies they need to graduate.

Student pathways through the individualized learning plan vary but not because certain competencies are required of one student but not of another. All competencies are required of all students, but some students may need two or three six-week classes to document sufficient learning while others may master learning (and document that learning at a level deemed proficient or above) in one class. The pathways vary in terms of learning and assessment possibilities, too, but that's getting ahead of this story.

Occasionally, we have to translate our ILP to a more conventional transcript that lists credit hours or time spent in classes. Sometimes we even have to indicate the grades a student would have gotten (they're always As or Bs, because that's the level the work needs to have reached to be declared proficient). More and more, however, colleges and universities are acknowledging the value of enrolling students who have graduated from high school according to demonstrated achievement of standards rather than seat time and grades.

A real dilemma occurs when schools move to a competency-based (or standards-based) system but are unwilling or unable to vary learning time. What do they do if a student does not master the competencies in the nine-month school year? What do they do if a student does not master the graduation requirements in twelve years? Retention has been addressed in many research studies; almost always, the conclusion is that retention is harmful to a student's future learning and that multiple retentions are disastrous. Many Eagle Rock students tell of the humiliation of being retained and their vow to "get back at" the school that retained them, usually only by hurting themselves. Many school districts are confronting this issue. Some require summer school for students who do not seem to be achieving the standards. Others are experimenting with extending the school year. If we think outside the box, we'll find many more ways that time can be a variable rather than an absolute for learning.

Curriculum Choices

At Eagle Rock classes are the vehicles for learning and demonstrating mastery of a competency and do not "count" in and of themselves. Student pathways through their ILPs vary because we believe students should pursue their own interests as much as possible. For example, all Eagle Rock students need to earn credit in the competency area of environmental science, but how they do so can vary considerably.

Student 1 may take a six-week class called Transportation and Environmental Issues, documenting learning through a composition and presentation on a global environmental issue and another composition and presentation on a national environmental issue. Because she does not achieve proficiency with these documentations, she may take an independent study under the guidance of the science teacher to continue to learn and revise her work. Then she may take Touch the Future and help elementary students from the Denver Public Schools learn about the local ecology; she designs a lesson for these students and achieves proficiency on a local environmental issue. Finally, she may take It's the End of the World—or Is It? and do an environmental impact project on recycling, later writing a reflective piece about her project, both of which are rated proficient. She earns her environmental science credit.

Student 2 may take Riverwatch to begin his work in environmental science, collecting and analyzing samples from local rivers and submitting data to a national center; he writes about both the local effort and the national effort and creates a multimedia project that shows the relationship between local and national river conditions and receives a proficient rating. Next, he may do a service project in a class called Designing the MacGregor Ranch Nature Center. This is his environmental impact project, but he does not at first achieve proficiency. He takes Plan It for the Planet and continues to work on his environmental impact project and also a composition and a project on a global environmental issue, achieving proficiency on all three. He, too, earns his environmental science credit.

Place of Learning

As long as students at Eagle Rock are working toward a competency, it doesn't matter where they do so. A "class" may be an internship in town with the pharmacist, accompanied by independent study of chemistry. It could be the site of a service learning project. Eagle Rock students have reported that they finally understood mathematics when they built a fishing pier for the handicapped at Lake Estes. In addition to mathematics, they learned a lot about civics when they built a playground at nearby Lyons, Colorado, because of the interviews they conducted with the mayor, town council, and other residents about how the town operated. They related mathematics to geology and climbing in a six-week class that took them through Wyoming. They practiced their reading skills by working with youngsters in a local elementary school. Our students, along with millions of others across the country, use technology to take them places they need to go to learn. They travel all over the world via websites to get the information they need. Their classroom may, in fact, be a computer with a modem. Some of our students take courses at nearby community or junior colleges.

Will all of these places of learning make schools as sites of learning irrelevant? Probably not, but educators may want to expand their ideas about where students can learn and be ready to be flexible as students are working toward mastering the school's competencies.

Style of Learning

Many of our students did not learn well in the typical "style" of their previous schools. In other words, they were not good auditory processors. They could not learn by sitting and taking notes even if the medium through which information was presented to them was a video or television program. Most tell us they can learn better if they try something out, work on it physically. They are kinesthetic learners.

It makes little difference which learning style theories you subscribe to—it is the *student's* learning style that determines how he or she will learn, retain, and transfer knowledge. Sometimes Eagle Rock staff members plan ahead, making sure that each learning experience can be accessed in a variety of ways. Other times, we simply offer lots of choices to students so that they can find their own best way to learn.

This does not mean that we ignore the most common learning styles. Because students' later learning experiences will require them to listen or read well, we continue to help students improve on those means to learning. However, we see no reason why one student can't learn about the Holocaust through reading about it, another by visiting a website on the Holocaust, another by interviewing survivors and survivors' families, and still another by watching several films about the Holocaust, all in the same "class."

Style of Assessment

Often attention to styles stops with how people learn. It needs to go further. How students are assessed is also an important variable. Some students would rather tell a teacher what they know. Others would prefer showing the teacher (or a whole class) what they know. Still others would prefer to write about their learning. And others want to make something to represent what they know. The best learning happens when students take on the role of teacher, choosing ways to present what they have learned to other students so that their own and others' learning styles are taken into consideration.

The documentations that attest to learning at Eagle Rock allow for variety. They are listed on our individualized learning plan and in our curriculum guide as projects or presentations or demonstrations. Sometimes they are described as a portfolio that might have a wide variety of material in it. Sometimes, we ask students to document learning in a specific way—write a composition, for example—but we are always open to alternatives.

The Effect on Students, Staff Members, and the System

Asking students to document their learning has a powerful effect on them. In their old seat-time environments they either didn't know what was expected and felt powerless or figured out that they could graduate by showing up and doing the minimum. Either way, they lost pride in themselves as learners. Why not just drop out? A documentation-based system gives students power and control over their learning. They own their ILP and can set their graduation date. They personalize their education.

Staff members like the way the ILP glues the whole curriculum together, from course proposal forms to learning experience records. They like how the documentations and rubrics clarify evaluation and focus instruction. Since courses are not the unit of credit, they can forget about seat time and grades and design exciting learning experiences for themselves and their students.

The documentation-based system works at Eagle Rock because students are not classified into grade levels and never reach a point when a decision has to be made about whether they pass from one grade level to another. Would it work in a system that was time based? Probably not, not even on the level of an individual teacher who establishes competencies for her course or grade level and varies the conditions of learning so that all students can achieve these competencies. What would happen to a student who reached the end of the year with some competencies not yet mastered? What about the student who mastered the competencies in March? In a time-based system, the solution to the former dilemma would be retention; the solution to the latter would probably be, "Too bad."

Could time-based systems become competency based? Some elementary schools cluster grade levels so that decisions do not need to be made about whether or not to move students from one grade level to the next until the end of the cluster. Could high schools abandon the four-nine-month-years march through learning? Could they imagine a three- or five-year block of time for learning? Would it be possible to do away with grades so that Pass and Not Yet Ready are the only indicators of progress? Could GPAs and class ranks be abandoned? Could a student, her parents, and the school set a graduation date according to how she is progressing with documenting that she has met the graduation requirements? Could universities and colleges grant special admission to students who have graduated with a diploma attesting to mastery of requirements? Do these students do better than students admitted because they have been in high school the requisite number of years and passed all their classes? This is perhaps a radical proposal, but one that is being considered and even implemented in various locations across the country. Changing to a competency-based system may be the hardest recommendation in this book to achieve— but it's also the most worthwhile.

Questions to Consider

1. Look at your school's graduation requirements and course descriptions (or if you teach in an elementary school, your scope and sequence outline), statement of purpose, accreditation report, or the accountability report you make to the district and community. On what basis do you promote and graduate students? How do you make decisions not to promote or graduate? What are students supposed to know and be able to do? How do you know they have learned? What do they show you, and in what ways do they make it clear they have or have not learned? How do you work with standards, either those handed down from the state or adapted by your district?

2. Is there any flexibility in terms of time for students to learn, the places they can learn, how their learning style affects how they learn and document learning? What room is there for students to set their own expectations? What are the conditions for learning in terms of time, space, learning style, assessment style, specific curriculum choices?

3. What would moving to a competency-based system mean to your school in terms of change? a major change? a minor change? a tweaking of things?

4. Who might support such a change? why? Who might not support such a change? why? What could you do to enlist the supporters, work with the nonsupporters?

5. Could individual teachers in your school move to a competency-

based system even if the whole school did not? Could grade levels do so? Could departments do so? What would be the problems? What would be the advantages?

6. What do various constituency groups know both about what students are able to do and how well? parents? the district administration and board? business leaders? colleges? students themselves? the school's faculty and administration? What do they need to know? How would they benefit if they knew exactly what students know and are able to do? How would they benefit if they knew how well students know and are able to do something? What would they gain that they do not now have?

7. How can state standards support your school's or district's move to a competency-based system? What state policies would need to be addressed and/or waived? What district policies would need to be addressed and/or waived?

8. What expectations or competencies would you set for students? Are these general enough for each student to find his/her interest? Are they truly challenging? Do you really believe that all students should achieve them? Are you ready to vary the conditions for learning so that all students can achieve them? Are you ready to commit resources so that they can achieve them? Do these expectations allow room for personalization? Are they likely to be meaningful and important to students?

9. What could you do to make time a variable? Can you reconfigure the school year or school day? How can you work with students who are able to proceed faster on achieving an expectation? How can you work with students who need more time and perhaps vastly different learning opportunities to achieve expectations?

10. Is needing more time a stigma in your school? Or is it accepted that people are very different in their learning needs, neither worse nor better than others? Is it understood that some students need more time with some subjects but less with others? When you give some students more time to learn, is that considered retention in a grade? How can you avoid retaining students in order to give them more time?

11. How can you allow students to learn in different places? at home? on the job? doing service? doing an internship? through the World Wide Web? What if students didn't come to school sometimes because they were learning somewhere else?

12. What curriculum choices can you offer students? Do all of them need to take the same course or unit to achieve mastery of an expectation or standard?

13. How can learning styles be accommodated through a variety of curriculum choices? Can some courses or units be offered that cater to particular styles, both of learning and demonstrating learning? Within required units or courses, how can students choose how to learn and how to document their learning according to their styles?

14. How would the school or district handle grades? GPA? class rank? transcripts?

15. How could the school or district rethink time for learning? How could high school be reconceptualized, for example, as a block of time from three to five years in length? How could the same rethinking be accomplished for a junior high or middle school block? an intermediate block? a primary block?

16. What kind of professional development would be needed to accomplish a move to competencies?

17. How will you know that your move to a competency-based system is working? What measurement devices can you put in place—both subjective and objective—to report progress as you move along? What data can you gather? How will you use these data?

18. How will you communicate with your constituencies about the progress you're making in moving to a competency-based system?

Chapter Six

Curriculum Helps Learners Become Self-Directed

James graduated from Eagle Rock in December 1996, but graduation was not at all what he expected in his life when he entered the school almost three years earlier. His name was different then, and his hair was curly and disheveled; he called it a "mop." An administrator in a Colorado school district had recognized in James a talent and intelligence no one else had recognized, and she worked hard to get him admitted to Eagle Rock. Other people saw a druggie who had somehow escaped the fate of two of his friends, who died of an overdose outside on a cold winter night. The anguish James felt about his friends dying while he lived was still deep within him when he came to Eagle Rock. So were the memories he had about being separated from his peers and put into special education classes for most of his educational life. He came to Eagle Rock convinced he was dumb, ugly, and unworthy.

In early August 1994, I had not yet begun to work at Eagle Rock but had been invited to be a panelist for presentations of learning. Like the other panelists, I had received a packet from James that included an autobiography that hinted at his past, but I was not at all prepared for his presentation. James began by talking about his career in special education and how he felt about himself. He said with some pride that he not only didn't need special education at Eagle Rock (we don't track students or label them, and we have open enrollment in all of our classes) but also hadn't needed it in his other schools. He described the philosophy books he was reading, inviting his panel members and audience to converse with him about Schopenhaur or Nietzsche.

Then he described and illustrated for us what had created the change in him. "I really wanted to learn how to compose music," he said, "but the school had no one to teach me. I talked Judy [the director of curriculum] into buying a computer program that would let me compose music, and she got one, but no one knew how to make it work. I was really frustrated, so I started to read the manual that came with the program. At first it made no sense, and I became even more frustrated. But gradually I learned enough of it to compose my first piece. Here it is." James played a tape of a very simple piece with one melody line, a simple rhythm, and lots of repetition. "I learned that I could do something on my own. Then I got back to that manual and read and reread sections of it until I could compose this piece." James played his next composition, a bit more complex. He told us he had repeated this sequence several times—reading and rereading the manual, trying to make sense of it, and then composing a more elaborate piece of music. The final piece of music he played—interweaving melody lines, pleasing changes in rhythm, and patterned repetition—had us all on our feet, applauding.

James grinned and then said something I will never forget: "I have discovered the secret to learning." He grinned again, moving his eyes to take us all in, especially those of us on the panel. "The secret is that we teach ourselves—that's how we learn. I used to think that learning was the teacher's responsibility. Now I know that it's mine." He smoothed back his curly hair. "I used to wait for the teacher to put learning into me, and when it didn't happen, I knew that there was something wrong with me. Now I know that I'm in charge of my own learning. Teachers just bring opportunities to learn to me, but it's up to me to learn. I need to be in charge of how that learning gets into me. That's what I did with the computer program; I took charge of learning it, and I did. I am a learner."

In his next POL, December 1994, James concentrated on two classes that helped him learn. In his geography class he said he was challenged to understand the world geographically—how it was formed, what makes people the way they are. He created an island country to illustrate what he was learning, a country called Capricornia, filled with landmarks named after his parents and closest friends. He told how it was formed, illustrating with his hands how two land forces came together and pushed the land up. At first hesitant, he warmed to his topic as he explained how his island had developed, why it had a desert, and why one area was tropical and the other tundra. He told the history of his land and how its invented economy helped humankind. A principled economy, it focused on free trade, making products, especially medicines, that were available to everyone. He grinned, "This is not communism but a big, huge community where everyone helps everyone else." He then moved on reluctantly to talk about a second class, the Culture of Science, through which students learned about chemistry and the humanities by exploring microchemistry. He didn't have enough time to discuss this class as thoroughly as he had the first class, but he showed a videotape and talked knowledgeably about chemicals.

As the staff facilitator, my job was to ask the first question to ease the transition from the presentation to the question-and-answer session. I complimented James on his depth of knowledge and understanding and then said, "You talked a lot about how you understood what real learning was in your last POL. You said it was teaching yourself; you said it gave you a sense of power. How did teaching yourself fit into all the learning you just demonstrated?"

James responded, "What we did was a very independent thing because we were all making our own countries, so I had to go look it all up, and by doing that, I got to teach myself out of encyclopedias and books. I was very involved in teaching myself. The teacher provided the structure, but we all got to do our own country. I actually had to figure out how to build Capricornia myself. I used papier-mâché and did levels of cardboard over it to build up the topography."

At James' April 1995 POL he sported a Mohawk. His focus was on his Washington, DC, Close-Up class, for which he had two weeks of preparation, one week in DC, and three weeks of follow-up to consolidate learning and write papers. He relished his chance in DC to express his views "to a lot of different people who counted. We got to ask the questions that liberals and conservatives would debate. Some opinions that I really wanted to know were taboo, for example, how [the congressmen] felt about Jocelyn Elders being fired. They didn't want to answer that question, but students got up and insisted on the answer." After the Director of Foreign Affairs of Sub-Saharan Africa had described America's threat to use firepower to stop a cross-canal fight between two countries as a nonviolent intervention, James countered that the solution was not nonviolent, because it was premised on the *threat of violence*. The director conceded, "You're probably right, but at least it's a less violent solution." James had written a paper about that event and read parts of it aloud to the POL panel.

James also wrote a paper about *Tinker v. Des Moines*—the Supreme Court case about the right of students to express themselves. In this case, students wore black armbands to protest Vietnam, and they got expelled. Although the lawyer defending Tinker said that an armband was in no way disruptive to students, James sided with Thurgood Marshall, who argued that if you're wearing a black armband to protest something, you are encouraging people to think about what you're trying to say. "So," James said, "it does disrupt people a little bit. But I think it's more important to express opinions. We need to express our opinions—the future of America will be affected by whether or not we pay attention to what's going on."

As in his previous POL, James went on for so long and in such depth about his Close-Up experience that he had little time to discuss his other classes. Again, however, he affirmed that he had learned because he pursued his own interests through the class.

In his fourth POL, August 1995, James sported a white chef's jacket and bright yellow hair. He had taken a class called Culinary Arts, and he chose to demonstrate knife skills. With a wry sense of humor, he described how to keep your fingers—the thumb, too—behind the knife. He shared what he learned about mathematics, especially how to convert measurements from metric to standard. "It's important to understand the math when you are exploding or imploding a recipe." He shared what he had learned about nutrition. He talked about the job skills he had learned and revealed for the first time his goals for the future: "Prep cooking—that's how I'm going to pay my way through college, all the way to a doctorate in philosophy."

Then he turned to the theme of being in charge of your own learning. He admitted that in a mathematics class on making tepees he had slacked off because he decided the class was lousy: "It wasn't teaching me what I wanted to learn. I just totally blew it off—I had an attitude: try to teach me. I got really disgusted. I was not learning anything from it. Finally, I just gave up on the teachers and decided I was going to learn and get credit by myself. I got some help from other staff, did some doodling, started to learn. I taught myself instead of tugging on [the teacher's] pant leg and saying, 'Can you help me?'" James grinned at us and waved his hand away from his body at hip level as he often did when making a point, "It was a paradigm shift. Everything. I just said I'm going to start learning things for myself. I worked really hard once I decided that. I had this notebook in which I wrote everything I'd need. I had to demonstrate what I'd learned, so I used video. I made an outline for my video and then I had the video and then my presentation of the video. So I learned it three times—once when I made the outline, once when I made the video, and once when I presented the video. I had a really firm knowledge base of the math that I learned, most of which I taught myself. I don't know whether I'll get credit on this but I just wanted to do it to learn. If I get no credit, I still learned something; it wasn't a total loss. I did a pretty good job."

In his April 1996 POL, James went high tech, organizing the presentation with the software Persuasion. He displayed graphics for each segment of his POL: "Outline: Meeting Math Requirements, Expressionistic Painting, and Peace in the Middle East." Meeting Math

Requirements was divided into "Running Into a Brick Wall," "My Math History," "Working on a Plan," "Using My Resources," "Learning," and "A CSU Math Professor." Frustrated about not having much credit in mathematics, James was sure he knew far more than the credit record showed. He could figure things out himself. He had completed a number of messy mathematics problems, some originating through interactive math projects like Crossing the River With Dogs and Go Figure. James felt he could handle college math, and Michael, James's math instructor, invited him to prove it. James began by utilizing his resources, especially email. "I had never used email before and I had a hard time using it—it's really cold and impersonal. But I decided that email was the way to do it, so I learned about email, and I began to correspond with a math professor at CSU [Colorado State University]. He hooked me up with a basic-level college math class for liberal arts majors—three math credits. This class was so simple, and I knew I could do it and go much further. We went to class and I met the professor and worked with him. Michael and I began to understand how I'd get credit for math. We wrote and both signed a letter that said, 'We can say with confidence and integrity that James has completed his mathematics work at Eagle Rock School.'" The letter began with a recitation of the six mathematics classes (or interdisciplinary classes that included mathematics) James had taken at Eagle Rock and noted, "His records indicate very little credit for all of this participation." Michael wrote, "My observations are that James has been an eager and committed participant [in classes] but has consistently failed to submit work for a final assessment. This was true even though James was observed doing work, engaging in the discourse, and responding to the prompts designed for the coursework. Throughout this time, James and I discussed his perception that the [credits] he had earned thus far did not adequately reflect his level of mathematics education. James has some clearly defined post–high school goals. He intends to apply to college to pursue higher education in philosophy. We agreed that his ILP did not adequately reflect his learning and we debated the value of pursuing additional mathematics given his obvious ability. To check out the accuracy of this perception, James arranged to visit a professor's class at Colorado State University. During this visit James also attended an applied mathematics course typical of the math that liberal arts major take. James took notes during these classes. He correctly identified the use of 'statistics, algorithms, surveying, probability, symmetry, and fractals' by the college students in this course. James's conclusion was that he was confident that the Eagle Rock mathematics program was at the same or a higher level of rigor. In fact, he was inclined to choose a more challenging precalculus course for his college education."

James next described the Expressionistic Painting class he took during which he learned to paint again, struggled with color (preferring to use a lot of black and grays), and painting his "dark side."

Then he focused on his Peace in the Middle East class. Again he used graphics to organize his presentation: "Understanding the Geography," "Understanding the History," "Understanding the Situation," "Using Your Information to Create a Peace Plan." He and his team, with a charge to develop a workable peace plan, researched the crisis through a number of different lenses: religion, the source of fresh water, why Israel and Palestine were fighting, why land is so important to them. "I studied Yasar Arafat. My opinion is that he is a national hero; he has tried to really help his people out. Yeah, he's definitely done some things I don't agree with, but he's done a lot for his people and gotten to where negotiations are possible."

In answer to a panelist's question, James reiterated his philosophy of learning: "The principle of education is that you don't drive things into students' heads; you teach them to love learning. Asimov says the fundamental reason for schools is to teach kids to teach themselves. When a school fails to do that, a school has failed. Kids can't become better at what they do or go any further than they have to if they can't teach themselves. They're stuck with expectations others have for them. I am committed to teaching and to peace in my life. I can make a difference; I know I can."

James' next POL, in August 1996, was especially significant. As it began James was on the floor gathering up a sheaf of papers that had scattered at his feet. He moved around erratically and finally stood up. As he leaned into the podium (a prop he had never used before) it was clear he had been crying. His first words were, "This has been my hardest trimester at Eagle Rock. I made the choice not to graduate because I need to learn how to write. I've grown the most this trimester. I'm still working on it, but I want to be a published writer. I left a little after the first six weeks, but I came back. A lot had to do with my fear with writing. I could have dictated to someone else I guess, but I chose not to; I chose to type it all myself and go through this [editing and proofreading] myself. I've got about eleven pages about conscientious objection somewhere around the school. I've taken from this experience that I really need better organizational skills. The next three weeks I'll be doing a lot on my senior research [on conscientious objection] and a college essay.

"I'm stressed out. There are other issues at home—my mother and grandmother are very, very sick. I'm using writing to put those problems in the back of my head." At this point, James broke into tears and struggled to speak through them. "I got picked on but my mother was always there for me, like a friend would be. She's the most important person in my life, and I'm scared—we don't know what's wrong with her. I think of Albert Camus' *The Stranger,* how he reacted when his mother died—he was cold and unfeeling. For a long time that was how it was; suddenly it blew up in my face, what my mother and grandmother have done for me."

It was absolutely quiet in the room as James bent his head over the podium and sobbed. A student brought him a handful of tissues. When he could, he raised his head to talk about his mother and grandmother and his life with them. When a staff member softly asked him if he'd like to forgo this POL, he shook his head and continued. "This has been occupying my time. I haven't been able to deal with stuff I need to deal with; I haven't been the best student I could possibly be. I'm feeling really lonely right now. I don't know why I'm telling all of you this. When I get that diploma it's going to mean so much more than any other diploma. My mother's going to be so proud of me. That's why I'm doing this. Why I didn't just decide to leave and say screw it."

Recovering, James moved to a splendid display against the wall. "I got to go to Washington, DC, for Learn and Serve America. It was a service fair and we were supposed to get ideas from others, and them from us. I couldn't figure out how to get all the service ERS does into the [poster] size [allowed for the exhibit], so we invented panels that turn like pages and show stuff on both sides. This is my legacy project: creating a culture of service learning in schools, passing it on to public schools. There's so much that can be taught through hands-on learning, and it's relatively inexpensive. Funding is not a problem." James moved each large panel as he talked about the service projects illustrated on each side: "Balarat [an outdoor camp for youngsters in the Denver Public Schools]; Touch the Future [our class wherein our students learn the montane ecology and teach it to inner-city second through fourth graders], the map of the U.S. we did on a school playground for students there. . . ."

A staff member asked the first question, "What is your commitment to learning?" James responded, "When I first got here, learning was learning, and education was education. Now, education is education, and learning is my passion. Not a whole lot has changed about education. I feel that I teach myself, I seek more knowledge than people teach me, with the exception of writing and English—that's still one of my biggest fears, a place where I still have to learn from others.

"I remember being told when I was a little kid in grade school—they told my mom that they thought I might be retarded in kindergarten. I was too slow for a lot of things, not able to cut it. And one thing that a lot of people don't know about me is that I wasn't able to read until I was like twelve. Now I read Nietzsche and Kant. I used to go to school with my shirts on backwards—I had a problem with dyslexia and didn't learn to write until ninth grade. This is the last thing that I really need to learn, what I need to conquer, is writing. I've found out that a lot of it is just my own fear of writing more than my actual writing.

"My real passion is reading. I read the back of shampoo bottles! I don't read novelists like Stephen King—except Kafka. I'm getting so much better with writing. I want to do a lot to change the world and make it a better place, and I think philosophy is the area where I want to work, help people get new ideas in their heads and make the world understandable. I want to write philosophical documents."

Another panelist asked James about Kafka's *The Metamorphosis*. James said, "[In the book] a man suddenly wakes up and he has become . . . a roach. I was the roach before ERS and then I turned into a butterfly or something; I turned into so much more of a complete person even though right now I'm feeling in a lonely spot with what's going on. I am a much more complete, well-rounded, well-educated person, learning how to write."

James focused intensely on his writing for another trimester and was at last ready to graduate. Here are some excerpts from the packet he prepared for his panelists.

- From his letter to panel members: "When I think about my learning since coming to Eagle Rock I am surprised at how afraid of my own intellect I was. I was not aware of my autodidactic capabilities. Eagle Rock School has taught me to teach myself, and that is quite possibly the greatest gift that anyone could give to another human being. . . . The three most important things I have learned since I have been at Eagle Rock are that I am an intelligent person capable of pursuing all of my dreams and hopes; that I have no reason to be afraid of what others think of me; and that I am able to teach myself better than anyone else. I can teach myself better than anybody else because I know myself better than anyone else, so I am able to adapt the criteria to my learning style. . . . Most importantly, I have been able to learn the things that I didn't want to or didn't think I wanted to. Now I am able to open my mind to new learning experiences."

- From his autobiography: "When we moved back to Grandma's for the last time, I was in junior high, and I started hanging out with the wrong crowd. I had only a few friends, and the ones I did have had similar interests such as music and just hanging out. They weren't into sports. Their main pastime was doing drugs. After a while, I started getting high too. It's hard to remember all that went on during this time. I was too stoned to care. It wasn't long before I started to look for any way to get high. One night I was staying over at a friend's house when we decided to look for some acid. One of the guys said he had heard that you could get the same effect from Dramamine if you took enough. We all went to the local grocery store and stole several packs of Dramamine. Outside the store we all took some. As we were walking back on a bike path, we started tripping. On the way back I was separated from the group, and the police found me sitting on the front steps of a bar after hours. I was taken home, and my folks let me go to bed thinking they would talk to me in the morning. The next day two of my friends were found dead, having overdosed on Dramamine. To say the least, this was a major turning point in my life."

- From his autobiography: "Eagle Rock also has an incredible learning environment. I have learned more than I have learned in all of my years of public school. The most important thing Eagle Rock gives is the passion for learning. Now that I have that passion for learning, I can teach myself anything I want to learn. One of the things that I want to learn is how to become a better writer. Since I have been at Eagle Rock, my perspective on life has taken a 180-degree turn. I have a new self-confidence that was never there before. My future after Eagle Rock is bright where before there was none. My family is proud of me but, more importantly, I am proud of myself."

- On his résumé: "Objective: Attend college and work towards a Ph.D. in philosophy."

- On his list of books read: Books by Aldous Huxley, Hunter S. Thompson, Tom Wolfe, Ken Kesey, Lao Tzu, Sun Tzu, Franz Kafka, Henry David Thoreau, John Kennedy Tool, Tom Robbins, Edward Abbey, Richard Preston, Albert Camus, William Burroughs, Philip Kaleau.

- On his *I Used to Be . . . But Now I Am . . .* personal growth sheet: "I used to be an introvert. I was intimidated by people and what they thought of me, but now I just don't care because I have enough faith in myself and what I am doing to know what is right for me." "I used to throw away knowledge, but now I crave it." "I used to be overly cautious, and it would stop me from doing what I wanted to do, but now I take risks and have fun doing it."

James devoted a large portion of his graduation presentation of learning to reflecting on himself as a learner. Speaking to about three hundred people in the Human Performance Center, James sported a bald head, a goatee, and several face rings that had accumulated one by one over the years.

"Well, here I am. One of my struggles has been a legacy of incompletion; it's my trademark. I'm here to show I'm not a quitter. I'm here to show you a legacy of *completion*. During the time we're spending with each other today, I'll be showing you some of my struggles, how I've developed throughout my education."

To thank teachers and people who helped him make his life a success, James read a passage from Khalil Gibran on teaching. This passage talks about how the teacher does not pass along his understanding but leads the student to his own understanding. The audience was quiet, and there were already a few tears.

James showed us what he was when he first came here. He introduced us to "Vern," with a mop of dark hair and an uncertain half-smiling face. "Three years ago, I walked like this [he demonstrates a hunched-over kid, eyes looking downward] and I had this big mop of hair going all over the place. I feel good about myself now; I'm confident; I walk tall; I speak with a loud voice; I speak to anybody to whom I can speak; I have beliefs that I vocalize; I'm relatively eloquent. . . . I'm very assertive in the way I speak even though I'm a pacifist.

"Another struggle I had was writing, so what I've done is present to you what I've written. The green folders are three different compositions—I got a lot out of doing these compositions. I can vividly remember sitting at my desk in first grade with a number 2 pencil in my right hand and a Big Chief tablet on my desk [he holds up a Big Chief pad] and a sentence written on the board that I'm supposed to copy. I sat there carefully copying each letter of each word, trying to make it as close as possible to what was on the board; I struggled to make all of the letters face the right way and not to turn words like *and* into nonwords like *nad*. Then I would turn to the teacher, and she would hand it back to me and tell me to do it again. I would repeat the grueling process over again. Then I would hand it in again just to get it back again. She would speak to me in front of the classroom, asking if I was just too slow. I continued to struggle through school, and in third grade I was tested for my IQ. I found out my IQ was around 145. They wondered why I didn't function in school, so they gave me more tests. They wanted to find out what was wrong. A kid like me with a 145 IQ should not be having this many problems with school. Through the testing they found out I was dyslexic, so naturally they put me in special ed classes. Soon I found out I could use dyslexia as a crutch to get through the hard parts of school. Special ed just makes that easier to do because they're your advocates, so I learned to manipulate them so I didn't have to overcome my difficulties. All I ever experienced from special ed is having my hand held and my work being done for me.

"So this went on all the way up to when I came to Eagle Rock, where I was asked to write all the time and every time I would find some way to slip through the cracks. Little did I know that it was catching up with me and I would have to confront it, this fear of mine, in order to graduate. When I was trying to avoid writing at Eagle Rock, I was missing at least fifty opportunities to write on subjects that interested me. Before I knew it, things were piling up on me at the end of my time here. I looked for ways to get around having to write things. I didn't want to have things handed back to me and be told to do them over again or that I'm stupid for not getting this. So I was forced to ask myself why I was still living this fear from years and years ago. And at one of the safest places I know. And if I wanted to get help, the help I need, I should get it while I'm here before I go to college, sinking and fading away. At first I was so angry—they were pushing me so hard—I left the community to see if could get my diploma a little easier, but I knew in my heart that the same thing would happen someplace else. One can only run so far before his or her problems rear their ugly heads again.

"I went back to my hometown and stayed about five days—it wasn't really leaving, but it was—I had five days to rethink what was going on with me and I found out that *this* is what I want to do. I didn't want to take the easy way out and I don't think I *could* have taken the easy way out. So I returned to finish what I had started for once in my life. When I returned, I was given the option to dictate my thoughts to someone and go through the revisions later on, after someone typed it for me. This was a tempting proposition for me but I thought, What would I do when I was in college? Who would hold my hand when I was doing a philosophy dissertation? I made the decision to do this for myself.

"Let me update you about what was going on during that time. I had two weeks left in the trimester—this was last trimester. I was supposed to graduate but decided to take the hard way out instead of having someone do my work for me. I knew I was not graduating that trimester so I decided to take my work home with me and do it over break so I didn't have to stay at Eagle Rock to get all the revisions done. Well, eight compositions, one senior research project, and three weeks later I was finished with these papers and ready to turn them in. I had this real fear of just turning in papers. Would I just get them back all red, and would people make a judgment about my intelligence because of the mistakes that are in that paper, which has happened before? They kind of blow you off. Alison [an instructor] asked me if I had actually written the papers myself. And I lost it, I was really angry. Oooh. I flipped out a little later. [Then I realized that I was better than Alison thought]—I was so down on myself—and if Alison thought I was better than myself, then I was better than myself. Then I was *definitely* better than I thought if Alison thought I was better than she thought. Do you understand what I mean?"

James proceeded to demonstrate his knowledge, concentrating on subjects that were hard for him, grammar and writing, and subjects that inspired him, philosophy, service, and art. He got two standing ovations, one when he finished his presentation and the other when he had answered all the questions the panel and audience had for him.

Perhaps James seems self-directed to you. Or perhaps you wonder whether he is as self-directed as he says he is. There is evidence that he is self-directed. He composed his own music after figuring out the software on his own. He pursued his own work in his geography class. He took it upon himself to pursue some issues related to his Close-Up class. After a struggle, he made the tepee class (a mathematics class) work. He challenged himself by taking a college math class. Finally, he took his writing—his most feared subject—and made it work for him. On a continuum of self-directed versus dependent learning, I would put him well along the self-directed side.

This type of student can be both exhilarating for a teacher and very frustrating. In the tepee class, for example, James may have seemed stubborn and even belligerent because he wasn't doing anything to meet the learning halfway. He had decided that he wasn't going to learn anything, so he didn't. What would I have done to help James make the leap from learning that wasn't happening to learning that was? Badgering him to get with it, start working, get his assignments done, probably wouldn't have done it. Maybe I would have tried to help him find his own interest in the class and pursue it. Leaving him alone until he, himself, got restless and took action to satisfy his own internal need, which is what his tepee instructor did, is risky, especially in a large class—but it is also perhaps the best, most constructivist approach to helping a student pursue learning.

It is part of our mission as educators to help all students become self-directed learners. That's what we mean when we speak of *lifelong learning*. Many schools say lifelong learning is their goal, but they don't help students become independent and self-directed, characteristics they need if they are, indeed, to be lifelong learners. Even very young students need to be helped to become self-directed. They need to practice self-directed learning on tasks that are appropriate for their age.

One thing our graduates have told us is that we have helped them become problem solvers. No matter what faces them in college or on the job, they know how to go about solving it. They've also told us that they have confidence they can solve anything that is thrown at them. They learned the problem-solving skills not by rote but through hands-on experiences, and they built their confidence as they were challenged to solve these real learning problems on their own (with some coaching when necessary). Our overall goal for graduates at Eagle Rock is that students "will have the desire and be prepared to make a difference in the world." Students need to be self-directed in order to accomplish this goal.

I don't want students in my classes learning just because I, with whatever authority, tell them to learn—and what and how to learn. I rejoice when students, like James, step forward and declare what they are going to pursue and how they are going to proceed. But this type of learning doesn't fit into all classrooms. It may be positively frightening to some teachers—imagine thirty students all pursuing their own learning. What does the teacher do? How is the classroom managed? One answer to these questions is smallness: the classroom should not contain thirty students. The school should be broken into smaller units, and each class should be smaller. The resulting smaller number of independent learners needs less management and more coaching, and so coaching becomes the strategy of the effective teacher. A classroom of thirty students, if they are all nurtured to become self-directed learners, can still work, however. The teacher can still coach all these students—with a little help: students coach each other, and parents and older students serve as coaches.

James wasn't always a self-directed learner. In his special education classes he played the system, using his disability as a crutch to do little or nothing. How and when did he change? I believe it happened when he had a keen desire to know how to compose music and couldn't get anyone to help him. That argues for some benign neglect on the part of instructors. His instructor in his tepee class also practiced benign neglect, and in both cases James stepped in to fill the void. He taught himself. Benign neglect is tricky. It may be hard to justify leaving students to their own devices, not rescuing them. But how else are they to develop their own internal (and external) resources? One of our teacher's favorite expressions is, *How could you find out?* He doesn't give answers. He requires students not only to discover an answer on their own but also to justify it for him. If they can justify an answer fully, he accepts their answer but does not pronounce it "right." If they can't justify an answer, he asks them questions that send them back to the problem.

Metacognition, thinking about thinking and learning about learning, is important at Eagle Rock. It starts with the first academic class new students take (see Chapter 2), in which the head of school, Robert Burkhardt, teaches $8 + 5 = 10$ at a deep level. He also talks to them about learning theory. The focus on metacognition continues throughout a student's career at Eagle Rock. In almost every class, the student is challenged to think about how he or she will learn in the class. Sometimes teachers do what is so obvious but so seldom done: they ask the students directly how they learn and what barriers to learning they might encounter in the class. Then they try to fashion the learning experience with the students so that it works. It is clear that James is very knowledgeable about how he learns. He also knows what he can do about his "soft spots." He has even found some success in attacking his own learning problems.

James was taking a detour around writing when he persuaded Michael to assess his mathematics skills aside from his portfolios. Although James knew what he was doing in math, he couldn't write about it and had a stack of unfinished portfolios to prove it. Communicating about mathematics has been an important part of the national and state standards for mathematics since the National Council of Teachers of Mathematics produced their standards in the 1980s. Requiring that learning be demonstrated through writing presents a dilemma. Is it appropriate to "fail" students in mathematics (or science or social studies or any other course) if they cannot adequately express what they know through writing but can do so through other means? To what extent do we base what students know in other subjects upon what they are able to learn through reading and express through writing? I don't have an answer, but I believe we must focus on communication skills, no matter what the subject is.

Did we do the right thing by offering James the chance to "dictate [his] thoughts to someone and go through revisions later on, after someone typed it"? In this case there was a happy ending: "This was a tempting proposition for me but I thought, What would I do when I was in college? Who would hold my hand when I was doing a philosophy dissertation? I made the decision to do this for myself." Another student might have taken us up on our offer, and we all would have lost. Perhaps we trusted James to resist our offer. Perhaps we knew he wouldn't succumb to his earlier avoidance tactics. Most likely, we knew that his stubbornness about his own learning would work for him as a writer.

Still, I wonder about the way he got all of his writing done: eight compositions, a research project, and other pieces. He did them at home, alone, by himself. He did not avail himself of a coach. We have evidence that he really did write (and rewrite many times) those compositions on his own. What brought about this change? Why could he suddenly do what he had been unable to do up to this point? Again, I think it was our appeal to him as a self-directed learner that did the trick. He stopped depending on anyone else and decided to teach himself. He weaned himself from others' evaluations of him (the red pen) and their possible judgments about his intelligence. He looked inside himself and struggled to find the resources he needed. I'm not sure this technique would work with all students, however, even at Eagle Rock!

We have never allowed a student who could not read or write on at least an eighth-grade level to graduate from Eagle Rock, but we came close with James. Despite standards, few schools and districts choose *not* to graduate students who have not met literacy expectations. They may issue such students a qualified diploma, but the students usually graduate. The sad truth is that students who have real literacy problems have usually dropped out by the time the school has to make a difficult decision about awarding them a diploma.

Finally, I'd like to comment on James's special education experiences. He is not the only student to tell us that he used his special education designation as an excuse for not learning (for not doing much of anything, in fact). He learned how *not* to be a learner. He says dramatically, "I learned to manipulate them so I didn't have to overcome my difficulties. All I ever experienced from special ed is having my hand held and my work being done for me." Obviously, James had problems with writing. Once he learned to read, however, he was fairly good at it, especially when he was interested in what he was reading. Not many people find philosophy tomes interesting, but James did, and consequently they were easy for him. His interest clues me into what halts many readers; they can read what they're interested in, but they cannot or will not read what bores them, often school textbooks. It may also have struck you in reading the transcripts of his POLs that James' oral language was sometimes random and unorganized. The sequiturs are there (sometimes only in his head) and can be discerned by paying close attention, but James sometimes wandered from idea to idea.

Do these problems require special education? I wasn't there when the decision was made to place him in a special program, so I don't know what resources were available to those making the decision. However, being placed in a special education program was damaging to James' sense of himself and to his self-confidence. James began to thrive when he entered Eagle Rock, where we have no special designations for any students and where the classes are small enough to accommodate all differences.

What Is Self-Directed Learning?

First, a self-directed learner follows his or her *passion in learning*. This puts the burden on the student and requires some flexibility on the part of the teacher. Eagle Rock student Abe declares, "It's taking a passion and following it and, through that passion, not only learning about what it is exactly that you feel passionate about (like music) but also learning about yourself and your opinions through that process. There has to be a passion there or expression or motivation for learning. You won't follow through, take the time to learn something, if you don't find the passion." Sixteen-year-old Darren adds, "I pursue my own interests, and that's what I mean by self-directed learning." One night at dinner I noticed Darren, oblivious to the noise and chaos of eighty teenagers eating around him, his nose in a book. I asked him what he was doing. "Oh, I'm reading about the Kreb's Cycle." It was a college-level textbook. Later he related, "Nobody could get through to me—I was so concentrated on that book. I wanted to learn more about where my food goes, how I get the energy to do the gate run, how I get the energy to talk to you. How does it work? I did this totally on my own, no prompting, no credit, just because I wanted to know. Scott and Craig [interns] heard about my interest, and they suggested the book I was reading." Similarly, Josh was reading *Napoleon at War* at a dinner table "just because I want to. We went to the Boulder Public Library to get books for our senior research paper—mine is on Martin Luther King and civil rights—and there were thousands of books, and I was just thinking there was a lot of stuff I wanted to learn about. So I got this book. It's pretty interesting."

Second, a self-directed learner is *curious*. Marchello: "A self-directed learner is someone who is curious to find out what things are." Matt offers an example of curiosity in learning a foreign language. "I'd noticed that I was writing poems in Spanish, trying to write them just to see if I could do it. 'I wonder what that looks like in Spanish,' I'd say. The class stuck to the basics of workbooks, but it definitely improved my Spanish trying to do poems."

Third, there is an element of *control* or *power*. Allie elaborates on this aspect of self-directed learning. "One difference is that you're more in control, making a conscious effort to be in control, not just letting the teacher give you the information and making an effort to take it in, not just having it sit on a piece of paper. It's finding your affinities and following them, covering the basic curriculum but finding what you have some kind of affinity for, at least some part of the subject if not the whole subject." Stephanie says, "I think self-directed learning is the power to take your education into your own hands." Power seems to be important for learning. When students feel as if all the power is in the hands of others (teachers, administrators), they often feel disenfranchised from what should be one of the most personal of human conditions—learning. Stephanie: "You have the power, but you also are accountable and stand by your word as a learner, and you're your own supervisor." Josh: "Power comes from seeing that you can learn in general about anything. You tell yourself to do something; somebody else doesn't tell you to do it. Nobody's talking at you; you're saying it yourself. My general interest in learning even helps in math. I might never really love math, but by me having a general desire to learn anything and everything, then I can learn math."

Conditions Required for Self-Directed Learning

Eagle Rock students offer some surprising comments on what classrooms must be like for self-directed learning to occur. Natalie is adamant about the need for *structure*: "Self-directed learning must be kinda structured in the beginning, and then students are able to pick their own topics at the end, what we want to work on." Darren elaborates on structure that supports self-directed learning: "Teachers can make a class more self-directed by encouraging self-direction. It's always good to have structure—structure works and I can push above it and do some of my own learning. Structure gets me started, motivated, inspired, ready—I like to look at it as a structured class and it gets me started. It preps me to do my own individual thing. I talk with teachers about having a hard time deciding what to do. They sit down and talk with me about options." Natalie muses, "What if classes were totally self-directed? I probably wouldn't have a problem with this if I knew what the topic was . . . if I had some background knowledge, I'd be okay. But, usually, the teacher should suggest generally what should be learned. If students are not self-directed after the teacher describes the learning that's expected, the teacher should throw out a hint or question. Especially when students come from regular high schools and are used to having teachers tell them what to do." She suggests, "Balance is important, half structured and half self-directed. We need to have some structure—know what to do—and then the teacher gives you a boost, thoughts to think about, then do, and go beyond. We can't just be thrown out by ourselves. We need structure with room to move—and then teachers should check in and then leave us to work independently. People need to have some boundaries."

Stephanie describes the appropriate role of the teacher as "walking with you." Natalie adds that self-directed learning "doesn't have to be alone, just yourself learning it. It's good to be working with other students and it's important always to have the teacher to go to for guidance." She says, "You need to have some guide outside directing the learning, where you could possibly go, show you the different paths. You cannot see all the topics yourself."

Another condition Stephanie is adamant about is *accountability and responsibility.* "Students need to know that what they do independently really counts. It's not just an add-on to the real work the whole class does."

Sometimes students don't see how they can pursue their own interests in curriculum without some *help with the process.* Here's Abe, thinking aloud about the connections between his passion, music, and academic subjects: "In a class called Recycled Reseen, we are making art out of trash and recycled materials—sculptures. We've been doing all these thematic sculptures, and I've been doing them but not caring about them. One day the instructors said, 'Come tomorrow with something you want to do.' I was struggling with what I was going to make in class, and it just came to me—I should make a guitar. It's sort of in a way its own protest against electronic instruments. I've crafted a guitar—out of tin cans! Fifteen Folgers cans and I made a guitar. I can do it. The only piece I had to buy was the tuning mechanism at the top. So, I guess I did. . . . I found room to pursue my own interest. Could I do that with the rest of my classes? I don't know. I guess I could learn about math through music. Maybe through music I could learn about history. Could it be done? It would take a lot of work. Could you learn anything through your passion? I guess I can pretty much learn anything through music."

Allie suggests that one of the conditions for self-directed learning is to have a *very open environment,* a class that "instantly can turn upside down, to different subjects, not what the teacher may be teaching, but related to that and to students' interests." She reflects on "visitors who ask why we know so much and act older than we are here. It's because our teachers allow us to have fun with what we're learning. If the environment is a fun place for learning, we're going to learn more—it's exciting and active. What makes an environment fun? Activities outside the classroom, outdoors, in museums, at the park; something to do with curriculum but it will give students more areas to expand in, juggle ideas, mix and meld them. Also it's the positive thinking of the teacher, always saying something can be done and encouraging it. Teachers who don't just say no or *We don't do that here.* They encourage us to go different ways, look for possibilities. Teachers who say, *Why don't you look into this and see if you can do this?* Creativity and imagination are a part of this. Absolutely necessary."

What Self-Directed Learning Means for Curriculum

What kind of curriculum do you need for self-directed learning? First of all, it should be *general* enough so that every student can find a way through it that makes sense and is satisfying to him or her. The graduation requirements on Eagle Rock's individualized learning plan

(ILP) are general enough—really just subject matter areas—so that students can pursue what they find interesting within them. Our documentations on the ILP are general enough as well: "a project on a hypothesis" in world history leaves a lot of room for students to explore what they are passionate about and express what they have learned through anything from a play to a paper, a diorama to a debate.

Sometimes it's through content that we can provide room for self-directed learners. Recognizing that we cannot cover all there is to know, we encourage *content options*. We choose "less is more" because we know two things: depth leads to some degree of breadth (as students go deep into their choice of content, they usually go broad as well) and we cannot hope to keep up with the knowledge explosion. (See Chapter 3 for more on this topic.)

Sometimes it's *organization of content*. Natalie needs to be able to organize content her own way to learn: "For myself, I like to have things organized my own way; I don't like things unorganized or organized the way the teacher organizes things. The typical high school is organized so that it's very predictable; it doesn't give students a chance to be self-directed. In my old public high school, we always did chapter-test-chapter-test. I didn't like learning anything or doing the work. I just took it in."

Sometimes it's *instruction*. The instructional conditions Eagle Rock students think are essential for self-directed learning include:

1. A structure wherein the teacher sets the scene, provides some basics, and guides students toward their own interests (process help); a structure that has the teacher "walking with" the student.

2. A chance to work with other students.

3. A way students can be in control, take responsibility, and be accountable.

4. An environment that supports self-directed learning. It communicates to students the possibility—even desirability—of pursuing their own interests; it promotes learning outside the classroom doors; and it conveys a spirit of imagination and creativity.

Sometimes it's *assessment* or how students show that they have learned. At Eagle Rock, students have a variety of ways to document learning and, if they want, they can petition teachers to allow them to select other, more fitting ways. Chapter 5 contains a list of the types of documentations we use at Eagle Rock.

If you are determined to enhance self-directed learning, you'll want to reconsider both curriculum and its corollaries, instruction and assessment. Natalie makes clear what the results will be: "I think I learn more and better if I can be self-directed. If I just wanted to do what the teacher says, even though I have my own ideas, I'm not personally learning. I can give them what they want, but I won't be taking it in in depth and learning it the way I want to learn it. I'll make the teacher happy, but I won't make myself happy. And I won't remember much because it won't have affected me personally."

The Value of Transparent and Coherent Curriculum

Two aspects of curriculum deserve special notice in terms of enhancing self-directed learning. First of all, the curriculum must be *transparent.* It must be accessible to everyone in the learning community, from staff to students, from parents to visitors. Thus, when we print iterations of our curriculum, we print enough for everyone, even students. It makes sense that those most affected by curriculum—the students—should have access to what they should know and be able to do. So ours is not a hidden or covert curriculum, a black book on the shelf of the department chair or principal. Our curriculum document not only describes what students should know and be able to do but also tells students how they can document their learning and, as much as possible, how good their work must be to represent mastery (rubrics). Our accessible curriculum helps students be in charge of their own learning.

Another aspect of curriculum that helps students function as independent learners is the curriculum's *coherence.* It makes sense to those who read it. At Eagle Rock the general requirements for graduation are noted on the one-page individualized learning plan, as are the documentations that will prove mastery. These match what's in the curriculum guide, which everyone has. The *order* of the requirements on the ILP matches the order of the pages in the curriculum guide. In addition, the curriculum guide supports what's on the ILP with detail: the big-picture goals, specific learning, and an assortment of rubrics. Everything fits.

Knowing what's required—in as much detail as possible—prevents students from experiencing the bewilderment common in most curriculum encounters ("I never knew what was required"; "I didn't know that was going to be on the test"; "I didn't know what to study"; "I did the questions at the end of the chapters, but they weren't on the test"; "I was always surprised by the grade I got—I didn't understand why the person next to me got a different grade"). A transparent and coherent curriculum is one more way to give students some power and control over their learning.

The Role of Choice in Self-Directed Learning

Eagle Rock students are very vocal about the role of choice in helping learners become self-directed. Natalie describes self-directed learning as *making choices,* "a very active choice to go out and find out what I want to know. In some ways this gives me specialties in some areas, makes me more of an individual as learner. There are areas in which I'm better at some things than others; this affects what I can share with peers, what my special knowledge is."

Self-directed learners sometimes *negotiate curriculum* in order to follow their passions. Natalie defines this aspect of self-directed learning: "There are two kinds. One is you get a chance to decide your own curriculum. The other is when you get a chance to have input on how things are taught." Marchello describes an experience negotiating curriculum: "[The instructor] gave me ideas of things he knew I was interested in. If he would have made us sit in class during those times and tried to teach us all about the same things, even if these were things he knew we liked, if he taught us about them rather than let us research them, it wouldn't have worked. It was like I was teaching him about what I was learning instead of him teaching me about what he knew. My main thing is curiosity. Teachers have to know students well to be able to stimulate their curiosity. If [the instructor] had done a lecture on X, Y, and Z, it wouldn't have helped. It's more fun to choose what you want to learn. It's okay that other students don't do all the same things."

Darren zeros in on input: "Having input is part of being self-directed. Where you draw the line is between what you want and what the teacher wants. I bring up what I want to learn, and the teacher helps me learn these things. So, I am learning what I want to know. In Act Out, although we had a voice, [the instructor] made decisions overall. But the important thing is that we got to bring up the options. We could propose ideas, and she would choose based on the interest of the whole class. I've been in classes in old schools, and we're told we're gonna study world geography and memorize countries in Africa. There's no attention paid to the student who might like to learn more than names."

Natalie says, "I talked with [the instructor] and suggested we should watch movies, read a book on our own, or read a chapter together and discuss it. [He] liked my suggestion. When you just tell the teacher what things you'd like to see changed, it's great when they take your ideas into consideration. When students are encouraged to come up with suggestions, and teachers pay serious attention to them, that makes the students feel good about learning."

Stephanie negotiated the curriculum in both science and mathematics. In science she took a class about birds and found herself turned off. "It seemed really confining, a box. I had to do a portfolio, and I asked if I could do something like the naturalist writers do—Lopez and Stafford, for example. Could I make my portfolio creative writing? I got the only accomplished portfolio in that class. I wouldn't have gotten as much out of the class if I hadn't taken on my own learning and decided how to express it, using my writing as a way to explore this brittle subject. I told [the intern] that I could meet her expectations and mine too with my creative writing portfolio. And I exceeded those expectations. I explored the scientific aspect and really learned science, the facts of it, choosing words to capture what goes on in flight. This has lasted more than mere facts for me. In a probability class, I also used my words to capture what I had learned. I made it creative writing instead of a really dry paper. I also added a chapter I wrote about math, 'My History With Math,' about my first math teacher and my last teacher and all the trouble I had had with math, all my struggles. I was really frustrated but the paper helped me embrace my frustration, and I ended up learning more."

Josh negotiated curriculum in Virus Hunters. "I could have given up in class and said screw it, but I really wanted to learn, so I asked [the instructor] if I could do my own thing. I made a process of reading a college book, writing down words I didn't understand, and looking them up and reading over again and taking notes and putting it in my head. At the end of the week I had five or six pages and a list of terms that I made and a picture of a process of what a virus does. I was able to expand this into a portfolio about bacteria. At the end it was pretty interesting. I didn't care much about credit; I just wanted to learn."

Ian, who is proud of his Gaelic background, tweaked his mathematics curriculum by adding an element to his problems of the week (POWs): "I always try to throw in history because it makes it more fun, mostly Irish history!"

Marchello and Ruth, whom you will get to know in Chapter 10, negotiated their way through the Eagle Rock requirements or competencies for graduation in very different ways, taking different amounts of time to reach mastery. Chello and Ruth are very different people—very different learners—and they needed choice in the curriculum to succeed. Another student expresses this idea as a quasi-syllogism: "Having choice is having options; having options is being able to choose; being able to choose is being able. For me this ability allows me to learn." A staff member adds, "I think choice is crucial to the learning process."

Although the choice that matters most is the one students make in the classroom, choice in curriculum begins long before it reaches that level. It starts with state standards. State standards are worthwhile documents—they usually express a consensus on what is important to know and be able to do. Often they are based on the best thinking of national groups such as the National Council of Teachers of Mathematics (NCTM) or the National Council of Teachers of English (NCTE). I have problems with state standards only when they take away local choice. If state standards describe exactly what students should know and be able to do at each grade level, they eliminate choice. If I know, for example, that all fifth graders must know the major battles of the Civil War, my curriculum will be the battles of the Civil War. But if the state standard says that by the end of eighth grade students need to know the causes of war, I have a lot of choice about what students need to learn, and how and when they need to learn it. I can work with other teachers to accomplish that standard by eighth grade. Each grade can do something different. I can choose what wars to study, based on my own enthusiasms and student interests. I can choose how students recognize the causes of war. And, I can pass those choices on to students, so that they'll choose what interests them and share it with others. And learn and remember. What matters more—knowing the battles of a particular, though important, war or knowing how and why wars start?

State standards that are tested in a high-stakes way also take away from the choice that is needed at the local level. If I know that students are going to be tested by the state at the end of fifth grade on the battles of the Civil War, I'll probably decide to teach to the test, especially if it's a high-stakes test—if the results are printed in the paper by school, or teacher, or district and my own or my supervisor's job depends on the scores. The better way is for the state to get a "snapshot" of compliance by sampling not only the standards but the students—one year testing a representative sample of eighth graders on the causes of war, the next year testing another representative sample of eighth graders on another standard. (See Chapter 5 for more about standards and testing.)

Choice at the school and classroom levels can be crushed by actions taken by districts as they adopt or adapt the state standards. Often the mandate requires adoption of the standards as they are or adaptation that exceeds state standards. If the state has been too specific at each grade level, the district has few choices unless it acts with courage and drafts more general standards at benchmark grades, such as 3, 8, and 12, and shows how these exceed state standards. However, many districts see as their mandate making the state standards more specific, both in terms of content and grade level. This makes curriculum choice at the school level even more difficult to accomplish.

And, of course, curriculum choice can be blocked by any school that decides to take the district standards—even if they are general and set for benchmark grades—and make them more specific as to content and grade level. Choices for the students in the classrooms are then limited.

One thing I particularly dislike about state standards that are set grade by grade is the isolation this engenders: "I'll teach toward my standards; you teach toward yours." Cooperation comes when fifth-through eighth-grade teachers work together to help all students work toward standards that must be attained by the end of the eighth grade. Instead of relegating the learning of all those standards to the eighth grade, each teacher takes some part of them, either developmentally appropriate or specific to an interest or passion, and says, "I'll help students by working on this in my grade."

What choices can students have? At Eagle Rock, these choices are wide ranging:

- Select a class from among a variety of offerings.
- Select within a chosen class the particular aspect of the subject they are going to pursue.
- Select how they are going to learn (reading, interviewing, using the Internet or appropriate software, writing a piece of nonfiction or an essay, etc.).
- Select how they are going to document learning (provide a demonstration, write a research paper, teach someone else, take a test, perform a skit, etc.).
- Select the categories and quality indicators for a rubric to judge their work.
- Choose with whom they are going to work—or decide to work by themselves.
- Identify how they are going to make use of the expertise and advice offered by the instructor and intern.
- Identify how they will get help when they need it.
- Decide how to use their time . . . and whether they need extra time.
- Decide where they are going to work.
- Modify their work as they go.
- Decide what they will do to follow up on their work.
- Decide how they will share or publish their work.
- Decide how they will reflect on their work and give feedback to the instructors and the interns about the class.

Staff members at Eagle Rock say that choice is very important to them, too. They not only recognize the benefits of choice to students—

"If you choose to learn about something, it will be more interesting to you than if someone tells you what you should learn"—but also recognize the benefits to themselves as educators. They feel respected as professionals, and they love the creative aspect of designing courses that provide many pathways for students to follow. One Eagle Rock teacher says, "I truly value the freedom I have to teach and create my classes. I don't think that would happen in many other places, but it should. Both students and staff are more focused and invested in the learning process when there is choice for both."

All students choose to come to Eagle Rock. All students choose to stay—or not. All staff members choose to come to Eagle Rock. This is the bedrock for all other choices, including curriculum. Someone who makes a choice—whether student (and the student's parents) or staff—has a real allegiance to the school she or he has chosen, wants it not only to survive but thrive. The more ways that can be found for students (and staff) to have choices, the more likely the learning will be engaging and enduring.

How can public schools get choices into their program and their curriculum? Ideally, they can declare a specialty, like magnet schools do. Barring that, there are ways to create programs of choice within a school. One of the best known is to create schools within a school. A lesson learned by the Coalition of Essential Schools is that a single school within a school does not work; it pits the "special" school against everyone else. But if all students and all staff choose one of many schools within the school, everyone is special. In an elementary school, grade-level or cluster (grades K–2) teachers can proffer a specialty. Ms. Jones and Mr. Rodriguez will teach fifth grade through the lens of medieval history. Mr. Becker and Ms. Smith will teach the same grade through the lens of space travel. Another set of teachers will teach fifth grade through the arts. Students and staff have choices.

Curriculum choices can work much as they do at Eagle Rock. Allow students to choose units to study and, within those units, the specific subjects they'd like to pursue. For example, in a history class students could choose to study any of a number of aspects of Revolutionary War America (the unit): culture, armament, religion, famous people, literature, science and technology, clothing and costume. If students share what they are learning with one another, they'll end up with a broad understanding of the Revolutionary War even though they have concentrated on their own interests. And they'll be much more likely to retain what they have learned.

You can also give students the opportunity to choose how to learn. Perhaps they'll choose to work in a group, reading reference works or primary sources. Perhaps they'll learn by watching videos about America in the 1770s. Perhaps they'll interview a collector of Revolutionary War weapons and have the teacher coach them in how to conduct an interview. They may want to memorize some fiery speeches of the times.

Students may also choose how to demonstrate their learning based on how they have learned. They might prepare a report as a result of consulting reference works or primary sources. They might show clips of various videos and explain their importance. They could replay parts of a recorded interview, show pictures of the weapons they discovered, and discuss what fighting was like during the Revolutionary War. They might deliver those fiery speeches of the times. Students might even create a rubric for themselves, their teachers, and others to use to evaluate their documentations. Even if they are all doing something different, there will be some categories on the rubric that will be the same for all students, something like, "Understands specific aspects of the culture of the country around the time of the Revolutionary War. Uses no anachronisms."

Finally, you can give students some choice regarding deadlines. (Staggering due dates will help your workload as well!) And students may want some choice in how they get feedback on their progress; perhaps they'll set up student review panels to look at work each is doing two or three times before the deadline. They may also want to do something with their work after it's finished, perhaps publishing it in a school, district, or local paper or setting up a display at a shopping mall. At the end of the course or unit, students can choose how to give you feedback about how the work went—both what they found difficult about the work as well as how they found success.

Eagle Rock students claim responsibility for their learning when they have choice:

- "When you learn by choice, you take it to heart more. You take it in, since you wanted it in the first place."

- "Choice gives you nobody to blame or depend on for credit but yourself."

- "I believe choosing your own class helps your education and helps you take responsibility for learning if you're the one who chose to learn about something."

- "It helps you be more responsible because if you don't hand in something on time you have no excuse. You chose that class. You chose that project. Maybe you even chose the due date."

- "If one has the choice to learn something one is passionate about, then one tends to learn more."

- "I think choice is absolutely brilliant—how at Eagle Rock each class is taught as a theme rather than an individual subject. I believe this way of presenting a class enables students to understand a subject much more thoroughly than if it was taught as a regular class you have to take. When individuals are given a base and then a variety of ways to go, they tend to learn, acquiring much more knowledge."

- "The process [choosing classes] is excellent. It's very good because it allows students to have more freedom at school. It brings a lot of color into my life here at Eagle Rock. If we were put into a system of classes that we had to take without any say in them, life would be colorless, very dull. I would probably drop out."

- "Choice affects learning because when you choose to do something you are most often interested in what you have chosen to do, and if you have interest in a situation, you will most likely be more focused and into what you are doing."

- "I like choice a lot because I am not being forced to take something I'm not ready for. It's good to start with something you're interested in."

- "If I have choice, I am learning at my own pace and have the desire to learn something I really care about."

- "I hold the choice to persevere at whatever level I am capable of, basically to work at my own pace."

- "I think that if you choose to learn you take on a big challenge on your own. No one is forcing you to do anything. You choose to learn. So, when you accomplish something that was your own choice to learn and you do what you said you'd do, you feel pretty good."

- "For me, choice makes me want to learn more, because I pick what I am learning. Choice affects learning 100 percent!"

Clearly, choice is essential to helping students become self-directed learners.

Questions to Consider

1. How do *you* want to study and move toward enhancing self-directed learning in your school?

2. Would most people in your school describe it as encouraging self-directed learning? What makes you think it does or doesn't?

3. To what extent do you think most people in your school would describe it as offering choices for learning?

4. Examine your curriculum guide, some units you've taught, lists of requirements, a few assessments. What do these artifacts say about the degree to which students can be self-directed learners at your school? What do they say about your beliefs about students? about teachers? about learning?

5. What do your students say about self-directed learning? How do they define it? To what extent do they think they are self-directed? What examples can they give of being self-directed, both within and outside school? To what extent do they see that they have choices in learning?

6. What do your colleagues say about self-directed learning? How do they define it? To what extent do they think they encourage self-directed learning? What examples can they give of times when they have encouraged self-directed learning? What have the results been? To what extent do they see that they can provide choices for learning?

7. What do parents say about self-directed learning? What do your administrators say? How do they feel about choices in learning?

8. What are the advantages of trying to inspire more self-directed learning? of offering more choices?

9. What would you have to change about curriculum? instruction? assessment? the environment? in order to include more self-directed learning opportunities in your school.

10. In what ways are you already incorporating choice into your program or curriculum? What evidence do you have that choice helps teachers teach and students learn?

11. What state, district, and school policies—including state standards and state testing—might affect self-directed learning and learning choices in your school or in your classroom? If you don't feel you have enough opportunities for self-directed learning because of these policies, what can you do to get them changed or get a waiver from them?

12. Who are the "change agents" already helping students become self-directed learners? Are they collecting data on the effects of their efforts? How can they share what they are doing and learning?

13. Who are the people most likely to raise a barrier against self-directed learning and more choices in the curriculum? What will be their objections? How can their objections be respected and, perhaps, overcome?

14. In what ways can you implement more choice in your own environment (school or classroom) if the system is reluctant or unable

to move to more choice to enhance self-direction? Consider the opportunities for student choice listed on page 145. Can you implement any of them?

15. Can your school become a specialty school that brings in avid teachers and students? If not, can you have several exciting schools within your school to which staff and students choose to belong?

16. How will you know that helping students become more self-directed learners is succeeding in terms of student learning? What data will you gather? How will you analyze it?

17. How will you communicate the results of your actions to help students become more self-directed learners? Who needs to know? What do they need to know and how will you present the information?

18. What professional development do you need in order to move to a more self-directed curriculum?

19. What are a number of ways your school could encourage more self-directed learning? Which would be easiest to implement? Which would be most effective?

Chapter Seven

Curriculum Is for the Whole Student

"Welcome. Thank you for coming to my personal growth presentation of learning. You've got my outline. What I've tried to do is set up the room so that we are close together, and I didn't want to have any big skits or fancy show-type things. I'm saving that for my graduation POL next week!"

Indeed, the reception area of the Professional Development Center is set up very subtly and personably. Melanie (Mel) is sitting in a wingback chair, her back to the fireplace. Arrayed around the flagstone coffee table are several other chairs and couches. About twenty people are present: the head of school, other administrators and staff, veteran and new students, Mel's adviser and her house parents. A batik cloth covers a portion of the table, and on it Mel has arranged pictures, a candle, some incense, and a basket of dried flowers. She has made coffee and tea for everyone.

"I didn't want to candy-coat anything. I want this just to be me, Melanie. A lot of people have told me they don't really know who I am. I'm going to keep it honest, and I just want this to be about who I am. Before Eagle Rock, my life was definitely heading downhill. I was having some serious rebellion problems with my parents, and the harder they tried to keep me in the house the more I just wanted to go out and experience what I thought was a great life. My friends were really important to me, and whatever my friends thought was cool was what I thought was cool. I was just learning so much. I went through about fifty different phases." She makes a face. "There was the big-hoop-earrings phase; there was the flannels-and-streaks-in-my-hair phase; there was the hanging-out-at-the-mall phase. I didn't know who I was, and I was very confused.

"And then, at the same time, I was going to church a lot, and I hung out with the youth group and so everything that I was doing in my life was contradicting what I was doing in church, but I was always glad I had my friends in church because a lot of people have had some bad experiences in church. With my church situation, my friends were always very accepting of me, and if I missed a couple of times they weren't like, *Where in the heck have you been?* They were like, *Hey, we're just glad that you're here.* They didn't really judge me, and so that was good.

"I got kicked out of the house when I was eighteen. I had been working while I was trying to succeed in all these different schools, but now I started working full time. My parents wouldn't let me take my car, and I was taking the bus around. I was a manager at a pizza place. I thought it was great to be a pizza manager because I was really needed. I knew the distributors, and I knew how to order the food, and I thought that this was probably the highest I'd ever get in life. I planned on working there forever. I worked there part time at first and then full time, and it was like the height of my career back then. I thought that was just great.

"I also had a serious problem with pleasing people. I always wanted people to like me. I didn't want people to think I was bad; I always wanted to be a *good person*. But I also put myself in situations where I wasn't doing the right things. I started getting all these drinking tickets where cops would come to parties and they would give everybody Breathalyzers and if you blew point one—like a *sip!*—then they would write you a ticket. So I got a few of these, and then my license was suspended, and I really had nothing. So then I decided I'm just going to totally stop, and I'm not going to do this anymore, and a week later I put myself in another position where I'd get in trouble again. So I was basically just setting myself up for failure.

"I went through several different schools. I went through tech school where I was doing nursing, and I felt that this was good enough—I went far enough, and I learned how to do this and that, but a week before I got my nursing certificate, I quit. Then, I tried private school, and I got kicked out of private school because my principal thought I was a bad influence on kids at this Christian school." There is some gentle laughter at this, given who Melanie turned out to be. "Then I tried home school, and working full time was not going well with home school. I was really tired when I got home, and there were these textbooks and these tests I'd have to take and I was just like . . . wsssssh," Melanie draws the palm of her hand from the front of her head to the back, "I'll do it later. Then I did a couple of papers, and I'd show Mom *[simpering]*, 'Look, I did some work today.' 'Great,' she'd say.

"I was always doing some, almost, kinda, sorta. But I was never completing anything in my life. So when I heard about Eagle Rock, for some reason it sounded really exciting. I'd moved back home—my mom let me come back home for a while because the people I was living with decided they didn't want me there. My sister had met one of the wilderness instructors, Anne, who told her about Eagle Rock. She came home and told me, and I thought, *Wow, this sounds really neat,* so we called and asked for the packet and everything. My parents said, 'Melanie, this is totally up to you. We are not going to push you to do anything in your life.' 'Cause they had tried that already, and it just was not working. So they said, 'This is up to you. You need to fill out the application. You need to figure everything out. For the most part, this is *your* deal.'

"So I did, and I was really excited. I did *not* want to get a GED. I did not want to just let things happen to me. So I wrote this poem. It really shows how I didn't know what to do." Mel opens her personal growth portfolio and reads: "'I cannot run,/I cannot hide./Is there someone in whom I can confide?/Is there anyone on my side?/I am caught in the pulling tide/And washed to shore./Worn and broken a little more,/Worse than the time before./I search for love, I search for/ Pride. I search for/Me in my soul/But I'm in the bottom of/A crashing hole./Where can I run, where/Can I hide? They are chasing/Me with guns on their side./No mercy, no slack, just/On me, ready to attack. I'm trippin'/Out watching my back./I long to be loved/By the one furthest away.'

"And this was just really showing confusion—this was in ninety-seven—and I was general in my ideas, over and over again. I had all these court dates coming up with these silly tickets that I kept getting, and I would write myself about what would make me feel really better. I'd list all the obstacles that I had to overcome. I think that helped me sort things out. Then I'd write another poem: 'A day to me is time to waste./Never plans made, just/Thoughts erased./There for a while then bored of/That taste./So many experiences I have faced./I wonder what the future holds—/I won't know until I unfold/The mystery of the years to come/Just based on where I'm from./Everyday, I pray for hope but there's too much/In my way. I'm sick of waiting./Oh, the price I will pay./I will finish something, not/Tomorrow, but today!/But, I am lost somewhere far away.'

"So, it's almost like Eagle Rock came at the right time, when I was frustrated with my life. I was sick of everything. I was sick of being around my friends. I was sick of sitting in their kitchens every single night, watching my friends drink and smoke their lives away. It was like, you know, I'm better than this! I can do so much better than this.

"I want to read you something I wrote my freshman year in high school: 'One in almost two thousand students, me. I don't feel known or recognized. Lost in a crowded hall, I search for my locker. Running to class I barely make it in time for the bell. It's lucky if I have a desk. I take a seat. My teacher asks questions with a cheat sheet or points and says, "You!" They see so many kids in a day, they can't seem to learn our names. With maybe one or two kids in the class I know, I try to work with them. Soon the bell sounds and again I shuffle down the hall. I want the faces I see to disappear so my path will clear, but the students grow. The school shrinks, and so do our hearts.'"

Melanie looks at her outline to remember what she wants to say next. "When I got here I struggled with my age a lot because I was eighteen. But, at the same time, I think that this was a plus because I knew what I wanted. I knew who I wanted to be. I knew Eagle Rock would work for me. Even though I had times where I kind of freaked out, I always persevered through it, I stuck to it, and I always learned a lot in my classes. My wilderness trip was really frustrating to me, however. Every single day, I'd write about problems. I'm like, I know how to order food from a distributor, and these kids just don't know anything about life, anything about being on their own. They're so young, and I thought this high school was supposed to be the high school at the end of the road. They've only been in high school a semester, and I've been to six high schools. I deserve to be here more, and why are they giving me such a hard time?

"Otherwise, I didn't have much trouble with my age. I had a little bit of a hard time with the rules. I knew I could follow them, but I also thought I could set my own rules. I could get my work done. I could be out after curfew. But then, at the same time, I realized why curfew was there—others were complaining about it—but I had good role models in my house, like Sita, who graduated a while ago. She was always really there for me and, whenever I was discouraged or upset, she would explain to me why things were the way they were. That was enlightening.

"I also started appreciating my family. I started realizing that the whole time I thought my parents were so against me!—the whole world was against me!—they were really not against me. I realized that my parents had been for me all along. They never gave up on me. Every time I had some new freaky-brained idea about what school I was going to try or what I was going to do next, they'd kind of say, *Uh, ooookay. We'll be there for you. You're gonna be a nurse now. Okay. You're in a Christian school. All right.*" There is lots of sweet laughter at this.

"They just went along with it and hoped that Mel would be something. And they knew that I would. They just didn't know quite what or when it was gonna be. They were getting a little worried about me when I was eighteen and things were still at the level of trying, like I'm gonna try this. *Okay, we'll see what happens to you.*

"They were really surprised and proud of me when I came to Eagle Rock. And then I just kind of started taking off—kind of stepping up. It's like you think that you're here." She places her hand out flat about waist high. "And the first time, you're lifted off the ground a little, like you're on a ride at an amusement park or something. It lifts you off and you're kind of swinging your feet off the ground and . . . whoaaa. And then it's like Eagle Rock keeps lifting you higher . . . and higher . . . and higher, and it's like right now I'm here." She raises her hand high above her head. "And I'm scared that, once Eagle Rock is gone, I'm just gonna go shwwwwwwwwww back down." Her hand descends rapidly to below waist level. "What I've failed to realize is that it's not Eagle Rock that has been lifting me. It has been me lifting me. I'm terrified. I get these cold feet. I don't want to do this. All these people have expectations. What if I get out there and I just totally mess up? I just have this fear there. I don't want to hurt my parents. I don't want to go back to where I was. But I also know that there is no way that I'm going to go back to the way I was. I've maintained myself—my credit, the years here. I've tried to coach other kids to understand what I've come to understand. Like Sita, when she coached me. And that's what Eagle Rock means, and that's what I've tried to be.

"It's cool that I'm going to be the only graduate. I think that happened for a reason. All I have right now is Mel. Me and Mel are gonna do it. I'll check in with Mel for everything. And that's really cool. Last break I went and ate dinner in a restaurant . . . by myself. I totally enjoyed it and I sat there and had a book and I read it, and I ate my grilled cheese and had some coffee afterwards. Why not! And sure, I'll have the peach pie! And I sat there in that booth, just totally okay, with people looking at me and wondering. I didn't even worry about it. I was just having lunch with myself. I also was taking drives by myself. I turned off the radio, driving way out to all these farmhouses, then downtown and parked and walked the mall, looking at the stores I wanted to and bought myself coffee. I had learned that it's okay to be by yourself. If I wanted to see a movie, why did I have to go call someone: *will you go see this movie with me?* And if they said no, then I couldn't go. Go to the movie!!! If you want to see the movie, see the movie. Why not? So that's been great for me.

"And then, my accomplishments." She has moved to the last item on her outline. "I never ever thought I would ever organize anything. I've always been athletic but I always kind of did it. I played basketball with my boyfriends when I was younger—I hung around with guys and played basketball. I really loved it, but then someone would say, *Go out for a team,* and I'd say, *Are you kidding? I don't want anyone to see me. I don't want anyone to watch me.* On the court I'd hide my face. Why? I really did have some problems there. When I joined that Christian school, I played a little bit. When I came here and played intramurals, that's where I started to shine. That's when I really felt what it was like to be on a team. I was on a team; I was in the gym four hours a night practicing my layups and really thinking this means a lot to me. And that's when I started taking personal fitness classes and realizing that I really wanted to go into sports medicine. I love to help people and I have helped people." Around the room, heads nod emphatically in agreement. "How can I still help people but have it be something successful? How can I make this into something? So that's when I decided that sports medicine would be a great way to help people.

"And the musical productions. I love to sing. I love it. I'll be in the shower just singing away. I can actually sing well. I can sing. Why not? If you can carry a tune, if you can open your voice cords and hum along, then you can sing. And I wanted to share that talent with others, and I never realized that I could do that until I came here. I was never okay with that until I came here. *Grease* was a blast. I had a blast being Sandra, and even though people made fun of me—oh, blond girl, Melanie, sure—I just had fun with it. And I made it my version of Sandra.

"That scholarship I got last trimester meant a lot to me because I felt like I deserved it. I felt like I had completed something here; I have a legacy; I've helped people. And I'm going to go on and I'm going to continue this. The excellence award felt really good too, so I was starting to get a taste of success. Success feels a lot better than failure. I just don't know how to deal with success like I know how to deal with failure, and that's one of my biggest struggles. Even a couple of weeks ago: *No way am I gonna graduate. There is something wrong with me.* And I wanted to screw it up. I really wanted to screw it up. It was like feeling pushed off the edge, and what are you going to do when someone's pushing you? You're going to rear up, and that's what I was doing, because I was afraid to jump. You know how birds swoop down and then up and then down? But I'm never going to hit the ground."

The purpose of this POL was for Melanie to describe her personal growth. When she gave her graduation presentation of learning a few days later, she wove academic growth into what she said about personal growth, the personal growth like the warp in a weaving—the strong part—the academic growth the weft. Although she proved that she had learned academically, it was clear that the amazing personal growth she had accomplished made the academic growth possible. Indeed, we have come to realize that personal growth must, to some extent at least, precede academic growth. Sometimes students must face up to their personal issues and deal with them in order to make progress academically. Often, what has proven impossible for them—academic learning—is only possible when they have dealt with those issues. Often what baffles us in terms of their academic learning becomes irrelevant once they have taken steps to grow personally. This phenomenon has caused us to wonder just how much of a "learning disability" is really related to impaired emotional growth and how much is related to real learning problems. Although Melanie did not talk about being labeled "learning disabled" in her personal growth POL, she did mention it in her graduation POL and stated soberly that knowing she was not going to be good in learning made her seek other ways to get attention.

Personal growth POLs, like any others, are designed by the students doing them. We encourage individualization—"Make this yours"—and creativity in terms of both the packet and the presentation. The assignment is this:

Portfolio 1

1. Pick a word or theme that describes who you are. For example, "courage," "strength," or "change." Explain your choice in a preface to your portfolio.

2. Collect fifteen songs, poems, or short prose pieces that relate to your theme. Five of those items must be written by you. Ten can be from other sources.

3. Finish with a short biographical statement describing yourself.

Portfolio 2

1. Document your personal growth from the time you started Eagle Rock until now (graduation trimester).

2. Include your latest autobiography, signed by your adviser. Also use letters, POL evaluation sheets, recommendations, awards, pictures, learning experience records, etc.

3. Include your written moral and ethical code.

4. Write a 250-word essay describing a moral and/or ethical dilemma and how your code would be used to resolve it.

Both portfolios are due two weeks before your personal growth presentation. Meet with your counselor three times prior to the presentation, presenting an outline of the presentation the week before it is scheduled. For your presentation, plan for a half to a full hour, choose an audiovisual person to videotape it, reserve video

equipment and a room, and invite panel members. In addition to
invited panel members, anyone else on campus (house parents,
advisers, instructors, family members) is invited to attend.

Students have included in their portfolios information from their
former schools—disciplinary letters, test scores, and report cards.
They've also included letters from judges, citations, even psychological
write-ups. Some have included early learning experience records (or
report cards from other schools) and compared them with later LERs.

Students shape their presentations in a variety of ways. Some have
invited former teachers, principals, friends, and neighbors (people who
knew them well during the "before" stage) to attend, asking them to
give testimonials on how much they've changed. (One invited the
judge who had sentenced him to boot camp and was persuaded to let
him go to Eagle Rock. This judge had kept in close contact with the
student.) Others have held a debate with their videotaped "old" self.
Still others have presented a dramatic monologue.

You may be wondering why we admitted Melanie, who was eighteen, when our usual age for admission is between fifteen and seventeen. Mel had been to several schools by the time she heard about
Eagle Rock—public high school ("One in almost two thousand students, me"), nursing school, a Christian school, home schooling. She
was pretty determined, and we admitted her. We make exceptions.

Melanie also blows away a stereotype or two about "at risk" students. Although I don't like labeling students "at risk" and would prefer
to call them (if anything) "students placed at risk," the connection
between student and family still applies. "Students placed at risk" often
come from families that neglect them or worse. *Broken homes, abandon-
ment,* and *abuse* are words often used in conjunction with *at risk.*
Melanie, however, came from a very attentive, warm, caring, and
loving family. Her particular angst came from somewhere else.

What if Melanie had "failed" her personal growth presentation of
learning—or, for that matter, her graduation POL? It is almost impossible for this to happen. Because we are a small school and our relationships with our students are so personal, we know how that student
is progressing—or not—toward graduation. Someone would almost
certainly have noticed a problem early on. If it had looked like Melanie
was not ready to give either presentation, she would have been ad-
vised to delay her intention to graduate, postpone both POLs. Only
once has a student been surprised by being told she was not yet ready
to graduate. And she quickly saw that she *wasn't* ready and needed
another trimester, largely for personal growth. And only once has a
student given a graduation presentation of learning that was unaccept-
able. This happened very early in the history of Eagle Rock, and we

were not clear ourselves about what was acceptable and what wasn't. We let her graduate, of course, unwilling to punish her for our slow development of expectations.

We do not yet have a rubric for the personal growth POLs, although we have one for all the others, including the one preceding graduation (see Chapter 5). The quality of the personal growth POL, and to a large extent the graduation POL, is in some ways unrelated to rubric criteria. In other words, students watch one another's presentations and determine what quality is themselves. The result has not been disappointing: students ratchet up the quality each trimester. Especially inspiring are the graduate POLs; we can almost hear students whispering, *Wow, when I graduate, I'm going to do that, only better!*

Personal Growth Is as Important as Academic Growth

Melanie's passion about her personal growth is not an anomaly. Almost all Eagle Rock students cite their own personal growth as the most important stride they've made. Sure, they're proud of their academic growth—especially because, for many of them, it was so elusive before they came to Eagle Rock. But most of them attribute the real differences between themselves before Eagle Rock and after to personal growth. Here are some typical *I used to be . . . but now I am . . .* statements from presentation of learning packets:

- "I used to need drugs to feel good, but now I feel good about myself without drugs."
- "I used to be angry, but now I know that anger is only a front."
- "I used to be a failure, but now I am learning the fundamentals of a successful future."
- "I used to be coldhearted, but now I am slowly letting people in."
- "I used to have weak morals, but now I am slowly devising my moral and ethical code."
- "I used to make a lot of excuses, but now I admit it when I am wrong."
- "I used to love violence, but now I am afraid of violence."
- "I used to never admit when I did something wrong, but now I can admit my mistakes and learn from them."
- "I used to never face my fears, but now I confront them."
- "I used to be undependable, but now I am someone you can lean on when in need of help."

- "I used to be satisfied with trying, but now I am unsatisfied until what I am doing is perfect."

- "I used to be a person full of animosity, but now I am honestly full of excitement and happiness."

- "I used to be unconscious sometimes, but now I am fully conscious of what I do and say."

- "I used to be a person who hid behind walls, but now I am a person who reveals my true self."

- "I used to be a person who thought my opinion didn't count, but now I am a person who knows that it does count."

- "I used to be a person with a negative attitude, but now I am working on that."

- "I used to act stupid to entertain people, but now I only perform on stage."

- "I used to be judgmental, but now I talk to people to see what they are about."

These statements are from the first *three* POL packets (out of eighty) from summer 1999. Fully 90 percent of the statements each student makes are about personal growth. How can we can ignore personal growth in schools?

And many schools don't. They have what is called *character education*. They present curriculum on emotional intelligence. They incorporate discussion of morals and values into literature and history. They may even have a set of known values that relate to personal growth. They may consciously model what they expect.

We don't believe in the efficacy of any prepackaged, prepared program of personal growth. The focus on morals and ethics—and personal growth in these areas—must be part of the culture. Educating the whole student and understanding the relationship between personal and academic growth is complex. It is not a matter of one value a day. It can't be something we do between 10:00 and 11:00 on alternate Wednesdays and Fridays. Didactic lessons don't do it. Teenage ears are not particularly attuned to moralizing. Personal growth is not something we add to the curriculum. It *is* the curriculum.

At Eagle Rock, we begin with the stated, learned, and lived principles that we call 8 + 5 = 10. (You've read about these in Chapter 1.) Many of these principles address personal growth. We purposefully construct courses that address these values through science, history, English, and other content. Course titles reveal the moral focus that accompanies the academic: Spiritual Geography; Transportation and Environmental Issues; Games and Culture From Around the World;

Building the Salud Clinic; Close-Up (a course on civic responsibility); Riverwatch; Civil(?)izations; Community Problem Solving; Eagle Rock Press (a course on preparing textbooks for young Spanish speakers); African Elf Project; Recycled, Reseen (an art course).

Service is one curriculum area that especially benefits personal growth. When students are building a fishing pier for the handicapped or finishing an office shell in a mall for a sliding-scale medical clinic or restoring a frontier cabin, they are learning the value of doing for others without expectation of compensation. Richard L. Curwin (1993) describes the effect of service on "at risk" students:

> For students with poor academic achievement, classrooms are breeding grounds for feelings of inadequacy and worthlessness. At-risk students are continually confronted with failure and told they are worthless. Many schools try to compensate by offering special programs to increase self-esteem. However, even the best activities do not significantly influence children who continually receive negative messages about themselves. Children are acutely aware of where they stand in the school community and how teachers and other students perceive them. Thus a "Catch 22" is created. Students will rarely be successful in school without hopeful attitudes, but they need to be successful before they can feel optimistic. One way to break this cycle is to actualize the basic human need to be altruistic. (p. 36)

Melanie discovered this principle when she initiated a project that had students helping other students when they were floundering.

It is hard for students and staff to ignore personal growth at Eagle Rock, written as it is into the individualized learning plan. It appears in several places:

- Civics (a project on citizen responsibilities; a report on citizenship; an action plan for change; a report on influencing public policy).
- Environmental Science (local, national, and global issues; an environmental impact project; a written reflection).
- ERS Orientation (a presentation on $8 + 5 = 10$; group-work journal entries; service projects).
- ERS Transition (success skills).
- Food Service (two trimesters serving as a crew leader).
- Lifeskills (a portfolio of possibilities; career development; independent sustainability).
- Personal Growth (portfolio 1; portfolio 2; presentation).
- Service Learning (portfolio of projects; written summaries of projects; statement of philosophy; legacy project).
- Wilderness Trip (journal entries; demonstrations of work ethic/attitude; solo "letter to myself").

Assessment often drives curriculum. Although some schools may be leery of assessing personal growth, assessing it ensures that it has a prominent place in the curriculum. Perhaps we cheat a little by not employing any kind of rubric and not allowing an opportunity for failure in relation to the personal growth POL, but simply knowing one needs to do such a presentation makes personal growth at least equivalent to academic growth, which is assessed in each classroom through documentations and at the end of each trimester through POLs. The requirement that students create portfolios for science and mathematics *and* personal growth also communicates importance. The personal growth POL reaches such a level of ceremony and ritual that it becomes a rite of passage. Students have their own concerns with personal growth recognized and legitimized. They feel valued and not just because they are learning about the causes of the Civil War.

Everyone at Eagle Rock must live its values publicly. So when a student breaks a nonnegotiable rule or fails to live up to one of the ten commitments in our code, it's usually a very public thing. The student who has transgressed sits on the hearth in the lodge and talks about what he or she did and why. This student also talks about what should happen next and the areas in which help is needed. Students and staff ask questions and consider consequences. They discuss how they can help the student in the future. They make recommendations to the director of students, who makes a final decision. Sometimes the student goes home for six weeks or more and writes a letter petitioning to reenter the school on a second chance. This letter, too, is considered very publicly at the hearth, and students may or may not recommend an interview by a mixed panel of students and staff who then make a recommendation to the director of students about whether or not the petitioner is ready to return.

Staff members do their best to model the values in 8 + 5 = 10, but we are far from perfect. What is modeled is not perfection but dealing with imperfection. It is more important for a staff member to say, *Oh, I goofed. I'm sorry. How can I make it up to you?* than remain unreachably perfect (even if they could).

Students learn what they observe. Above all, they learn honesty when a staff member is honest about shortcomings.

Democracy prevails at Eagle Rock. Anyone can write a proposal to change anything, and that proposal is considered publicly. Most classrooms try to model a democratic process about curriculum, instruction, and assessment: *Here's what you need to learn. How will you learn it? How will you show me you've learned it?* Peace mediation and peer council continue the emphasis on the values of a democratic society. Students practice what they need to do to live within such a society.

Incorporating Personal Growth Into Public High Schools

Even schools that say they do not touch on personal growth do. Theirs is a hidden curriculum and as such may not represent what the school would wish it to if it decided to examine and explicitly address values and principles. It may not be as effective as an examined personal growth curriculum could be. When we preach democracy but through our actions disenfranchise a whole set of people (usually students), our hidden curriculum is in contrast to our espoused curriculum. We may preach fairness but are biased toward some students and against others. We may espouse respect but treat students as if they were inferior human beings. We may teach thinking skills and then assign students mindless busywork. Students notice such disjunctures. They lose faith, become cynical. They see rules as silly and get angry about their disenfranchisement. Many of the students who come to Eagle Rock have issues about power and control, often because they've watched adults say one thing and do another or because they have been treated as part of a herd, not as individuals.

Some schools say they cannot deal with values, morals, ethics, and personal growth: their communities won't allow them to. Many education writers dispute this as an excuse and argue that if brought into the process early enough, all communities are willing to unite behind a set of common values, "those values we share, not those that divide us," as Etzioni (1993, p. 15) puts it. Some communities reference the Constitution, the Bill of Rights and other cherished documents to find the values they'll support in their schools. Who can argue with "such values as respect, responsibility, trustworthiness, fairness, caring and civic virtue" (Lickona 1993, p. 9)?

Questions to Consider

1. How do you think your school currently addresses personal growth? What do you think students? staff? parents? others? would say about the importance of personal growth at your school?

2. To what extent is expectation of personal growth explicit? implicit? (Perhaps this is a statement you send home to parents at the beginning of each school year, a self-study report from an accreditation process, or an accountability report you make to the district and community.)

3. What aspects of curriculum, instruction, and assessment support personal growth? What aspects of the school as a whole support

personal growth? What aspects of the district or state support personal growth?

4. What would be your ideal personal growth curriculum? How far away is what you're currently doing from that ideal? Are there some pioneers in your school or district who are already incorporating aspects of a personal growth curriculum? Do they have evidence (objective and subjective) that it is working with students? Do they have any evidence that personal growth is related to academic growth?

5. Are there likely to be some resisters? Who are they and what are their positions (both actual and perceived) within the system?

6. Could individual teachers? grade levels? departments? in your school incorporate a personal growth curriculum even if the whole school did not? What problems might arise? What are the advantages?

7. What do you think the various constituencies in your school community would think about a personal growth curriculum: parents? community members? business leaders? teachers? school administrators? district administrators? state administrators?

8. How could you present your ideas about a personal growth curriculum as well as its benefits and liabilities to your constituencies in a way that will help them understand? How could you use students and teachers already engaged in a personal growth curriculum?

9. What barriers might various constituency groups raise if a whole school or the district wanted to incorporate a personal growth curriculum? How could those barriers be overcome?

10. How could the school (or individual classroom teachers) represent the personal growth curriculum (as Eagle Rock does on the ILP)?

11. To what extent do you want the school or individual classroom teachers to be accountable for personal growth? How can this accountability method have low stakes but still be meaningful? Would displays of personal growth learning (through portfolios or presentations of learning) be useful?

12. What kind of professional development is needed? What kind of ongoing support would teachers and administrators need? What professional development will they need to measure success of a personal growth curriculum?

13. How will you know that your incorporation of a personal growth curriculum is working, both in terms of actual personal growth and its effect on academic growth? What measurement devices can you

put in place—both subjective and objective—to report progress as you move along? What indicators would come from teachers? from students? from parents? from others?

14. How will you communicate with your constituencies about the progress you're making in incorporating a personal growth curriculum?

Chapter Eight

Curriculum Encourages a Constructivist Approach

Danny graduated from Eagle Rock in December 1996. When I talked with him in July 2000, he said, "In [the schools before Eagle Rock] I was not there. I just wasn't interested in anything that was going on in school, I never wanted to follow what the teacher was telling me. I wasn't challenged at all in high school. The only challenge was could I get there enough days not to get kicked out. And eventually I didn't. That's what led me to Eagle Rock. It was weird. I got kicked out of school and was doing drugs and painting houses, and my mom read a tiny article in our local newspaper, one paragraph, about this school in Estes Park. This article commended Eagle Rock for its service learning, and it included a telephone number. Fortunately, I was accepted. At first I was a real jackass; I think I kind of picked on people, had an ego. I had to learn to deal with that. I had to leave and came back. This time I was ready."

Danny remembers one particular learning experience he had at Eagle Rock. "A bunch of us were sitting in the lodge after a meal and Michael [the mathematics instructor] said, 'If you have twenty-five hundred photons of light hitting your hand at one unit away from the source of the light, how many photons would hit your hand two units away from the source, and three and four and five?' I don't know why that caught me! We started talking about whether light spread in pixels like on an LCD screen, so the pixels would be further and further apart as we moved away from it, or did it spread like butter, thinner and thinner?

"I did a proposal and petitioned Michael to do independent study. Then, it took me awhile to get my thoughts together and figure out how to attack the problem, logically. Michael was really good at asking questions and at arousing my mind. Nobody knew the answer off the top of their heads, but as I went through the process, the lightbulb went off in Michael's head before it went off in mine. It turned out to be the inverse square law. The intensity of the light goes down proportional to the increase of the radius squared. I remember that! Wow. I also remember going through the whole thing, making spheres. Twenty-five hundred photons of light one unit away, two units away. Units could be anything—inches, miles, meters.

"Before I built the spheres, I remember I got a bunch of data, numbers and stuff, did charts, saw patterns in them. I simplified by telling myself that I was dealing with a thousand photons one unit away. It could be any number, but the pattern always seemed to be the same. Then, I did a two-dimensional model and then went back to the initial question—do photons get scattered evenly across a bigger area? Going through the process again in my mind now, I realize that I've got a problem—the same problem I had when I did this in independent study! I'm thinking like I did then. It doesn't work two-dimensionally. Surface area grows in a different way than a linear measurement.

"I figured it out by surface area—the first sphere broke down into sixteen parts, so my hand was one-sixteenth of that sphere for one unit away. At two units I kept it in sixteenths, and I remember I figured out the exact surface area at one unit and then two units, swelling up to twice from the first to the second unit, so the diameter of the sphere doubled, but the third I added one more unit to the diameter, so I tripled the first one, so I didn't keep the relationship of doubling. That would have thrown it off because it's not exponential. I may have messed that up one time, doubled it one time. I realized that I skipped a unit—I went one, two, four. I had to go back and make three.

"I collected data from the spheres—I found a formula and plotted it. The patterns matched the earlier patterns, but I don't think I'd figured out what the law was by then—the inverse square law. I remember doing some sort of exercise with cubes—fifteen cubes were supposed to be twenty-five hundred. I laid them out and they were a trigger to something in my mind, and when I was playing with those blocks I figured out it was the inverse square law. I could have stared at the numbers forever and not seen it, but when it was in front of me in three dimensions I saw it. It went beyond light. I didn't know anything about the inverse square law when we started, and until I figured it out, I didn't know what it was I was trying to figure out. I was learning it inside out, not getting the textbook definition. It was like I started from the back of the chapter and got back to the beginning. I learned that rule from the inside out for sure.

"I got a light meter, and we had calculators that could measure pH and temperature and light intensity. I went into the dark room and I used a slide projector. I made some kind of cover for it, so only pin-hole light would come out. I set up the floor from one foot, two feet, and called that the distance from the point source. By the time I did that, I think I had figured it out already, trying to do a real database, and the numbers didn't line up perfectly but the curves were the same. It was an imperfect simulation.

"What I really started thinking about was that this phenomenon happens with sound—if you have an explosion, the sound decreases as you get further from the source. With waves and water, the wave-length decreases as it gets further away from the wave's beginning. It spreads out. Vibrations spread . . . all these are applications of the law. Not just light. If you had some way to measure sound, like if you lit a firecracker, and you measured sound at ten, twenty, thirty feet, the curve would be the same as what I discovered with the light.

"It's hard to learn everything this way, but there are definitely advantages. Look at all I've remembered! The way it all started it was unique. When Michael asked questions, he had no intention in lead-ing me there. We were kind of blind. On his side, he didn't know what he was doing any more than I did when we started. Michael played along really well; if he realized something before I did, he didn't tell me. He let me figure it out. He might have been one step ahead of me the whole way, but he didn't take it over. He never got frustrated that I couldn't figure it out. He never just told me. He waited until I fig-ured it out. It really takes away from the process when teachers just tell you the answer and you forget it. If you went back to somebody who learned inverse square law in tenth grade, they couldn't have told about it the way I have. They wouldn't have really learned it.

"The answer to the question? It does disperse itself. By three or four units, the gaps between light are so big, you don't see it with your naked eye. Light actually gets spaces between it. They don't really understand how light behaves; sometimes it's a wave, sometimes it's a particle. If you think in purely particle terms, spaces between par-ticles get larger and larger the further away you go.

"I had to think about whether the light was a point source with constant light coming out of it. That would be different from a point source that flashes. If you think of a lightbulb on all the time with light coming out constantly, when you turn it off, you already have light coming out of it to your eye. The tail end of the light comes to you, and then it's dark. The light's off before the eye sees that it's dark. That's about a wave more than a particle. If you have a light source that only flashes once for a split second, think of it sending out par-ticles of light. When it's on all the time, it's like a wave. Think of an explosion where all the matter travels away from the source and, as it travels away, it spreads; it gets thinner and thinner, broader. I thought of it like that. As the matter gets further away from the source, there are gaps. It spreads way out.

"The question I didn't raise then was the Big Bang theory. Now I think about how the universe spread. Are the stars where they are because of the inverse square law? Does that have anything to do with where they stopped and the space between them?

"My feelings during the process? I had days of frustration with the independent study. Sometimes I couldn't mess with the problem; I did other homework and was frustrated and needed to let it sit and let my head sit. There were definitely times of exhilaration and ecstatic discovery. At the same time I was discovering answers to this problem, I was doing a little bit of self-discovery. I realized that all the things I learned, someone had to figure out in the beginning. Galileo and Newton and all those guys spent their whole lives going through the same frustrating processes. It makes you appreciate the people who figured out all the things we learn. I got a little taste of how they did it. The feeling of wanting to know—I got a lot of that. I wasn't just doing it for credit; I really wanted to find out the answers. Lots of what people learn in their science and math books, they don't give two thoughts about how it was discovered. Someone had to spend a lot of time figuring out those things. I imagine the process I went through is what someone else did to figure it out initially, or close to the same way I did. You don't just hear a question and have an answer pop into your head. Some of this is the miracle of discovery. You really do retain it so much better when you discover it on your own.

"As a learner, some of my problem-solving skills improved. I had the ability to figure out where to start and ask myself leading questions. My curiosity is naturally piqued about things, and I don't give up, usually. There was one problem that I worked on for awhile, and I never did figure it out so I gave up. I think that, as long as I can see the light, so to speak, I'll keep on.

"I could see some next step or some meaning in this inverse square law problem; it wasn't so far away. The initial discussion we had about it motivated me. Nobody knew or had any idea. It equalized things; we were all curious and ignorant. Ego had something to do with it. I personalized the problem; I had to do it! I had this superiority issue, you see, and I had to take this on and prove it! I took that question and said, 'I'm gonna figure this out.' No ifs about it. Dare and double dare."

It is amazing that Danny could remember these details four years later—not only what he had learned but how he had learned it. He also remembered—poignantly—how he felt about his learning: some frustration as well as the exhilaration of discovery. As he says himself, few students remember much of what they learned after they have learned it (which brings into question whether they *have* learned it). It was also clear that he saw other applications of his learning, not only at the time, but later, during our interview, when he wondered if it applied to the Big Bang theory.

Danny's reminiscence suggests a special relationship between him and his teacher Michael. This relationship can be characterized in several ways:

- Michael respected Danny and talked to him as a thinking human being.

- Michael was unafraid of "not knowing." During Danny's work to discover the answer to the puzzle about photons, Michael may have discovered some answers prior to Danny's own discoveries, but he had no need to take away from Danny's process of discovery. He didn't deliberately withhold from Danny a key he had already discovered, but he offered the key in the form of a question that Danny could take up as he liked.

- Michael had a lot of respect for Danny as a learner. Danny respected himself as a learner.

- Michael was flexible. He was content to let Danny find his own way through the problem even if it differed from how Michael himself had done it. He continued to ask Danny to explore and write about his answers in order to clarify them for himself.

There was also something about this learning situation that appealed to Danny's ego. Here was a problem his teachers didn't know the answer to. Maybe he could solve it! He was curious, challenged, determined, ambitious. We shouldn't dismiss the effect of ego on learning. When students guess at answers already in the teacher's mind, work on something the teacher already knows the answer to, or solve a problem that is already solved in the textbook, their egos are thwarted. Their deeper selves are not involved.

Danny spent one and a half hours four days a week for six weeks in his independent study. He'll never forget the inverse square law or the process that helped him learn it or how he felt about that learning. He may not have learned everything in mathematics, covered all the chapters in a succession of mathematics textbooks, but he *uncovered* mathematics. Especially poignant is his realization that he was doing what Galileo and Newton did. He was engaged in the process of discovery. He was thinking mathematically and scientifically. He was doing what every great thinker and inventor has to do to come up with something universal. He exulted, "Lots of what people learn in their science and math books, they don't give two thoughts about how it was discovered. Someone had to spend a lot of time figuring out those things. I imagine the process I went through is what someone else did to figure it out initially, or close to the same way I did. Some of this is the miracle of discovery." That's worth any number of formulas learned from a textbook any time!

Two aspects of Danny's process are especially interesting—his need to try out a real-life model and the breakthrough he experienced when he used the blocks. Much of Danny's work was abstract, finding patterns in numbers, doing charts, using a calculator. For many, that may suffice, but when Michael challenged Danny to apply what he'd learned to a model, Danny was eager to do so, especially since Michael left making the model entirely up to him. And when Danny moved the blocks around to make different patterns that matched his number tables, he saw the solution clearly. We often relegate the use of manipulatives to primary and elementary grades, but they are important for teens and adults as well. Danny circled completely around the problem, using all means of learning he could think of (or that were suggested to him), so that he had real confidence that he *knew* the answer.

Finally, a word about the idea of relevance. Usually something is relevant in education when it has some bearing on the student's personal life. We go to great lengths in classrooms and in textbooks to figure out what that elusive element might be, as if we could guess right for any one student, let alone a very diverse set of students. At no time did Michael relate photons to Danny's personal life, unless you count specifying his hand as the object that the light shines on from increasing distances. Danny stays with the idea of "hand," but it's clear that he doesn't need relevance in the typical sense to keep him engaged in the conundrum.

The Theory of Constructivism

Constructivism isn't a curriculum; it's a theory about learning. Yet it has much to say relative to the broad definition of curriculum (curriculum plus instruction plus assessment) I am using in this book. Constructivism posits that we construct our own learning, whether we are learning from a teacher, a textbook, an experience, or on our own. Brooks and Brooks (1993) suggest that "we construct our own understandings of the world in which we live. We search for tools to help us understand our experiences. To do so is human nature. . . . Each of us makes sense of our world by synthesizing new experiences into what we have previously come to understand" (p. 4). They contrast mimetic learning (repeating or miming what has been heard, seen, or presented) with constructivist learning: "Deep understanding, not imitative behavior, is the goal. . . . We look not for what students can repeat, but for what they can generate, demonstrate, and exhibit" (p. 16).

Newman, Griffin, and Cole (1989) focus on the social aspect of constructivism. "The situated nature of learning, remembering, and understanding is a central fact. It may appear obvious that human minds develop in social situations, and that they use the tools and representational media that culture provides to support, extend, and reorganize mental functioning" (p. vii). They emphasize that "cognitive change must be regarded as both a social and an individual process" (p. 1). Danny's learning was both social—as he worked with Michael, especially, but also as he tried to explain what he was doing to others—and individual.

Brooks and Brooks present some very helpful ways to think about curriculum and constructivism:

1. "Curriculum is presented whole to part with emphasis on big concepts."

2. "Pursuit of student questions is highly valued."

3. "Curricular activities rely heavily on primary sources of data and manipulative materials."

4. "Students are viewed as thinkers with emerging theories about the world."

5. "Teachers generally behave in an interactive manner, mediating the environment for students."

6. "Teachers seek the students' points of view in order to understand students' present conceptions for use in subsequent lessons."

7. "Assessment of student learning is interwoven with teaching and occurs through teacher observations of students at work and through student exhibitions and portfolios."

8. "Students primarily work in groups." (p. 17)

They also identify specific teacher behavior that lends itself to a constructivist approach:

1. "Constructivist teachers encourage and accept student autonomy and initiative."

2. "Constructivist teachers use raw data and primary sources, along with manipulative, interactive, and physical materials."

3. "When framing tasks, constructivist teachers use cognitive terminology such as 'classify,' 'analyze,' 'predict,' and 'create.'"

4. "Constructivist teachers allow student responses to drive lessons, shift instructional strategies, and alter content."

5. "Constructivist teachers inquire about students' understandings of concepts before sharing their own understandings of these concepts."

6. "Constructivist teachers encourage students to engage in dialogue, both with the teacher and with one another."

7. "Constructivist teachers encourage student inquiry by asking thoughtful, open-ended questions and encouraging students to ask questions of each other."

8. "Constructivist teachers seek elaboration of students' initial responses."

9. "Constructivist teachers engage students in experiences that might engender contradictions to their initial hypotheses and then encourage discussion."

10. "Constructivist teachers allow wait time after posing questions."

11. "Constructivist teachers provide time for students to construct relationships and create metaphors."

12. "Constructivist teachers nurture students' natural curiosity through frequent use of the learning cycle model." (pp. 103–16)

Finally, Brooks and Brooks include some suggestions for creating constructivist educational systems:

1. "Structure preservice and inservice teacher education around constructivist principles and practices."

2. "Jettison most standardized testing and make assessment meaningful for students."

3. "Focus resources more on teachers' professional development than on textbooks and workbooks."

4. "Eliminate letter and number grades."

5. "Form school-based study groups focused on human developmental principles."

6. "Require annual seminars on teaching and learning for administrators and school board members." (pp. 121–25)

Many of these ideas, behaviors, and suggestions were at play as Michael and Danny worked together on what turned out to be the inverse square law.

Applying Constructivism at Eagle Rock

As with all theories, constructivism can be applied to learning situations in a variety of ways. Danny's experience was close to a pure application. His mind was piqued by a puzzle, and he pursued it by proposing and completing an independent study. Here are some other structures we've used to create classes that implement a constructivist approach to curriculum, instruction, and assessment:

1. The instructors have a general concept of the content of the class, such as the Holocaust, but let students follow their own interests as they pursue the general concept. They share what they are learning so that learning is deep for them and as broad as possible for the whole class.

2. The instructors begin a class by asking students to write questions about the general concept of the class. These become the questions the instructors—and the students—pursue. Additional questions invariably arise as students and instructors pursue the original ones.

3. Students suggest a class and take an active part in teaching it. (For example, Matt went to Thailand and Vietnam on a Global Routes scholarship and returned enthusiastic about sharing all that he had learned and having students look into a variety of political systems.)

4. The instructors pose an essential question or problem to the class, not knowing the answers themselves. The class pursues the questions and presents answers or solutions to one another (or outsiders). (For example, in Peace in the Middle East, students formed teams to propose workable solutions to the myriad problems between Arabs and Israelis.)

5. Instructors ask students to help them design classes. They meet beforehand to prepare the course proposal form, and the students help teach the class, doing research as needed and inventing activities and projects. They also help develop an assessment rubric and give feedback on portfolios.

6. Students map what they know about a subject. They identify areas on their map that they can share with others as a primary resource and areas in which they think they'd like to continue their learning.

And here are some more specific examples of classes or activities that have followed a constructivist philosophy:

1. Instructors and students create a way to remember Eagle Rock students and staff members. (For example, an art class began a tile

wall in the Human Performance Center. Each student and staff member designs and creates a tile that represents his or her life, and that tile is added to the wall.)

2. Instructors and students partner with an inner-city elementary school, learning all they can about the students and the staff. Then they make books ("big" books and regular-sized books) for the school's library, doing all the research and finding or making the pictures, laminating and binding the books, reading them aloud to test audiences, and presenting them to the school. (This course was called Eagle Rock Press.)

3. Students in a class called See Me, Know Me, Read Me prepare art and written work of their choice to express themselves. They may pursue autobiography or epic poetry, representationalism or abstraction. They may make a book and illustrate it or do a mural for one of the (few) blank walls at Eagle Rock.

4. Instructors make contact with businesspeople and others in and around the town of Estes Park. Students choose an internship with one of these contacts and then design a course of study that fits the work they are doing. This class, Learner's Guild, has been offered during the past few summers and is very popular with people in Estes Park.

5. Students and instructors form a class called Community Problem Solving to identify a problem on campus and come up with some solutions. Along the way, they learn democratic principles, leadership skills, and how to run meetings.

6. Students write their philosophy of life. On the basis of their writing, the instructors suggest original sources and summaries of philosophical ideas. Students rewrite their philosophies at the end of the class and make a presentation to one another about what they have learned from the world's philosophers.

7. In a class called Civil(?)izations, students explore a variety of government structures throughout history, looking for a definition of the term *civilization*. The essential questions are: Do we truly know what the term means? How do we determine which society is civilized? What do we use as our measurements? Is our own civilization truly civil?

8. In an art and environmental science class called Recycled, Reseen, students survey the state of recycling in the local community, learn some statistics and issues surrounding global consumerism and waste by-products, and then construct art with throwaway items. They present their art as "restored beauty" and make some kind of commentary on the environment.

9. Students propose using our bioshelter to raise tomatoes hydroponically. Through research and field trips, they set up the system and manage plant care so we have fresh tomatoes for the lodge.

Many of the examples above are founded on essential questions or problems to be solved. The key to an essential question is that it is authentic or real, not a "teacher question," for which students suspect there is a right answer. It needs to be broad enough to allow for a variety of responses. It needs to engage students in some way, but—as we saw with Danny—it does not need to be "relevant" in the traditional educational sense of personally meaningful. The questions that guide the Civil(?)izations class fit these criteria pretty well. Problems can be both personal (as in Community Problem Solving) and global (as in Peace in the Middle East).

The key to all these approaches to a constructivist learning environment is the role of the teacher. The teacher cannot be the expert—indeed, she or he should have as much curiosity about the question or the problem as the students. The teacher becomes, truly, a coach or mentor to students who are struggling to understand the question or problem, find resources and make sense of them, and present their learning in some meaningful way.

Can a classroom, school, or district apply constructivist theories and still be standards based? The key, it seems to me, lies in three aspects of the descriptor *standards based.* As always, I would prefer that standards be created at the school level, with the whole community participating in the process. Second, I would prefer that standards be as general as possible and therefore workable within a constructivist approach. Third, relative to state testing, I would prefer sampling both students and subjects in various years rather than testing every student on every subject every year. High-stakes testing has serious validity problems and, because it forces teachers to focus on known outcomes, almost certainly gets in the way of a constructivist approach.

Eagle Rock is standards based in the broad sense; we are responsible for the state's standards and our students graduate on the basis of having met them, but we do not break those standards into specific, detailed elements of learning. We document achievement of standards with actual performance. (See Chapter 5 for more information on how Eagle Rock is standards based.) Since we have kept our graduation competencies as well as our documentations general, we allow room for students to design their own learning. Danny was able to work on an algorithm in mathematics that interested him and produce a portfolio to document learning.

Questions to Consider

1. What do you know about constructivism? What is your understanding of how this theory can be applied?

2. How are teachers in your school teaching? How are learners learning? What generalizations can you make? What patterns or themes emerge as you consider the teaching and learning process? How would you label most of the learning experiences: mimetic or constructivist? On what basis do you make that judgment? What aspects of curriculum, instruction, and assessment lean more to a traditional approach? What aspects lean more to a constructivist approach? Are there some subjects that lean more one way than the other? Are there some teachers who favor one over the other?

3. How distant is what you are currently doing from a constructivist approach? Are there some pioneers in your school or district who are already teaching in a constructivist way? Do they have evidence (objective and subjective) that it is working with students? Are there likely to be some resisters? Who are they and what is their position within the system (both actual and perceived)?

4. Could individual teachers in your school move to a more constructivist approach even if the whole school did not? Could grade levels do so? Could departments do so? What would be the problems? What would be the advantages?

5. Do the various constituencies in your school community—parents, community members, business leaders, teachers, school administrators, district administrators, state administrators—know about constructivism? If so, what do they think about this theory?

6. How could you present your ideas about constructivism as well as its benefits and liabilities to your constituencies in a way that will help them understand? How could you use students and teachers already engaged in constructivist learning?

7. How can state standards be accounted for if the school moves to a more constructivist approach? How about state testing? district testing? How can individual classroom teachers be accountable for learning? How would public displays of learning—exhibits or demonstrations (like our presentations of learning) help? What state policies would need to be addressed and/or waived? What district policies would need to be addressed and/or waived?

8. What kind of professional development is needed to start the process (Brooks and Brooks suggest study groups)? to implement a constructivist approach? to know whether or not a constructivist approach is making a difference in student learning?

9. How will you know that your move to a constructivist approach is working? What measurement devices can you put in place—both subjective and objective—to report progress as you move along? What indicators would come from teachers? from students? from parents? from others?

10. How will you communicate with your constituencies about the progress you are making in moving to a constructivist approach?

Chapter Nine

Curriculum Is Meaningful*

Every summer Eagle Rock puts on a major musical. The production involves most of the staff members and almost the entire student body; in one way or another, everyone in the community contributes to its success. The instructional staff always develops some curriculum in connection with this musical.

The 1999 production was *Grease*. A couple of problems surfaced as we considered this musical. First, it did not lend itself easily to becoming a direct source of study. Also, it depicts a predominantly white high school in the fifties but doesn't touch on any of the historically critical events of that time. What's more, its main message can be interpreted as, *If you can't get the guy by being yourself, change.* Consequently, we chose to provide a fifties curriculum focused on all the issues so casually *avoided* in the play—racial tension and the civil rights movement, the feminist movement and the era of the Norman Rockwell family, the Cold War.

The more we discussed the possibilities, the more excited we became. Ideas abounded for learning experiences that would dig deeply into the roots of the civil rights movement; study some of the era's best literature, poetry, music, drama, and visual arts; pinpoint the inception of many modern technological advances; and relate the climate of world politics then to the world political climate now. Working as

---

*The description of the fifties unit was written by Alexander Hamilton Head, first an intern and then an assistant in the Professional Development Center. Alex took the lead in designing and managing this unit, even though all Eagle Rock instructors and students participated.

an entire staff through many brainstorming sessions, we grouped the multitude of ideas into four courses:

- Technological Advancements
- Pop Culture
- Us Versus Them: The Pot Begins to Boil
- Global Citizenship

In Technological Advancements, the teachers focused on the impact of the automobile through four "essential questions":

1. Why was the automobile suddenly so popular after World War II?
2. What was the impact of the automobile on fifties society?
3. What was the significance of the automobile in the development of modern technology?
4. How did the popularity of the automobile permanently affect/change the culture of the United States?

Throughout the week, students worked on one group project and one individual project. The individual project was to write a short research paper addressing one of the essential questions. The group project was to create an advertising campaign to sell a car in the fifties. Both projects required the students to understand the nature of the culture at the time—what people valued and what people desired. Students learned about the culture through class discussions, often prompted by video clips or old *Life* magazines. Each of the group projects included visuals, and some included mock television commercials. At the end of the week, the class voted on which ad campaign was most successful, based on what they knew of fifties culture.

Pop Culture was a week of immersion in the fifties. Each day of the week had a theme. On Music Monday, the students watched a documentary of the history of rock 'n' roll. This opened the students' eyes to both the racial and cultural struggles during this era. On TV Tuesday, the students watched clips of Westerns and other popular television shows from the time. The instructors facilitated discussions about what the students knew of the political and social climate in the fifties and how that contrasted with what was being shown on TV. The students then acted out skits, one group portraying the television families as seen on the shows, the other portraying a real family. On Wha'cha Wearin' Wednesday, the students dressed up in fifties garb. Everyone, instructors included, did their best to capture the styles of the decade. The women wore poodle skirts and saddle shoes, sweaters and kneesocks, while the men, their hair slicked back, wore blue jeans with the cuffs rolled high and white t-shirts with fake cigarette packs rolled up in their sleeves. They talked about the fashions and what they represented (rebellion, conformity, innocence, etc.). Thirsty Thursday dealt with the era's thirst-inducing convenience food: TV dinners, fast food, frozen food. Students also considered the roles of women in the house and the advent of appliances designed to ease kitchen chores. Freaky Film Friday used the recent film *Pleasantville*, in which two teenagers cope with being transported from the present to the fifties, to tie together everything from the four previous days. Students discussed morals and values of the times, family life, roles for males and females, and self-expression.

On the first day of Us Versus Them: The Pot Begins to Boil, the students were seated at long tables loaded with books and videos and old records and posters, all from the fifties. The instructors asked the students to write down words they associated with the fifties on pieces of precut paper. The students then taped the words to the board and discussed what certain words had in common, ultimately defining two categories, *us* and *them*. Many students were surprised to find out that many of the struggles and movements associated with the sixties and seventies actually had their roots in the fifties, a decade associated with muscle cars, poodle skirts, TV dinners . . . and some stability. Over the next few days, the students watched videos and read from books that depicted the conflicts and struggles facing people in this era. The finale to this course was a "living museum." The students became figures they had learned about in their exploration and put on skits for the rest of the class and then talked about the skits as they related to the political/domestic climate at the time.

Each week of Global Citizenship was different. The first week's students delved into the years 1948–60 (each student researched one year and presented that year to the rest of the class). During the second week, a new group of students studied world figures from the time, including Kim Il Sung, Stalin, Teller, Batista, Nixon, McCarthy, Oppenheimer, Mao Tse Tung, and many others (each student researched two people and presented their findings). The students in the third week investigated events and concepts such as the Suez Canal in 1956, the 38th Parallel, NATO, the Domino Theory, Dien Bien Phu, etc. During the fourth week, students looked at specific people as they related to specific concepts (particularly the Korean War, colonialism, and Vietnam). The students were given assignments in advance and began their presentations on Monday. On Monday, the class was split into two teams. Led by an instructor, each team explored topics that they would debate later in the week. On the second day, the teams met together and decided on a debate topic. For the rest of that day and on Wednesday, the students searched the school library and the

Internet for information that would support their arguments. On Thursday, the debates were held. On Friday, the each team presented the material they had debated to the other team.

Each course was taught by between four and six Eagle Rock instructors or interns, all from different disciplines, all bringing to their classes not only their expertise in their discipline but their shared knowledge and, often, their personal experiences from the fifties. For example, Us Versus Them: The Pot Begins to Boil was taught by instructors in English, art, social sciences, and human performance. The students looked at racial and socioeconomic issues as they were depicted in fifties literature, arts, sports, and politics. They read Kerouac, Burroughs, and Ginsberg; compared Norman Rockwell and Jackson Pollock; reviewed the impact of Jackie Robinson and Willie Mays; and reenacted moments from history in "living museums."

We struggled with how best to engage all students in all four study areas so that they all participated in a comprehensive, interdisciplinary curriculum. Each of the four sections was important, and each section related to the others, with overlap and repetition of themes throughout. And there were only six weeks for the overall unit. To ensure that each student received some exposure to all four areas, we decided to teach the first four weeks as a "survey," with students rotating through each course, one after the other. The students had the equivalent of four brief one-week courses, a total of five ninety-minute sessions each. For the last two weeks, the students could choose from other courses that built upon the four-week courses and allowed students to investigate specific areas of interest. Some of these more specific course offerings included How We Learned to Love the Bomb, a close examination of the Cold War; Beatitude, which studied the writings and music of the beat generation; We Shall Overcome, a closer look at the civil rights movement and its impact; and And the Beat Goes On, an examination of the music of the times.

Students received credit for their courses in a number of ways. In We Shall Overcome, students put together oral presentations and delivered reports and research to receive part of their American history and government credits. In Technological Advancements, students researched and wrote papers about the impact of specific inventions and developments through to the present. In Beatitude, students wrote essays of explanation, essays of opposing ideas, and their own poetry. In From Bobby Socks to Leather Jackets, students designed costumes for *Grease* and received an art credit for their portfolio. In And the Beat Goes On, students learned musical scores from the era, studied the musical genres then in their infancy, and learned to play instruments using the I–IV–V progression found in most rock 'n' roll songs.

One Student's Fifties-Unit Experience

Jena was born in Boulder, Colorado, but moved around a lot as a child: a year in Florida, a year in Stag Island, Canada, less than a year in Michigan. She returned to Boulder when she was eight. During her first couple of years of high school in Colorado, Jena received "straight Ds and Fs. I used to have competitions with friends to see who could get the worst grades." When she was sixteen she moved again, to California, to live with her aunt and uncle. "This was the first step towards taking my life and my own learning into my own hands." In California, Jena had a 4.0 grade point average; she was academically "successful."

Jena came to Eagle Rock when she was seventeen "because it was better than where I was. And because I wanted something more out of my education . . . for it to be more whole. Even though I was getting good grades in California, I hated school. It wasn't very human. I wasn't learning anything, or at least I didn't think I was. Now I know I was learning that I wasn't interested in what was being taught or how it was being taught." She graduated from Eagle Rock in April 2001.

Jena has a very clear idea of what she wants to do with her life. "I want to start a school," she says very confidently. "I have always been critical of the [school] system and always felt like there was a better way to do things." In her two years at Eagle Rock, Jena was able to work with third and fourth graders in Touch the Future, a class in which Eagle Rock students learn to become outdoor and environmental educators and counselors for grade-school children from all over the Denver-Metro area. She says she "learned a lot about what to do—and what not to do—through this experience. Teachers can do the smallest, most insignificant thing to students, and it matters, either negatively or positively to the students. That's scary."

In her second year at Eagle Rock, Jena proposed that she be allowed to take a trimester off to travel and look at schools; this proposal was approved, and she looked both at colleges she might want to attend as well as at a number of progressive high schools "to take notes and collect ideas." During this trimester, Jena also worked as a teacher's aid in an inner-city middle school, an experience from which she "learned and grew so much."

What will be the key components of Jena's school? "A big emphasis on community. And the curriculum will be interdisciplinary. It won't be compartmentalized—not broken up into math, English, etc., but based on a project that brings in a lot of different disciplines. Life isn't broken into chunks for you. Life is a fully integrated course."

The fifties unit was required. Like other students, Jena was a little upset about this at first. "I hate the idea of required classes and walked into this unit with a bit of a negative attitude," she said on an evaluation at the conclusion of the unit. A year and a half later, Jena looks at the class differently. "I can't remember what other classes I took that block, but I do remember the fifties unit a great deal more than I thought I would."

In Technological Advancements, Jena's first class, she remembers "looking at the impact of the car on the family structure, on the geography of the United States . . . especially how far people could live from work . . . which has now lead to urban sprawl." She thought the old ads were informative and funny. "It was painfully clear how obsessed with security and image the nation was. And what their values were. There were these Sears ads where women were dolled up and curled, made up with pink lipstick, wearing aprons and clutching a duster in their hands . . . and, of course, always a smile. And they would be posed up against the latest, fanciest, new and improved washing machine!" She learned about the new era of consumerism and convenience. "Everything was supposed to be easy and 'drive-in.' Even Jesus was readily accessible at the drive-through churches. One commercial kept emphasizing the spaciousness of the back seat."

In Pop Culture, Jena began to understand the sexual mores of the decade, largely through examining the controversy generated by Elvis Presley and other rock 'n' roll stars. She came to see that the family-oriented television shows then did not really depict what was happening politically and socially in America. She concluded that she "would've hated to be a girl in the fifties" after trying to dress like one. And she realized how limited roles were for both men and women more than fifty years ago.

About Us Versus Them: The Pot Begins to Boil, Jena said, "History is best when you can trace its impacts to present day." She was excited to discover that the social repression she identified in Technological Advancements and Pop Culture was "getting ready to explode. It was such a complex time ridden with so many ideals and fears." For the "living museum" finale, Jena and a friend "dressed up as crazy housewives turned beat poets." Dressed in black, smoking fake cigarettes, they read passionately from Marge Piercy and others. "I've never been that into a skit before—we yelled in some poems, almost cried in others. If I could relate to any part of the fifties, it was to these women."

Jena was enrolled in the fourth week of Global Citizenship. Her team chose the question, "Was colonialism beneficial to Africa?" and the other team debated whether or not U.S. intervention in the Korean conflict was necessary and justified. "The debates were a great way to understand both sides of what was going on," Jena wrote in her evaluation. "The more you knew about your opponent's argument, the more prepared you were to counter it, but really, the more you knew about the whole picture."

For the last two weeks of the unit, Jena focused on technological advancements. She took an in-depth look at the impact of the automobile, researching not only its effects on the urban sprawl of the United States but also the cultural epoch of individuality and the deterioration of our nation. In one essay, Jena remarked that "the more man seeks comfort and security, the more detached he becomes from the environment and other men. The less reliant people are on one another, the less they care for one another." Commenting on the role of the car in the capitalist economy and the "disposable generation," Jena noted "a relentless pursuit of growth" was promoted by the automobile industry. "The advertisements ranged from 'What's good for General Motors is good for America,' to 'To live is to consume.'"

Was the Fifties Unit a Success?

Throughout the unit staff members solicited regular written feedback from students and met with them to address their needs as learners. Overall, feedback was positive. Students and staff alike wished for more time but were happy with the survey structure. Many of the students commented on the multidisciplinary instruction: "It was a great schedule and diversity of teachers/teaching styles." "You all contributed so much in your individually gifted ways." "Thank you so much for making [this unit] fun and educational." All in all, the unit was a success. With the support of the administration and because of the open minds of the students, the instructional staff was able to implement a curriculum that involved the entire school, made connections between disciplines, and was not only educational but fun.

One of the most important questions to ask about any unit of instruction is, *Did the students learn?* Here is some of what Jena did during the unit:

- Completed a group project for Technological Advancements.
- Completed an individual project for Technological Advancements.
- Discussed the political and social climate in the fifties.
- Participated in skits portraying the political and domestic climate of the time.
- Dressed up in fifties garb.
- Listed and categorized words associated with the fifties.
- Became a figure in a "living museum."
- Prepared debate notes on colonization in Africa.

- Participated in a debate.
- Wrote one or more essays on a technological advancement.

Here's what Jena said she had learned:

- The impact of the car on family structure and geography in the United States.
- Some of the causes of urban sprawl.
- Fifties values as depicted in advertisements.
- Concepts of consumerism and convenience.
- The racial and cultural struggles during the era.
- The political and social climate in the fifties versus television portrayals of society.
- Dress and makeup in the fifties.
- Characteristics of the time.
- Categorization techniques.
- The roots of the various movements usually attributed to the sixties and seventies.
- Manifestations of social repression.
- The complexity of the time: ideals and fears.
- What women were like in the fifties.
- Issues on both sides of colonialism.
- How to debate an issue.
- The cultural epoch of individuality; the deterioration of our great nation.
- Reliance and community; self-sufficiency and detachment.
- The implications of pursuing growth, consumerism, and disposability.

Is that sufficient? Is it efficient? Could our students have learned more and learned better in a standard learning environment, one not interdisciplinary and experimental? These are good questions, and there's probably no way they can be fully answered.

When Jena felt disenfranchised from her own learning, she got back by getting poor grades. A lot of Eagle Rock students describe that action as the only one they can take when they have no control over their learning. They refuse to be learners in the conventional sense, even though they might, in fact, be learning. Later, Jena takes things back into her own hands and gets good grades. She wants her education to be more whole. She describes her learning prior to Eagle Rock as not very human. Jena clearly values school as community (see Chapter 2), and she wants curriculum to be less fragmented than it usually is. She says strongly, "Life is a fully integrated course." That's a statement to use as a basis for any thinking about curriculum.

Particular aspects of Jena's learning style and preferences are worth singling out. She was not happy that the fifties unit was mandatory—she likes choices (see Chapter 6)—but she found that there were sufficient choices within the requirement to satisfy her. She has a natural curiosity about people and society . . . and a sense of humor about life that gives her a lens for looking at both. She likes to relate what she's learning to her own values and beliefs. She personalizes learning ("If I could relate to any part of the fifties, it would be to these women"). She sees the big picture (history) but also likes looking at the details (especially when they present inconsistencies or anomalies). She likes to see connections. She likes to see both sides. She searches for the themes and meanings that come from events.

Jena's ambition to start her own school causes her to be critical of both Eagle Rock and the other schools she attended or researched. She wants students to have much more say in what—and how—they learn. She is wrestling with the idea of "privileged knowledge." To what extent are teachers the experts? To what extent is their job to share their expertise? To what extent are students experts in the making? To what extent should teachers facilitate others' expertise? Her questions are ones that Eagle Rock struggles with constantly.

The Eagle Rock staff would probably say that what matters most in learning is student engagement and that engagement takes time. Does depth matter more than broad coverage? The Eagle Rock staff would argue that broad coverage is a much less efficient use of time than depth. Should students have more say in what—and how—they learn? Eagle Rock struggles constantly with the idea of "privileged knowledge."

A dilemma that surfaced during and after the fifties unit was that of credit. Students complained that they did not get much credit for the four weeks they cycled through the four general fifties courses. They got credit for the final two weeks when they focused on their interests, but they didn't see that the first four weeks were preparation for the work they did during the last two weeks. Staff members were torn. The first four weeks certainly included activities that could have been used for credit. However, there wasn't time for the revision and polishing required for students to get credit. The dilemma remains.

Also, each time they taught their area, instructors changed what they did. They learned from their students, from their coteachers, and from themselves. The subunits got better and better each time they were taught, but students in each of the sessions learned different things. At Eagle Rock, we sometimes have to struggle to remember that no particular content is sacred. Students always learn different things, depending on their interests and experiences.

Curriculum Is Interdisciplinary, That Is, Meaningful

This chapter was originally called Curriculum Is Interdisciplinary. As I considered this title, and the concept that underlies it, I realized that what is critical is not that curriculum be interdisciplinary but that it be meaningful, and an interdisciplinary approach is one very good way of helping make curriculum meaningful. There are many other ways to make curriculum meaningful, and I've already talked about many of them: base it in the school's culture, make it learner centered, allow choice, provide variety in learning conditions, let students find their own pathways through it, be as constructivist as possible, fit curriculum, instruction, and assessment together so that they make sense, help students become self-directed.

If it is meaningful, discipline-based curriculum can also be an effective way to help students learn. In fact, in some cases—music classes, for example—discipline-based curriculum may be the *best* way. Hands-on active and interactive learning can happen in a discipline-based classroom. Students can be self-directed in a discipline-based class. They can be given the opportunity to choose. However, an interdisciplinary approach is a very immediate way to infuse meaning into the curriculum and it is an important practice at Eagle Rock. Therefore this chapter concentrates on an interdisciplinary approach to making curriculum meaningful.

Types of Interdisciplinary Approaches

The Appalachia Educational Laboratory (AEL), in Charleston, West Virginia, has come up with a good taxonomy of interdisciplinary styles (Burns 1995), which they see as "evolutionary stages of curriculum integration." The first two stages—*parallel* and *multidisciplinary*—focus on the "content of the disciplines." The remaining three stages—*interdisciplinary, integrated,* and *transdisciplinary*—focus on "essential concepts and skills." The differences largely have to do with how embedded the disciplines are. In the first two, the "content and procedures of separate disciplines" reign. In the latter three, there is both more integration and a higher level of organization. For example, *interdisciplinary* curriculum focuses on "generic and metacognitive concepts and skills."

Integrated curriculum focuses on "real-life skills, issues, concerns and questions." *Transdisciplinary* curriculum focuses on "students' social-personal concerns and questions."

The fifties unit was most probably an *interdisciplinary* curriculum according to these definitions. A teaching team decided what students were to learn and "blended content that emerges from disciplines." The teachers were as much generalists as specialists in their content areas, and they saw themselves as facilitating learning.

At Eagle Rock, we have featured discipline-based learning as well as all of the AEL stages of curriculum. For example, we have what director of curriculum Linda Sand Guest describes as "timeshare." Teachers in this type of curriculum may share a general idea that unites them but they each cover their own content and learning processes. One teaches one day, the other teaches the next. Both may focus on helping students with work or projects, but essentially they have merely combined their disciplines around some common topic. AEL would describe this form of curriculum organization as *parallel disciplines* because each teacher is focused on his or her discipline, and they have united under one concept. An example of this form of curriculum at Eagle Rock is the course Tessellations, in which students learn both art and mathematics, exploring Escher's (and other artists') tessellations as well as the mathematics of tessellations and fractals. The instructors mostly teach their own subjects, the art teacher helping students develop their own tessellations as an art form, and the mathematics teacher helping students understand the mathematics of fractals.

Sometimes, we are *multidisciplinary*. We find a theme and slightly revise content to fit that theme. However, individual teachers still take turns teaching the content and processes of their disciplines. An example of an Eagle Rock *multidisciplinary* curriculum is a course on the Renaissance that students were offered in the fall of 2000. They approached the course through history, art, music, and drama, and the instructors tailored what students were to learn so that it fit the theme of the Renaissance, with the art teacher, for example, focusing on art techniques of the period.

As I said, the fifties unit was probably *interdisciplinary* because the content was blended in new ways. The focus was less on the traditional disciplines and more on the overarching ideas of the fifties and what they have to do with today. While instructors addressed their disciplines, they also crossed the border into being generalists, sharing whatever they knew about any part of the fifties. They were more inclined to be facilitators, interested in what students could make of the fifties in relation to the present day, and less likely to want to be sure that students "got" the particular content of their discipline. They focused on having a cooperative and collaborative classroom as well as active, even constructivist, learning.

At times, Eagle Rock students have experienced *integrated* curriculum. What's Love Got to Do With It? in particular could be called *integrated* curriculum because the instructors focused on real-life skills (personal relationships) and ventured into whatever discipline the real-life issues demanded. Sometimes students read poetry; sometimes they looked at the history of relationships (Cleopatra and Anthony, for a start); sometimes they studied science (pheromones); sometimes they even did physical activity (yoga) to approach the theme, or mathematics (problem solving), or art (paintings depicting love), or music (songs about lost love and betrayal).

Finally, I believe we have also had what AEL calls *transdisciplinary* curriculum. The class called Community Problem Solving is an example of curriculum based on "students' social-personal concerns and questions." Students explored their various communities (the community in their houses or dormitories, the school community, the larger Estes Park community), looking for what worked and what didn't. When they discovered some part of any of those communities that was not working well, they designed a problem-solving process to reach some conclusions about what could be done to ameliorate the situation. And then they did the necessary work to solve the problem. The students were in charge of the content and the processes, with the teacher serving as mentor.

AEL describes the five stages of curriculum integration as a hierarchy, proposing that transdisciplinary curriculum is the highest form of curriculum integration. I'm not sure that there is a hierarchy for meaningfulness. In some ways, a parallel disciplines curriculum can be as meaningful as a transdisciplinary curriculum. Both can engage young people in learning, one from the point of view of a theme to which they may relate (and thus be able to learn concepts related to that theme) and the other because the premise begins with their lives.

Conditions for Linking Curriculum

There are lots of ways to link curriculum. What makes linked curriculum work? Here are some thoughts from our director of curriculum, Linda Sand Guest:

1. Not all learning needs to be interdisciplinary. Some things are better taught as a single discipline or as parallel disciplines. Areas best taught alone are usually preliminary or prerequisite to other learning, such as beginning band or first-year Spanish.

2. Not everyone in a school can teach within an interdisciplinary structure. The worst thing a principal can do is arbitrarily say, "You and you, be a team. Teach an interdisciplinary class together."

3. Sometimes, team teaching an interdisciplinary unit is a matter of gradually becoming a team, perhaps starting out with a simpler form of interdisciplinary teaming—the parallel disciplines structure, for example.

4. If at all possible, let teachers choose teams. In a large school, it may be enough for teachers to indicate a willingness to team; someone who knows all of them can suggest the most likely teams if the teachers themselves don't know with whom they might team.

5. Have teams choose a leader, and provide training for the leaders so that they understand how teams work. The team leader needs to facilitate more than lead and help with decisions more than decide. This person also needs to be the person through whom others initiate contact with the team.

6. Let teachers (if at all possible, in conjunction with students) identify the topics they'd like to study. Encourage them to work together to develop the theme or unifying concept and discover the connections between or among their disciplines. Sponsor curriculum conversations.

7. Beware the elephantine topic. Work to limit the subject so that it won't be too big for the team or for students.

8. Involve students in any way possible—as consultants, researchers, coteachers, reviewers, project heads, etc.

9. Provide time for teachers to work together to develop their ideas and learning experiences. It is so much easier for teachers to do their own thing, especially if they've been teaching a long time. It's much harder for them to collaborate with someone else.

10. Provide time for debriefing—at the end of each day as well as the end of the unit or class.

11. Help team members work on outcomes for the whole unit, not just their own discipline within the unit. It's important that team members understand the whole focus first and then their part in it. Also, have them create team rubrics, not just rubrics for the individual outcomes or products. They should all know the whole unit and they should all know how to evaluate all the work of the unit.

12. Provide a sounding board for ideas—in department or grade-level meetings, for example.

13. Have some way to evaluate the interdisciplinary class or unit. Teachers can keep journals. Students can complete a survey.

Consider having an outside observer sit in on the classes as well as the debriefings. Also, be sure to review the evaluations. Don't let them sit on a shelf somewhere. Draw up a list of lessons learned for the next time you design an interdisciplinary unit or class.

14. Repeat the unit. Learn from prior iterations and make it work better.

How to Build and Implement an Interdisciplinary Unit

The steps below can start you on an exciting journey toward interdisciplinary learning but should be modified to fit your own particular situation:

1. Brainstorm themes, connections, interesting topics. Draw arrows to connect possibilities.

2. Select a likely theme. Be willing to go with it until it doesn't work anymore.

3. Brainstorm all the possible subtopics related to the theme. Review and expand those subtopics. Add subtopics under subtopics.

4. Connect the subtopics to outcomes, standards, or requirements that could be accomplished during the unit or class. At the end of the unit or class what kinds of products or outcomes would prove to you (and to students) that they had learned? What could students do?

5. Once you have all the possibilities, begin to limit them to what is realistic. Perhaps your theme is too broad for the time you have. Perhaps you have too many topics or subtopics, perhaps too many products or outcomes.

6. Pare away again. There is nothing worse than trying to cram too much into a unit—you'll end up with breadth (and be out of breath!) rather than depth.

7. Begin a rubric for each product or outcome. What does it have to look like to be good enough? What are two or three characteristics that would indicate mastery or proficiency? Finish this process, perhaps with students, when you make the assignments—but definitely before they begin their projects.

8. Decide what needs to be taught directly and what students can learn on their own or in small groups. Keep the direct instruction to a minimum and look for ways to coach individuals and groups. Look for ways students can work together and teach one another.

9. Decide on learning experiences that will help students learn what they need to know and be able to do. Phrase these, if possible, as essential questions, problems to be solved, or inquiries.

10. Decide on the resources you'll need. Find or make them. Do not depend on a textbook as your entire resource; use relevant pages if necessary.

11. List the experiences in the order that will work best for the learners and decide the roles each team member will play during those experiences.

The roles team members play in an interdisciplinary unit or class are very important and deserve special mention. The whole team should plan together, both before the unit and during the unit. The whole team should also debrief together daily as well as at the end of the unit or class. However, every member of the team does not have to be in class every day.

Generally, there should be one lead instructor on any given day. Any other approach will probably be confusing to both students and staff. If you are working toward a more integrated unit, you may consciously *not* select the most likely instructor to be the leader. In other words, if the day's topic is art in the Renaissance, select someone other than the art teacher to take the lead. Purposeful role switching pushes the boundaries for both students and staff.

A pair of instructors who have been working together for a long time and feel comfortable with each other can share the lead-teacher role. I have observed skilled dual presenters finish each other's sentences without creating animosity! They had worked together so closely and for so long that their presentation was seamless and lots of fun to watch. Sometimes they even spoke in tandem; occasionally, with good humor, they inserted something new into their presentation. However, I've also seen team-teaching fail miserably, with inevitable repercussions on learning. I've watched team members step on each other's lines, making both of them unhappy and wary of each other. I've seen one member go off on a tangent, making it impossible for the other to get the class back on track. I've listened to them contradict each other about what should happen next or what something means, creating palpable tension in the classroom. Learning how to be a team is an important skill in interdisciplinary teaching.

While one or a pair of instructors is working as the lead instructor, other instructors can:

- Listen and observe and take notes (especially noticing what *students* do but also commenting on what the instructor says and does).

- Work with individuals or small groups.
- Prepare materials for later use.
- Give feedback to the primary instructor(s) during a break.
- Be on the lookout for difficulties.
- Intervene if it seems critical to do so.
- Work outside the classroom (visit other classes or conduct research, for example).

Questions to Consider

1. What makes your current curriculum meaningful? What do your curriculum guide, units you've taught, a video of a class, or class evaluations say about how you currently make curriculum meaningful in your school? What do the assumptions underlying these artifacts say about your beliefs about students? about teachers? about learning?

2. What might others (students, parents, administrators, community members, others) say about how meaningful your curriculum is?

3. How could your curriculum be made more meaningful?

4. Is an interdisciplinary approach (of whatever variety) an appropriate way for you to make curriculum more meaningful?

5. What should continue to be taught as a single discipline? In what ways can your single-discipline classes be made more meaningful?

6. Using the Appalachia Educational Laboratory taxonomy as a guideline, what kinds of interdisciplinary learning would you like to see at your school?

7. Who is already doing some form of interdisciplinary teaching and learning? How could these teachers share what they are doing? What evidence do they have that students are learning better through their approaches to curriculum? If you currently have no one who is doing some form of interdisciplinary learning, who might be the pioneers in your school's effort to make curriculum more meaningful?

8. Who might be most resistant to more interdisciplinary curriculum? What would be their objections? Would it be all right if some teachers chose not to participate in a more interdisciplinary curriculum? What would be the repercussions if this were not an all-school effort?

9. What outside constituencies will need to know of the plan to make your school more interdisciplinary? What are the likely reactions

of other schools? the school board? the central administration? parents? community members? others? How will you communicate with them, address their concerns, and continue to keep them informed?

10. Do any teachers in your school team-teach? How have these teams worked? What can you learn from current teams about teaming?

11. What professional development might be important for staff considering a more interdisciplinary curriculum? What professional development might be necessary for staff learning how to team? learning how to lead a team?

12. What ongoing support will staff need as they make the move to interdisciplinary teaming? How would coaching help?

13. How can staff involve students in the move to a more interdisciplinary curriculum?

14. How can the school provide adequate time for planning, executing, and debriefing interdisciplinary classes or units?

15. What roles can team members play with one another?

16. How will you evaluate the effect of more interdisciplinary curriculum? What data can you collect about student achievement? How can you share what you are learning?

17. What steps could your school take to encourage a more meaningful, possibly interdisciplinary, approach to curriculum? Which steps would be easiest to implement? Which steps would be most effective?

Chapter Ten

Curriculum Is for Learning

Marchello Before and During Eagle Rock

Chello grew up with his family in the Chicago projects. His mother was featured in a *New York Times* article as a single mother who refused to go on welfare and found a job to survive and help her family thrive. The author of that article knew about Eagle Rock and helped Chello (and later, his cousin) apply. After he was admitted, a very close family, especially his mother and grandmother, supported him as he struggled to graduate.

In his first POL autobiography Marchello wrote: "My life at home is unlike others. First of all, I had to look after my brother Andrew who is only five years old and my two sisters who are only two years old. I had to take them to school every day. I remember walking home one day in the middle of a gang war, not knowing where the bullets were flying. For all I knew one of the bullets could have hit me or my sisters or brother. The next thing I knew, here came my mother running out of our building, hollering and screaming, 'Run, my babies!!!' and me feeling her pull me is what got me to the house and safety. I knew for sure I wasn't going outside that day. At night I thought I was going outside, but it was the same thing going on all night."

Chello's first trimester was the winter term 1996. These are the learning experiences (not always classes) he engaged in before he graduated (one of a class of two) at the end of the Winter 2000 trimester:

First Trimester (Winter 1996)

ERS 101 (Orientation to Eagle Rock School)

Group Work (Orientation to ERS)

Wilderness Prep

Wilderness Experience

ERS 201 (Transition to ERS)

ERS Enterprise (Math, Service)

A Midsummer Night's Dream (Literature, Performance, Music)

Building the Challenge Course (Physical Education, Math)

Mythology (Literature, Performance)

Second Trimester (Summer 1996)

Write for the Rock (Writing)

Building the Telescope (Science)

Exploring Estes (Civics)

A Midsummer Night's Dream (Performance)

Atlanta to Estes (History, Physical Ed)

Hamlet (Literature, Performance)

Building the Playground (Mathematics, Service, Civics)

Third Trimester (Fall 1996)

What's Love Got to Do With It? (Literature)

Chemistry (Science)

LRC Aide (Library Media)

CPR (Health)

Terrific Technology (Library Media)

Patterns (Mathematics)

Fourth Trimester (Winter 1997)

The Game of Pig (Mathematics)

Hoop Dreams (Physical Education)

Newton's Law (Science, Mathematics)

French for the Fearless & Flamboyant

Shadows (Mathematics)

Act Out (Literature, Performance)

Fifth Trimester (Summer 1997)

Mas Espanol (Spanish)

To Use or Not to Use (Environmental Education, Service)

Love and Foreign Affairs (World History, Literature)

Turn the Poet Out of Doors (English, Literature)

World Map Mural (Geography, History)

Fun in the Sun (Physical Education)

Sixth Trimester (Fall 1997)

Personal Fitness

Instant Gratification (Art)

French II

Can Lines Talk? (Art)

Write for the Rock (Journalism, Writing)

Building Santa's House (Mathematics, Service)

Seventh Trimester (Winter 1998)

Solve It! (Mathematics)

Portfolio Construction (Mathematics)

Close-Up (Government, Civics)

Cookies (Mathematics)

Hydroponics (Science)

Give Me Liberty or Give Me Credit (American History)

Eighth Trimester (Summer 1998)

Freedom Summer '98 (History, Literature)

Sink or Swim (Physical Education)

Tessellations (Art, Mathematics)

Hail, C. J. (World History, Literature)

Back to the Basics (Mathematics)

Calculus (Mathematics)

Ninth Trimester (Fall 1998)

Pit and Pendulum (Mathematics)

Touch the Future (Environmental Science, Service)

Going Places, Making Choices (Science, Geography)

Back to the Basics (Mathematics)

Othello (Literature, Performance)

Tenth Trimester (Winter 1999)

The Game of Pig (Mathematics)

Let the Games Begin! (History, Physical Education, Music)

Independent Study

Physics (Science, Mathematics)

Act Out (Literature, Performance)

Revolutions (History)

Eleventh Trimester (Summer 1999)

Fifties Unit (Interdisciplinary)

Advancements (Science)

Learners' Guild (Internship)

The Play's the Think (Literature, Performance)

It All Makes Sense (Music)

Independent Study

Twelfth Trimester (Fall 1999)

A Slice of Pi (Mathematics)

Independent Study

Write for the Rock (Writing)

Astronomy (Science)

Independent Mathematics

Math Through Technology

Thirteenth Trimester (Winter 2000)

Eagle Rock Press (Writing, Service, Art)

Independent Study

Fractals (Mathematics, Art)

Going Places, Making Choices (Science)

Chello sent the following letter to the members of the panel who would evaluate his graduation presentation of learning:

March 14, 2000
Dear Panel Members:

I want to welcome you and thank you for being on my panel. I would like you to know that I put this packet together to share myself with you, not that you don't all know me already. Who am I? What do I want to be? What's my purpose in life?

I'm writing this letter to give you a taste of what's in store at my presentation of learning (POL). I am a student who has been climbing from rock bottom all my life. I'm a person who will not allow himself to wallow in a shallow pool of knowledge. I feel every day spent here on earth is a blessing, and I've had many of them. I've been at Eagle Rock for four long years, and I feel as though I'm reaching the dream.

I've been looking forward to walking across the stage of success and completion. I haven't given up on going to college and succeeding in life. I've only gotten stronger and more determined.

This trimester has been one of the most contemplative times in my life. I've chosen to do all the work I could and learn as much as possible before I move on to that special club [Eagle Rock graduate] that Robert [head of school] always mentions. I know for a fact that I expanded my knowledge base this trimester by learning about different muscles, the circulatory system, the respiratory system, fusion, fission, trigonometry, math through technology, astronomy, English structure, and how to dissect a cat. This list goes on like a fractal. I've also been studying how to use a plethora of new computer programs on my own. Within all of the subjects mentioned I know I had many academic struggles, but I stuck it out and enjoyed the outcome of my learning.

Aside from all my academic learning, I feel my biggest struggles were personal. I know I must work on being compassionate, and I've taken a big step this trimester. I am a very compassionate person but scared to show it because it makes me feel vulnerable. Now I am definitely over that. I have also been working on not pushing away the people I care about. I push them away because I know I might hurt them if I get too close.

These are just a few things that I will be presenting to you in my POL. Please feel free to ask any questions and give me advice.

Sincerely,
Marchello

P.S. I really love all of you. You all are the reason I'll be on that stage.

And this is Chello's graduation autobiography:

I Had A Dream

This is what I consider a true dream. I've spent a fairly good amount of time here at Eagle Rock and during this time I've learned beyond my expected quantity and quality of learning. I expected to learn a fairly small amount, compared to the things I actually have learned here.

This trimester I worked on my personal moral and ethical code. I've been reading two very good books in the last two trimesters. They are *Values* by Bill Bradley and *The Road Less Traveled* by M. Scott Peck, M.D. *Values* is mainly a book about basketball and the values of the game. These values are things like leadership, perspective, teamwork, selflessness, commitment, the agony of defeat, responsibility, courage, and respect. I've taken these from the book and applied them to my everyday life. In the book *The Road Less Traveled,* I mainly learned about commitment. In this book there's a sentence that says, "Whether it be shallow or not, commitment is the foundation of any genuinely loving relationship." The way I apply what I've read is by looking at that sentence and making a connection between it and my life. This book also has helped me to continue to put both feet in Eagle Rock. I also decided to look at my life in such a way that I am committed to learning forever and to do what Chello needs to do to become that successful, handsome young man he wants to be.

I've had plenty of struggles this trimester, but I feel I've worked through them. One struggle that I have faced more this trimester is my lack of compassion. The first thing I had to do was admit to myself that I needed to work on it. The reason I had to admit this to myself was because I knew if I didn't say it, nobody else could say it to me. That was a part of that titanium-coated Teflon armor that I used when I hid my feelings. The reason I have this lack of compassion is that I feel very vulnerable when I show feelings for someone. I feel it puts me in a position to be used. I didn't care about people's feelings for a long time, and this trimester is what brought the truth to the surface. I knew deep down inside that I wanted to care, but I forced myself to show no feelings toward people who were hurt by me or just hurting inside. I have been working on being compassionate and caring by not hurting people's feelings. I'm scared to show people who I really am because I used to get close to people easily and I would always be the one to get hurt. That is when I found the invisible titanium-coated Teflon shell. I know that this is now history, but it is something that I must continue to work on for me.

My other big struggle was the fact that I hurt both of my knees and had to have surgery. I am thankful that I went through this experience here at school. I always feared needing people or depending on them, so this was like a big awakening for me. I couldn't walk, so I had to let people help me and try not to feel worthless. I always felt like less of a man if I needed help. That is mainly why it took me so long to graduate. I never was willing to ask for help on anything. I never asked Jason for help in math, never asked Dave for help in science until this last year of my time here. If someone offered help nine times out of ten I wouldn't accept their help. From me realizing how important it is to have help now after hurting my knees, I don't hesitate to ask or accept help if needed. But, I'm still very independent.

I've been worried about a lot of things in the past like graduation and future plans. These thoughts consumed most of my thought space, and, honestly, when I realized I was not graduating last trimester, I gave up on everything and everyone. I know it's wrong, but that was my first reaction. I then thought about it and decided what I could do with my life. That is mainly why I came back to finish what I've started and to be successful throughout my life.

Academics is the golden key to my future. I feel this trimester was a big advancement in my academics also. I studied more about the difference in muscle tissues. I learned about smooth, cardiac, and skeletal muscles. I learned about how the heart and the lungs work together and the different compartments in the heart. I studied the basics of fusion, which is the joining of atoms at very high temperatures, and fission, which is the separating of atoms. I also learned how to do trigonometry. *Sine, cosine* and *tangent*—these were things that I never thought were valuable to learn until I took Slice of Pi. I learned how to incorporate math and technology. I did a computerized portfolio, and I did most of my learning of algebra on the computer. I've taken a math class that taught about fractals, which is a new form of mathematical understanding, emerging around 1980. These are just a few of the classes that I've chosen to expand my knowledge base. They were good choices for me.

I know the struggle will not stop here, so I'm preparing to fight for the rest of my life. As I get older and mature, I realize what I need to do more often and that is count my blessings and take action and control of my education. As of right now, I am content with my decisions in life and plan on being true to myself.

Einstein said, "He who doesn't live a life for others doesn't have a life worth living." My life is lived for my family and me.

Ruth Before and During Eagle Rock

Ruth came from a middle- to upper-middle-class family in a town that was largely middle- to upper-middle-class. Here is an excerpt from her first POL autobiography:

At the beginning of my freshman year, I was on top of all my work, but as the school year progressed, distractions became a huge problem. I began to party with friends every day. This partying usually consisted of taking all sorts of drugs and partaking in illegal activities. I began to lie to my parents just so that I could continue to have the fun I thought I was having. I also stopped listening to them and, in a sense, rebelled. I continued to disrespect my parents, first, by having a party in my house while both of them were out of town. During this party, my friends and I managed to consume all of my parents' liquor and I betrayed most of the trust they still had in me. I didn't comply with the punishment of grounding my parents gave to me, therefore causing more friction within our family.

When New Year's Eve of 199_ rolled around, I decided to have another one of those great parties, but this time at the house of a family whose children I was babysitting. My friends and I managed to intake much of the expensive alcohol in the house as well as to take the family's car out to get cigarettes and engage in other illegal activities. I was very lucky to be only grounded for these illegal acts. After this situation, amazingly, my family dilemma improved, mainly because I became a good liar and could deceive my parents on how well my school work was going.

On January 28, 199_, I was arrested on charges of second degree burglary for stealing alcohol from a bed & breakfast. I was blind to the consequences of my actions and reached a point of not caring enough to change my lifestyle. Fortunately, this was my first arrest, so I was offered a unique six-month program, quite like probation but called diversion. In complying with diversion, I was put on a bond that forced me to attend school full time, not be able to use public transportation, and to have no contact with my co-defendant until after my court date.

After my court date, I was paired with a mentor and we established a contract, in which I had to agree to complete certain requirements such as a letter of apology to the complainant, $102 in restitution, 65 hours of community service, regular urine analyses (UAs), family counseling, and individual counseling.

Luckily, keeping my record clear meant enough to me that I successfully completed the diversion program. My case was legally dismissed on August 25, 199_. Since that time, I have continued to stay out of all legal trouble.

Ruth's first trimester was Winter 1998; she graduated with Marchello at the end of the Winter 2000 trimester. These are the learning experiences she engaged in:

First Trimester (Winter 1998)

ERS 101 (Orientation to Eagle Rock School)

ERS 201 (Transition to ERS)

Group Work (Orientation to ERS)

Journey Into the Human Body (Science)

Wilderness Prep

Wilderness Experience

So Much Depends on a Red Wheelbarrow (Poetry)

Second Trimester (Summer 1998)

Freedom Summer '98 (History, Literature)

AIDS Awareness (Health)

Write for the Rock (Writing)

Mas Espanol (Spanish)

Mas, Mas Espanol (Spanish)

Garden of Eagles (Science, Art)

Conceptual Calculus (Mathematics)

Third Trimester (Fall 1998)

On Eagle's Wings (Music, Performance)

Touch the Future (Environmental Science, Service)

Glass Blowing (Art)

Journey Into the Human Body (Science)

Let's Make a Racket! (Physical Education)

Fourth Trimester (Winter 1999)

Close-Up (Government, Civics)

Memoirs (Writing, Literature)

Books: It's What's for Dinner (Literature)

Just for the Health of It (Physical Education, Health)

Act Out (Literature, Performance)

Fifth Trimester (Summer 1999)

Fifties Unit (Interdisciplinary)

Sports Safety (Physical Education, Health)

Art on the Rocks (History, Art)

Israel Study Tour

Sixth Trimester (Fall 1999)

Affinities (Art, Literature)

Touch the Future (Environmental Science, Service)

Paper Making and Book Binding (Art, Writing)

Solve It! (Mathematics)

Vietnam: The Longest War (History, Literature)

Seventh Trimester (Winteer 2000)

Eagle Rock Press (Writing, Service, Art)

Recycled/Reseen (Art, Service)

Fractals (Mathematics)

Here's Ruth's letter to her graduation panel:

March 14, 2000
Dear Panel Members,

Thank you very much for taking the time to read my packet. I have titled my packet Just Me because that is just what this is. I am presenting you with all that I am and want you to know that there is no more and no less than what is presented here. I have put my all into this packet, and I am very proud of what has accumulated here. I hope you enjoy it as well.

About a year ago, I took a class with Alison named Memoirs. For me, this class was not about telling my memoir but, instead, learning how to write from the depths of my soul and getting so deep in my mind that I lose direction of where reality really is. Some may say this is a bad thing, but I think this is how I discovered who I am. So I decided I wanted to show you in my autobiography who I am and where I came from and maybe give you a glimpse into the depths of my mind. I began writing this autobiography as a journal entry in which I wanted to capture my time at Eagle Rock and, somehow, it developed into the piece it is today. It may not show you how far I have come in learning how to write properly, but it will show you how far I have come personally and who I am today. If you struggle with reading it, I suggest reading it aloud because, as a silent piece, the meaning sometimes gets lost.

Thank you again for taking the time to read through my packet, and I look forward to seeing you at my graduation presentation of learning.

Warmly,
Ruth

This is Ruth's graduation autobiography:

Just Me

A new page in my book of life opens with waking up at sunrise to run and a large rock that somehow resembles an eagle. My ruined lungs and hurt soul barely hang on. I find relaxation in solitude. I go off to the desert where it's supposed to be hot, but, instead of worrying about heat stroke, we worry about hypothermia and the rain beats down on us day in and day out. I become a we but stick with my comfortable solitude. Anything you can do, I can do better . . . and I'm not going to let you ruin *my* day. High school is about getting credit and graduating, not how much you know or what you can learn. I can get credit and I can graduate, just don't look at me and push that personal growth bullshit my way.

I am a hard worker, and Jason excites me with math. I don't know what he's talking about with "the learning is the important thing." Yes, I will learn it and I will excel, but you better give me the credit. I get an Eagle Rock Excellence Award. Yes, I have excelled, and I have put on an act. But no one knows. They all just think I am this good-willed-down-to-earth type of gal, but I still go home on breaks and ruin my body and my morals. I miss the only place where my solitude can't exist: I miss my house wing and all the unique girls who really love me for *me*. I return happy and excited to be back, but I still would rather be ruining me in [my hometown].

Alison gets me really interested in writing from my soul and tells me if I do, the credit will come later. And I do; I write from my soul and don't worry about credit. I write about me and the awful situations I wish I never had to remember. And I am no longer at Eagle Rock, but in the depths of my mind where it is a very scary place and the words on paper don't come nearly fast enough. I do come back to sitting in the library on the blue chair which I left so long ago. And the credit does come, but my journal, my precious journal, from the depths of my mind means more than any credit or any graduation plan. Alison taught me this, and every class from there on was about making that mind of mine a little stronger and maybe not so scary.

Papa Bear [the students' affectionate name for the director of students] pushes thoughts of my mother everyday and I can't figure out why he doesn't understand that it's really not an issue. But all the other issues come from him and his tough love and why can't he just be like [I'm] his daughter and trust that I really do know how to run my life. Cause I do, yes, I really do . . . I think I do. . . .

Each day something new clicks in my mind and I'm an inch smarter, with miles and miles to go. Then one day a new girl doesn't deal with her issues, and I remind her in my very solemn way, "Personal growth is half the Eagle Rock experience." And I wonder why I never take my own advice. The beginning of when I listen to myself is born and I hear more than I ever thought was there. Some people say the voices in the back of your head are your conscience, but my conscience isn't the voices; it's what I make myself think.

Words like responsibility and trust mean something to me. And I know with those traits, I can do and have whatever I want, except, of course, when Papa Bear interjects. I begin to play, and I learn to learn, and I also learn to help others as they struggle with life. But I am not perfect. No, by no means am I perfect, but I try really hard to be that good Eagle Rock student that I want to be.

I remember my Judaism and go to Israel. I kiss holy soil and am welcomed *home*. I learn about a life I never knew before but one that feels so familiar and welcoming. And I return to the States and wish I never had to, but make it my plan to return some day very soon. Savio calls me "Miss Eight Plus Five Equals Ten," and I'm not, but I try really hard to be. I know I have become a role model, and it excites me. I want to be a role model for anyone who can't deal with daily life at first at the Rock. And I care more than ever about the new students and who I am welcoming into *my* community. And it really becomes *my* community and I love it openly and dearly. I decide that you better not f— it up and ruin the greatness and, if you do, you should be expelled and I hesitate ever wanting you to return. But those who make it a better place should stay and cherish and give back, because we are all blessed.

I try to graduate and fail miserably. But in my failure I succeed and I am better today because of it. And now I get to graduate with just Chello and feel all special because the class of April 2000 is just two people, and I am half the class. And I am special and not conceited for saying so, because I am smart and intelligent and going to make it in life and be happy. My life will be filled with all I want to fill it with and I have already begun. My tool box is full and it's time to get a bigger one that I will soon fill to the brim. And now that I am going to be a high school graduate I know life is about learning and high school should be, too. Now I get to accomplish all my hopes and dreams and I get to kiss holy soil again. Also, I will go to college and not for the diploma and credit, but to learn to be an animal doctor and fulfill my childhood dreams. And more dreams will come and will be fulfilled because, G-d Almighty, isn't that what life is about? Most importantly, I am going to continue to discover what *my* meaning of life is and I am going to live it to the fullest.

I am going to remember Eagle Rock and how it has helped me more than I could help myself and I am grateful, very grateful. And one day I am going to be able to help others as everyone has helped me and then I will be exactly where I want to be and I will be able to die with a clear conscience. But, for now, I am going to just live: I am going to follow my dreams and be successful and stop once in awhile to feel the cool breezes on my cheeks and the fresh air in my lungs, because that's what my life is about. For now, I am going to close one chapter in my life but always go back to it because, when you read a book, you have to remember what came before the page you are reading today. I always turn back the pages in books to understand the chapter I am now reading, and the same goes for my life. I am finishing one page and moving on to open a brand new one that shines. But soon enough that shiny page will have that good worn-in feeling that really makes me that good-willed-down-to-earth type of gal that I love and I know others love, too.

Marchello and Ruth are very different people. Their backgrounds and previous learning environments are very different. It took thirteen trimesters for Chello to graduate, seven for Ruth. They learn differently, and they took different classes to graduate. They want to do different things with their lives. Both are in college as this is being written, Chello in Chicago and Ruth in Israel.

As a former English teacher, I notice differences in their "before" and "after" writing skills. Chello, for example, improves his vocabulary, syntax, and voice. Here's a "before" sentence from an early autobiographical essay: "That's how it use to be but now, since I've been at Eagle Rock, things have been going good at home." Look again at his graduation autobiography. It is vastly improved in terms of vocabulary (he uses words like *contemplative* and *plethora*) and syntax (especially sentence variety). He has developed a voice that allows him to display his sense of humor. I enjoy his reference to himself as the "successful, handsome young man he wants to be," can hear him emphasize that word *handsome* with a wide grin and a little swagger. I also enjoy his description of himself as outfitted with "titanium-coated Teflon armor." He employs metaphors: "wallow in a shallow pool of knowledge"; "walking across the stage of success and completion"; and "this list goes on like a fractal." He uses quotations.

Ruth's writing, although stiff, is more mature than Chello's when she enters Eagle Rock. Her vocabulary in that first POL autobiography includes words like *partaking* and *relapse*. Her syntax is straightforward. Her writing in her graduation panel letter and autobiography is more fluent and personal. She lets the reader know who she is and how she feels. She is conscious of her audience: "If you struggle with reading [my autobiography], I suggest reading it aloud because, as a silent piece, the meaning sometimes gets lost." She begins with a metaphor: "A new page in my book of life." Her syntax sometimes comes very close to poetry: "I become a we, but stick with my comfortable solitude." Her line, "I'm an inch smarter, with miles and miles to go" is rich. She weaves sentences with statements and exclamations, short and long. Her writing has drama and personality.

I especially appreciate Marchello's honesty about his struggle with both being the man in his family and needing and asking for help. The excerpt from his early autobiography—the story of his caring for his younger sisters and brother while his mother worked—is particularly poignant. So is his struggle with lack of compassion because he has felt both used and "scared to show people who I really am, because I used to get close to people easily and I would always be the one to get hurt."

When Chello entered Eagle Rock, he brought in almost no transfer credits. (Eagle Rock gives credit for grades of C or better in high school–level courses.) Chello had not been to school much before he found Eagle Rock. Ruth, on the other hand, had been part of a good school system, had attended good schools, and in her own words, "ended up being able to struggle my way through middle school without doing too poorly. As I completed my eighth grade year, I felt as if I was ready to take on the challenge of [the high school]. . . . At the beginning of my freshman year, I was on top of all my work, but as the school year progressed, distractions became a huge problem." She talks about procrastinating, not prioritizing, and not completing her work, but at least she was in school and could transfer in a number of credits. Chello begins almost from scratch; Ruth proceeds further, faster, because she not only is able to transfer in a number of credits but also has some skills in writing, mathematics, and other subjects.

As with most graduates, Chello's and Ruth's autobiographies blend what they say about academic growth and personal growth. First autobiographies and POLs tend to be segmented: *Now I will talk about academic growth. Now I will talk about personal growth.* As students mature at Eagle Rock, the two become inseparable. So it is with Ruth's and Chello's comments about personal and academic growth.

Chello and Ruth took some of the same classes, sometimes at different times. We do repeat classes that serve a real learning (and possibly service) purpose and work well for students—Touch the Future is an excellent example. Ruth and Chello also repeated some classes.

For Chello, it was mostly because, when he first took them, he was not able—yet—to achieve mastery of one of the documentations required for credit on a competency. The important word is *yet*—he was not punished for failure; indeed, there was no failure; he just wasn't ready. So he took the same—or a slightly different—class later to work again on the competency.

It was partly because of his struggle with writing that Chello took so many mathematics classes. In order to get credit in mathematics and science classes, students need to produce a portfolio, writing what they understand about the math or science. We believe that manipulating numbers is not enough, that true understanding comes when students can express what they know both orally (by teaching others) and in writing. Chello struggled with putting his understanding into written English but emerged knowing more about writing and mathematics—and how to do both better.

Physical education was a must for Chello; he chose to go above and beyond our requirements. For Chello, physical education is a personal enterprise, something that sometimes saves him from his frustrations. We seldom give credit for physical education prior to Eagle Rock because our philosophy is so different from the philosophy in most high schools. We believe that physical education is a lifelong pursuit, so we're more interested in students seeing the personal value of physical education than in their learning a particular sport or activity.

Beginning in his tenth trimester at Eagle Rock, Chello had a lot of independent studies. He had begun to recognize his own learning problems and became an activist in seeking remedies for them. It was very powerful for him to say, "I need this," and write a proposal for an independent study, find an intern or volunteer to help him learn, and dedicate himself to learning what, previously, he'd chosen to ignore.

Ruth's pathway through the curriculum was a little more direct and straightforward. One class she took for a second time was Touch the Future, not because she needed a second learning experience to earn credit but because she liked the class so much, especially working with the children. Her learning difficulties were minimal—she had to work on procrastination—and she quickly understood how to graduate at Eagle Rock. In fact, instructors—and eventually Ruth herself—were worried that she was pushing toward earning credit and graduating as soon as possible rather than focusing on learning. She recognizes this in her graduation autobiography, with a little bit of sarcasm: "High school is about getting credit and graduating, not how much you know or what you can learn. I can get credit and I can graduate. . . ." Later she writes, "And now that I am going to be a high school graduate I know life is about learning and high school should be, too. . . . Also, I want to go to college and not for the diploma and credit, but to learn to be an animal doctor and fill my childhood dreams."

Neither Chello nor Ruth graduated when they first applied to do so. Chello applied for graduation a number of times before he finally completed all he needed to. His was a drawn-out process of learning that he had to master something to get credit; he couldn't just sit in class and be charming. He had to learn and document that learning. His disappointment built each time: at the end of the trimester before he actually graduated, he almost quit Eagle Rock. He had been here, after all, four years; he deserved to graduate. Only his grandmother, and his own realization of all he would throw away if he left, brought him back. He was very angry—mostly at himself—and then realized some growth from that anger.

Ruth expected to blitz through her requirements. As she got closer to graduation, she discovered that she was being held to standards of learning, not just earning credit. She wasn't allowed to do something that represented less than what she could do. As she expressed in her graduation autobiography, she, too, felt "better today because of it."

Putting These Ideas to the Test

Were the curriculum concepts I present in this book at work in the curriculum Ruth and Chello experienced? Well, let's see.

How Did Curriculum and Culture Relate?

Both Chello and Ruth had experiences before coming to Eagle Rock that affected them personally. Chello lived with fear every day, and Ruth tested the limits in every way she could, perhaps seeking a way to get back at people in her life. *Living in respectful harmony* was probably a very important aspect of being at Eagle Rock for Chello, while *devising an enduring moral and ethical code* was as important for Ruth.

In his final autobiography, Chello wrote about *expanding his* knowledge and working on his *moral and ethical code*. In fact, he oriented his reading toward his goal of building a moral and ethical code and wrote extensively about the values he was working on. While he may just be using the vocabulary of $8 + 5 = 10$, his continued reference to the school's principles indicate to me that he has internalized them and is trying to live with them.

Ruth's autobiography rings with spirituality, a subtle but important component of $8 + 5 = 10$. Her everyday actions and how she writes about them approach the spiritual: "The beginning of when I listen to myself is born and I hear more than I ever thought was there." She has also awakened her spirituality in terms of her Judaism. Ruth says she has been called "Miss Eight Plus Five Equals Ten." She denies that she lives each of the principles but adds that she tries to. "I know I have become a role model, and it excites me."

Has Eagle Rock been a learning community—the phrase that best defines our culture—for Chello and Ruth? While Chello does not directly address community, he does address important roles in community—being compassionate and accepting help—in depth. Ruth addresses community more directly. She recognizes her role; she loves the community and wants to protect it. She has definitely discovered herself as a learner. Neither graduate has put *learning* and *community* together in their writings, although they may understand that the two-word phrase has a deeper meaning than the two words alone. Nevertheless, both Ruth and Chello have made 8 + 5 = 10 theirs and expect to live it even when they are no longer at Eagle Rock.

How Did Curriculum Include Instruction and Assessment?

It is very hard to determine if Chello and Ruth realized whether or not the curriculum was coherent, whether or not curriculum–instruction–assessment fit together. This concept may not be on our students' radar, but Chello and Ruth experienced the coherence in many of the classes they took. Let's examine a few.

- *Building the Playground:* The curriculum was, on the surface, building the playground in a nearby town; students were supposed to learn how to do that. Along the way, however, they had to learn mathematics. The math curriculum was taught hands-on. They also had to work with residents of the town and thereby learned something about how a town works. The finished product was the successfully completed playground; that was the real assessment, although students had to make correct mathematics calculations along the way for the playground to be realized. They evaluated their work leading up to the completion of the playground, and they evaluated the playground, as did residents of the community in which they did their building.

- *So Much Depends on a Red Wheelbarrow:* The curriculum was poetry. Students read, wrote, and shared poetry and responded to poetry others shared all day, in all sorts of settings. They learned how to select good poetry; they learned how to read poetry with expression; they learned some techniques for writing poetry; they learned how to deliver an effective critique. They learned these things by actually doing them. For the assessment, students read poems they'd selected and written around a theme; they also responded to the selections others had chosen and written.

- *To Use or Not to Use:* The curriculum was environmental education and service. Students investigated use of paper, plastics, glass, and aluminum around the campus. They learned about the materials, labor, and power sources related to each, getting into some chemistry. They researched recycling possibilities for each and, as a final project, made a recommendation to the director of operations about what we should use (one large bottle instead of five small bottles of shampoo, for example) on the basis of its impact on the environment. They also presented their findings and recommendations at a gathering, and the community changed how it was using and disposing of a variety of products.

- *Let the Games Begin!* The timing was right for this class: the 2000 Olympics were around the corner (too bad they were also on the other side of the world). The end product was to be our own Eagle Rock Olympics, building on history as well as the present, featuring the national anthems of the participating countries. In order to design the Eagle Rock Olympics, students researched the Olympics of the past (locations, cultures, political problems). They learned the music (and its meaning) of selected countries. They then presented their findings to one another and decided how they would organize an Eagle Rocks Olympics around what they had discovered. They designed a number of murals to convey what they had learned about past Olympics, led the community in the national anthems, and then staged several Olympic contests (both historical and present-day), complete with awards ceremonies and more music. They wrote reflective journals about their learning.

It seems to me that there is a fairly close fit among curriculum, instruction, and assessment in each of these examples, something that Ruth and Chello might not have detected but something that if it hadn't been there might have made a difference in their learning. One way I arrive at that conclusion is through considering the alternatives. Sometimes the alternatives approach the ludicrous: What if students hadn't built the playground after all that work? What if they had just taken a test on building a playground? Or written a paper on how they would have built the playground? What if students were expected to critique a poem as part of an assessment but they never learned what a good critique was (curriculum) nor practiced giving critiques and hearing others give critiques . . . and critiquing the critiques (instruction)? What if the curriculum in the Olympics class omitted the national anthems? It seems a small thing, but the moment when bronze, silver, and gold medals are placed around the necks of the winners of an event is made more meaningful and poignant when the national anthem of the winner's country is played.

How Was Curriculum Learner Centered?

Ruth gives the best example of a learner-centered experience in her description of the class called Memoirs: "For me, this class was not about telling my memoir but, instead, learning how to write from the depths of my soul and getting so deep in my mind that I lose direction of where reality really is. . . . I think this is how I discovered who I am." The academic purposes of the class meshed with the personal growth purposes of Eagle Rock. The class also let Ruth understand herself better as a learner.

Her mathematics instructor challenged her to think about herself as a learner. Was it enough just to get credit? graduate? What about *learning*? She describes herself as a learner: "I always turn back the pages in books to understand the chapter I am now reading, and the same goes for my life. I am finishing one page and moving on to open a brand new one that shines. But soon enough that shiny page will have that good worn-in feeling. . . ." She has united the academic and personal.

Ruth writes (and speaks) with confidence that she didn't have when she entered Eagle Rock. She has come into herself as a learner; she feels power and control over learning.

Chello is very focused on himself as a learner. He does not want to "wallow in a shallow pool of knowledge," for example. He writes a lot about expanding his knowledge base, knowing that that's one of his goals as a learner: "Academics is the golden key to my future." He tries to take power and control over his learning each time he tries to graduate. He finally realizes that he has to do the learning (and prove it) himself. He also states that he needs to "take action and control of my education" in the future. One important lesson he learns is that he has to ask for help and accept it when it is offered. This realization as a learner helps him, finally, to graduate. Although he separates his personal growth learning from academic growth in his autobiography, he is aware that both are important to his success.

How Was Curriculum Competency Based?

Again, Ruth and Chello do not talk directly about graduating according to a competency-based system, but they did. They both completed their ILPs—they produced documentations of learning that indicated mastery, and they had those documentations checked off on their ILPs.

When they had all documentations accounted for, the boxes for our graduation requirements or competencies were darkened. When enough had been darkened that they thought they could apply for graduation (signifying that they thought they could complete the remaining documentations in the trimester of graduation), they did so. Also, Ruth and Chello both made presentations of learning at the end of each trimester. Chello did twelve before he gave his graduation POL. Ruth did six before her graduation POL. Although POLs are not meant to document learning of specific competencies, they do document learning. They also document speaking ability.

At first, Chello just didn't get it—and many students new to Eagle Rock don't. He had not thought through what it meant to move from a system in which he just sat and got credit to a system in which he had to document his learning, actually *do* something until he'd mastered it. Also, he had a number of personal growth issues to deal with. Eventually (especially by watching his friends graduate), he got it. Later, however, he kept applying to graduate and then not completing documentations he still had to master. Graduation may have been very scary for Marchello, the future very scary. Sometimes students sabotage themselves when they cannot face the unknown. The letter and autobiography he submitted to his panel indicate that, perhaps, Chello has finally turned a corner and learned what it means to "take action and control of my education." He exults in the learning he did during that final trimester. He indicates that he is excited by a possible future.

Ruth got it from the beginning, and she received credit in almost all of her classes for documentations that represented mastery. What she needed to realize, as Jason indicated to her, was that learning was what mattered. She said, "I can get credit and I can graduate. . . ." He challenged her to consider that "'learning is the important thing.'" She still resisted, "Yes, I will learn it and I will excel but you better give me the credit." It's only after she works through some personal issues that credit becomes less important. Her journal, in particular, is part of the transformation. "And the credit does come, but my journal, my precious journal, from the depths of my mind, means more than any credit or any graduation plan." Ruth gets it at a deeper level than how to get credit and graduate. She understands the internal learning behind those outside indicators.

How Did Curriculum Encourage Self-Directed Learning?

Both Ruth and Chello are strongly oriented toward self-directed learning, though I suspect they weren't when they entered Eagle Rock. Both of them write strongly about themselves as learners, both in their personal and academic lives. Chello writes, "I've chosen to do all the work I could and learn as much as possible before I move on to that special club [Eagle Rock graduates]." He continues, "I also decided to look at my life in such a way that I am committed to learning forever. . . ." In his autobiography he writes, "I realize what I need to do more often and that is . . . take action and control of my education."

Ruth knows she's a hard worker, but doing is not always the same as learning. It seems to me that she learns, perhaps reluctantly, that one important result of doing is learning. She moves from putting on an act to being authentic. That's an important step in becoming more self-directed; she's not letting outsiders (whom she can influence through her acting) motivate her. She becomes more self-motivated. She also realizes that failure is an opportunity to succeed, and that kind of thinking is important to self-directed, lifelong learning. She declares that she knows "life is about learning."

These are words. What about the actions? Will Ruth and Chello be lifelong learners? Their ability to get themselves together enough to graduate is a good sign. They are both in college; that's also a good sign. Contact us in about four years and we'll tell you how they're both doing!

How Did Curriculum Provide for the Whole Student?

Both Chello and Ruth had to assemble two personal growth portfolios and make a personal growth POL in order to graduate. In each of their regular POLs, they were required to discuss both personal and academic growth. In addition, they needed to discuss personal and academic growth in their POL packets. Much of what they wrote in their graduation letters and autobiographies addresses personal growth.

Chello is very explicit about two aspects of personal growth he needed to deal with: learning compassion and letting people help him. Although he doesn't use the word, issues surrounding *trust* are big for Chello, affecting the degree to which he can open up to people and let them see his compassion and the degree to which he can trust people not to reject him when he asks for help. He also focuses on devising a personal moral and ethical code, something that most adults haven't formalized.

Ruth confesses to anger and belligerence in her autobiographies: "I'm not going to let you ruin *my* day . . . just don't look at me and push that personal growth bullshit my way." She fights with Jason: ". . . but you better give me the credit." Inside she knows her accomplishments are all an act. She can't keep the act going when she goes home. It's only when she takes the memoirs class that she breaks through. The journal that is part of the academic requirement in the class lets her write from her "soul." Her ability to unite personal and academic growth continues: "Each day something new clicks in my mind."

The key to providing for the whole student is the interrelationship between personal growth and academic growth. Did the personal growth both Ruth and Chello accomplished at Eagle Rock affect their ability to learn, earn credit, and graduate? You bet it did. Both came to see personal growth as being as important as academic growth. Chello realized his trust issues were blocking his learning when he couldn't ask for help. Ruth's perception of her personal growth was so interwoven with her perception of her academic growth that she couldn't separate them. She discovered her soul and thus was able to shed new light on knowledge and learning.

How Did Curriculum Encourage a Constructivist Approach?

Deciding whether or not the classes Ruth and Chello took encouraged a constructivist approach requires both looking at the classes and at what Ruth and Chello say about themselves as learners. As Chapter 8 suggests, there are a number of ways of implementing a constructivist approach.

As I look at the classes Marchello and Ruth took, I notice that a number of them encouraged a constructivist approach: ERS Enterprise, Journey Into the Human Body, Exploring Estes, Garden of Eagles, Conceptual Calculus, What's Love Got to Do With It?, Patterns, On Eagle's Wings, The Game of Pig, Newton's Law, Flamboyant Shadows, Memoirs, Books: It's What's for Dinner, To Use or Not to Use, Love and Foreign Affairs, Turn the Poet Out of Doors, Art on the Rocks, Can Lines Talk?, Affinities, Touch the Future. We can trust that both Chello and Ruth were exposed to a constructivist approach to learning.

They also perceive themselves as self-directed learners, one important result of taking a constructivist approach to learning. They take responsibility for their own learning. They don't think someone else is supposed to fill them with knowledge. They must do that themselves. Chello is determined to not to let himself "wallow in a shallow pool of knowledge." Ruth knows that "life is about learning," and she seems determined to pursue her future as a learner.

How Was Curriculum Meaningful?

Many of the courses Chello and Ruth took were meaningful in the narrow sense of being interdisciplinary. In the larger sense of meaningfulness, we need to check the letters and autobiographies that Ruth and Chello sent in their packets to their panelists for their final POLs.

Chello felt he advanced considerably in his academics during his last trimester. He lists not just his courses or what he did in them but what he learned. He learned enough about fractals to use the term in a simile: "This list goes on like a fractal." He's pretty impressed with himself and all his learning.

Ruth's most meaningful class, Memoirs, was not interdisciplinary other than that it was both a reading and writing class. It was meaningful in that it touched Ruth personally. She learned to write from her soul. She risked going into the "depths of [her] mind where it is a very scary place and the words on paper don't come nearly fast enough."

As I hope I made clear in Chapter 9, courses that are interdisciplinary are usually meaningful because they are more realistic; they represent the real world better than single-subject courses. As Jena put it, "Life is a fully integrated course." However—and it certainly is the case with Ruth—a single-subject course can also be meaningful if it makes use of some of the other ideas of good curriculum—if it addresses the culture students live in, helps the students find power in learning, allows students some variation in the conditions of learning, provides opportunities for self-direction and plenty of choices, addresses both personal and academic growth, encourages a constructivist approach, etc.

Questions to Consider

These are the *big* questions related to school change. They are questions you can consider by yourself, but eventually you'll need to invite ever-widening groups of people who care about what happens in your school to consider them with you.

1. Why would you want to change your school? What is the "pain" in the system? What is not working as well as it should?

2. What data do you have (or can you collect) that substantiate the need to change? How can you communicate what you have learned from your data and why the data suggest a need to change?

3. Who are the people who would not want to see your school change? What reasons would they give? Before anything is done to initiate change, how can you initiate a dialogue with people who do not want change?

4. What concepts of curriculum—from this book or from other sources—suggest a powerful way to help everyone at your school learn and succeed?

5. What policies might affect your implementation of change? How can you address any state or district policies that might block the change you want to make? Are waivers possible? under what conditions?

6. What incentives are there for making the change? Who will support the change? Who will be the first to implement it?

7. How will you communicate with everyone interested in the welfare of the school (various constituencies) as you progress with your change?

8. What professional development will be needed —for staff? administrators? others? What ongoing support will be needed?

9. How will you know that the change is affecting learning? What data will you gather and how will you analyze and use your data?

10. How will communicate what you are learning about the effect of your change?

Afterword

As I finish writing this book, I am aware of so much that we are not doing or not doing well enough at Eagle Rock. I am painfully aware of what we still don't know about how to help young people learn and succeed. I am aware that there are questions we haven't even asked. Perhaps the word I should add to these sentences is the word we use with students when they haven't mastered a documentation—*yet*. We don't *yet* know all we need to know. We haven't *yet* been able to do all we can to support learners. We haven't *yet* asked all the questions that will help us move forward. I hope you have read this book with the realization that Eagle Rock is not perfect—and never will be.

I'm aware, however, that while there are some things we aren't doing as well as we would like, there are things we *are* doing that help our students learn and succeed. What I hope most fervently is that something you've read here will help you work toward the goal of helping all students have "the desire and preparation to make a difference in the world."

References

Armstrong, T. 1994. *Multiple Intelligences in the Classroom*. Alexandria, VA: Association for Supervision and Curriculum Development.

Brooks, J. G., and M. G. Brooks. 1993. *In Search of Understanding: The Case for Constructivist Classrooms*. Alexandria, VA: Association for Supervision and Curriculum Development.

Burns, R. 1995. *Dissolving the Boundaries*. Interdisciplinary Teamed Instruction Program. Charleston, WV: Appalachia Educational Laboratory.

Caine, R. N., and G. Caine. 1991. *Making Connections: Teaching and the Human Brain*. Alexandria, VA: Association for Supervision and Curriculum Development.

———. 1997. *Education on the Edge of Possibility*. Alexandria, VA: Association for Supervision and Curriculum Development.

Calfee, R. C., and C. Wadleigh. 1992. "How Project READ Builds Inquiring Schools." *Educational Leadership* 50 (1): 28–32.

Christensen, C. R., D. A. Garvin, and A. Sweet, eds. 1991. *Education for Judgment: The Artistry of Discussion Leadership*. Boston: Harvard Business School Press.

Curwin, R. L. 1993. "The Healing Power of Altruism." *Educational Leadership* 51 (3): 36–39.

Cushman, K., ed. 1994. "Less Is More: The Secret of Being Essential." *Horace* 11 (2): 1–10.

Dale, E. 1946. "The Cone of Learning." In *Classic Writings on Educational Technology*, ed. D. P. Ely and T. Plomp, 1996. Englewood, CO: Libraries Unlimited.

Duckworth, E. 1987. *The Having of Wonderful Ideas and Other Essays on Teaching and Learning*. New York: Teachers College Press.

Easton, L. 1999. "Tuning Protocols." *Journal of Staff Development* 20 (3): 54–55.

———. 2000. "If Standards Are Absolute. . . ." *Education Week* 19 (31): 50–53.

Elias, M. J., J. E. Zins, R. P. Weissberg, K. S. Frey, M. T. Greenberg, M. H. Norris, R. Kessler, M. E. Schwab-Stone, and T. P. Shriver. 1997. *Promoting Social and Emotional Learning: Guidelines for Educators.* Alexandria, VA: Association for Supervision and Curriculum Development.

Etzioni, A. 1993a. *The Spirit of Community: The Reinvention of American Society.* New York: Simon and Schuster Touchstone.

———. 1993b. "On Transmitting Values: A Conversation with Amitai Etzioni." *Educational Leadership* 51 (3): 12–15.

Gardner, H. 1985. *The Mind's New Science: A History of the Cognitive Revolution.* New York: Basic.

———. 1993. *Multiple Intelligences: The Theory in Practice.* New York: Basic.

Glasser, W. 1975. *Schools Without Failure.* New York: HarperCollins.

Goleman, D. 1995. *Emotional Intelligence: Why It Can Matter More Than IQ.* New York: Bantam.

———. 1998. *Working with Emotional Intelligence.* New York: Bantam.

Heath, S. B. 1983. *Ways with Words: Language, Life, and Work in Communities and Classrooms.* Cambridge, UK: Cambridge University Press.

Isaacson, N., and J. Bamburg. 1992. "Can Schools Become Learning Organizations?" *Educational Leadership* 50 (3): 42–44.

Jensen, E. 1998. *Teaching with the Brain in Mind.* Alexandria, VA: Association for Supervision and Curriculum Development.

Langer, E. J. 1997. *The Power of Mindful Learning.* Reading, MA: Perseus.

Lazear, D. 1991. *Seven Ways of Knowing: Teaching for Multiple Intelligences.* 2d ed. Palatine, IL: Skylight.

Lewis, C. C., E. Schaps, and M. S. Watson. 1996. "The Caring Classroom's Academic Edge." *Educational Leadership* 54 (1): 16–21.

Lickona, T. 1991. *Educating for Character: How Our Schools Can Teach Respect and Responsibility.* New York: Bantam.

———. 1993. "The Return of Character Education." *Educational Leadership* 51 (3): 6–11.

McDonald, J. P. 1996. *Redesigning School: Lessons for the 21st Century.* San Francisco: Jossey-Bass.

Meier, D. 1995. *The Power of Their Ideas: Lessons for America From a Small School in Harlem.* Boston: Beacon.

Newman, D., P. Griffin, and M. Coyle. 1989. *The Construction Zone: Working for Cognitive Change in School.* Cambridge, UK: University of Cambridge.

O'Neil, J. 1995. "On Schools as Learning Organizations: A Conversation with Peter Senge." *Educational Leadership* 52 (7): 20–23.

————. 1997. "Building Schools as Communities: A Conversation with James Comer." *Educational Leadership* 54 (8): 6–10.

Peck, M. S. 1987. *The Different Drum: Community Making and Peace.* New York: Simon and Schuster Touchstone.

Philips, D. C. 1995. "The Good, the Bad, and the Ugly: The Many Faces of Constructivism." *Educational Researcher* 24 (7): 5–12.

Prawat, R. S. 1992. "From Individual Differences to Learning Communities— Our Changing Focus." *Educational Leadership* 49 (7): 9–13.

Schaps, E., and D. Solomon. 1990. "Schools and Classrooms as Caring Communities." *Educational Leadership* 48 (3): 38–42.

Senge, P. M. 1990. *The Fifth Discipline: The Art and Practice of the Learning Organization.* New York: Doubleday Currency.

————, ed. 2000. *Schools That Learn: A Fifth Discipline Fieldbook for Educators, Parents and Everyone Who Cares About Education.* New York: Doubleday.

Senge, P. M., C. Roberts, R. B. Ross, B. J. Smith, and A. Kleiner. 1994. *The Fifth Discipline Handbook: Strategies and Tools for Building a Learning Organization.* New York: Doubleday Currency.

Thompson, S. 2001. "The Authentic Standards Movement and Its Evil Twin." *Phi Delta Kappan* 82 (5): 358–62.

Vygotsky, L. S. 1962. *Thought and Language.* Cambridge, MA: MIT Press.

————. 1978. *Mind in Society: The Development of Higher Psychological Processes.* Translated by M. Cole, V. John-Steiner, S. Scribner, and E. Souberman. Cambridge, MA: Harvard University Press.

Wiggins, G. 1989. "Coaching Habits of Mind: Pursuing Essential Questions in the Classroom." *Horace* 6 (2): 7–8.

————. 1990. "Secure Tests, Insecure Test Takers." In *The Prices of Secrecy: The Social, Intellectual, and Psychological Costs of Current Assessment Practice,* ed. J. L. Schwartz and K. A. Viator. Cambridge, MA: Educational Technology Center, Harvard Graduate School of Education.

————. 1998. *Educative Assessment: Designing Assessments to Inform and Improve Performance.* San Francisco: Jossey-Bass.

Wiggins, G., and J. McTighe. 1998. *Understanding by Design.* Alexandria, VA: Association for Supervision and Curriculum Development.

Wood, G. H. 1990. "Teaching for Democracy." *Educational Leadership* 48 (3): 32–37.

Zahorik, J. A. 1995. *Constructivist Teaching.* Fastback No. 390. Bloomington, IN: Phi Delta Kappa Educational Foundation.

Index